The Seer's Dictionary

Your A-to-Z Guide to Understanding Seer Language

By Jennifer LeClaire

Best-selling author of The Seer Dimensions

The Seer's Dictionary

Permissions Department
Awakening Media
P.O. Box 30563
Fort Lauderdale, FL 3330

E-mail support@jenniferleclaire.org

Table of Contents

What is *The Seer's Dictionary?* 1
How to Use *The Seer's Dictionary?* 3
A 5
B 21
C 39
D 53
E 67
F 85
G 97
H 107
I 117
J 123
K 133
L 139
M 147
N 157
O 163
P 169
Q 183
R 187
S 195
T 217
U 231
V 235

W 245
X 251
Y 253
Z 255
All the Visions in the Bible 257
Every Dream in the Bible 265
Resources Used in this Book 275
About Jennifer LeClaire 277
Other Books By Jennifer LeClaire 279

Why *The Seer's Dictionary*?

Many may wonder, why do we need a seer's dictionary—a dictionary for seers? The reason is clear. As I wrote in *Power Seers* and *The Seer Dimensions*, as we step into a new era in the prophetic movement, God will showcase seers and seeing believers in an unprecedented way. We've witnessed a restoration of seeing eyes in the Bride.

The Hebrew years 5770-5779 set the stage for power seers—and seeing believers everywhere. Indeed, as the Body of Christ entered into the Hebrew year 5780, we completed a significant period of restoration of seership. If you weren't paying attention, it's likely you didn't see it. Consider this: The number seven in Hebrew correlates to seeing or vision. In 5770 God began unearthing a new generation of seers to carry the torch and light the way for the Body of Christ to enter into seer dimensions some weren't sure existed.

Just as God restored and emphasized nabi prophets with a striking ability to hear beginning in the 1980s, seer prophets will be a central focus of Spirit-filled churches in the new prophetic era. Seer prophets and hearing prophets will partner together to go further into revelatory dimensions than either could go alone. This is part of the "times of restoration of all things, which God has spoken by the mouth of all His holy prophets since the world began" (see Acts 2:21).

In writing several books on seers and teaching the *School of the Seers* for many years now (www.schoolofthespirit.tv), I've compiled a list of terms seers know or should know—and discovered language to help seers better understand their calling and express their prophetic revelation.

With seers being so misunderstood, *The Seer's Dictionary* helps give a common vocabulary and understanding to issues related to the seer dimensions. Any seer or seeing person will find their comprehension of seer realms expanding as they browse through definitions and will adopt a language that helps define and demystify what they are experiencing. Coupled with *Prophetic Ethics & Protocols*, *The Seer's Dictionary* not only informs but educates seers in vital topics related to the gifting.

How to Use *The Seer's Dictionary*

As I mentioned, this reference book is not only valuable for learning and growing your spiritual vocabulary but there are lessons peppered within many of the definitions to help guide you in the proper—or improper use of the gift. Although this book is no substitute for the highly recommended *Prophetic Protocols & Ethics* or other teaching books I've penned, it does offer a blend of definition and instruction.

You can read *The Seer's Dictionary* like a book if you choose to. This is not primarily a book to help you interpret dreams or symbols you see in visions. There are other books that serve that purpose. This reference source aims to help you develop spiritual language around your gift, familiarize yourself with important seers in the Bible, and explain concepts of the seer dimensions with which you may not have clarity.

You may hear people speaking this lingo and lack understanding about what people mean. This reference guide will fill in the gaps. You may have heard about certain concepts written in books in which the authors did not give a clear definition. This dictionary will go deeper in defining the intended meaning.

I've purposely spent time defining specific concepts around false encounters, time, seasons, the names of the Father, Son, and Holy Spirit, angelic beings, and anointings because I believe understanding the seer dimensions through these lenses is part of the healthy development of a seer. If you want to go deeper, also pick up *Prophetic Protocols & Ethics* and *Seer Activations*.

This is an extensive list, but not an exhaustive one. That's because seer language is evolving and growing. We may revise and expand this dictionary as the years go on, but feel this is a strong starting point in an area that's sorely lacking definition.

A

Aaron: a prophet, high priest, and elder brother of Moses

Abba: an Aramaic term for our heavenly Father. Both Jesus and the apostle Paul use the term Abba in Scripture, which is used as an intimate term akin to *Papa* but it does not mean Papa or Daddy (see Romans 8:15, Mark 14:36, and Galatians 4:6)

Abbadon: an angel at the bottomless pit described as a king in Revelation 9:11: "And they had as king over them the angel of the bottomless pit, whose name in Hebrew is *Abaddon*, but in Greek he has the name *Apollyon*. *Abbadon* literally means ruin, destruction, the place of destruction, the name of the angel-prince of the infernal regions, the minister of death and the author of havoc on the earth, according to *The KJV New Testament Greek Lexicon*.

Abide by: to submit to the laws of the Spirit; to operate according to the laws of the spirit dimensions; to work within the protocols of the ministry in which you are exercising your seer gift

Abide in Christ: to remain or make one's home in Christ; a heart posture of moving, living and having one's being in Him (see Acts 17:28)

Abode: a place one lives in the spirit; Father, Son, and Holy Spirit make their abode in believers who love Jesus and keep His Word (see John 14:23)

Abomination: something detestable in God's eyes. God may show you visions or you may have dreams of abominations. Ezekiel 8-11 reveals the visions of abominations the prophet had in his day. Here's a sample from Ezekiel 8:7-13 (NASB):

"Then He brought me to the entrance of the court, and when I looked, behold, a hole in the wall. He said to me, 'Son of man, now dig through the wall.' So I dug through the wall, and behold, an entrance. And He said to me, 'Go in and see the wicked abominations that they are committing here.' So I entered and looked, and behold, every form of creeping things and beasts and detestable things, with all the idols of the house of Israel, were carved on the wall all around.

"Standing in front of them were seventy elders of the house of Israel, with Jaazaniah the son of Shaphan standing among them, each man with his censer in his hand and the fragrance of the cloud of incense rising. Then He said to me, 'Son of man, do you see what the elders of the house of Israel are committing in the dark, each man in the room of his carved images? For they say, 'The Lord does not see us; the Lord has forsaken the land.' And He said to me, 'Yet you will see still greater abominations which they are committing.'"

Abraham: a prophet, an intercessor, a friend of God, the father of our faith. God changed Abram's name to Abraham, which means father of many nations

Abstract: difficult to explain. In the spirit world, some things we see are clear and definable. Other things are more abstract, which means they are more difficult to understand and to explain. It can be difficult to give language to some of what seers see in the spirit.

Acceptable Time: the manifestation of God's desired will. Psalm 69:13 reads, "But as for me, my prayer is to You, O Lord, in the acceptable time; O God, in the multitude of Your mercy, Hear me in the truth of Your salvation."

Access: also called a gateway, access is a point of entry into the seer dimensions. You can access the seer dimensions legally or illegally. Legal access is through the Door of Jesus (see John 10:9) with the guidance of the Holy Spirit. Jesus gives us access, or permission and ability, to see what He wants us to see in the spirit. The Holy Spirit shows us what is to come as Jesus opens the door (see John 16:13).

Account: to give a report or describe what you saw in the spirit or in a dream, understanding with the fear of the Lord that you are accountable for every idle word (see Matthew 12:36)

Accurate in the Spirit: freedom from error or influences that would breed error; a state in which one is careful to weigh what one sees in the spirit realm against the Word of God, the ways of God and the law of God; precise in describing or explaining what one sees and hears before sharing prophetic insight

Accuser of the Brethren: a name for Satan, who accuses believers day and night (see Revelation 12:10)

Activation: turning on one's spiritual gifts through exercise or release; Activate means "to set up or formally institute (as a military unit) with the necessary personnel and equipment; to put (an individual or unit) on active duty," according to *Merriam-Webster's Dictionary.*

Activation comes from a charge. Jesus activated the disciples in their impartation in Matthew 10:7-8: "As you go, preach, saying, 'The kingdom of heaven is at hand.' Heal the sick, cleanse the lepers, raise the dead, and cast out demons."

Acuity: the sensitivity of a seer's spiritual perception

Adonai: a name for God that means Lord, Master. This name for God first appeared in Genesis 15:2: "But Abram said, 'Lord God, what will You give me, seeing I go childless, and the heir of my house is Eliezer of Damascus?'"

Adversary: another name for Satan (see 1 Peter 5:8)

Advisor: a function of some seers in the Bible. Gad was one of David's seers who advised him in matters of the kingdom.

Advocate: another name for the Holy Spirit seen in John 14:16: "And I will ask the Father, and He will give you another Comforter (Counselor, Helper, Intercessor, Advocate, Strengthener, and Standby), that He may remain with you forever..." Also, another name for Christ seen in 1

John 2:1, "My little children, these things I write to you, so that you may not sin. And if anyone sins, we have an Advocate with the Father, Jesus Christ the righteous."

Affirm: the act of an elder seer validating a younger seer and welcoming him into the seer community

Agabus: a prophet in the Bible who foresaw a famine in the Roman world (Acts 11:28) and who prophesied Paul the apostle's arrest (Acts 21)

Age: a period of time marked by a prominent person, breakthrough, or event

Agent of Darkness: a term used to describe Satanists

Ahijah: a prophet in the days of Solomon who carried a kingdom-impacting message through a prophetic act (see 1 Kings 11)

Allegorical: a dream or vision with a hidden meaning that goes beyond the surface level revelation that is obvious

Allegory: a symbolic representation. At times, God may show seers allegories in either dreams or visions. *Baker's Evangelical Dictionary of Biblical Theology* explains: "A popular form of literature in which a story points to a hidden or symbolic parallel meaning. Certain elements, such as people, things, and happenings in the story, point to corresponding elements in another realm or level of meaning."

In fact, Dream Allegory, also called Dream Vision, describes the allegorical tale presented in the narrative framework of a dream, according to *Britannica.com*. In dreams or visions, objects can be personified. In Psalm 80, a vine is personified as Israel. In Ezekiel 17, we see an eagle capture the vine, representing Israel's exile in Babylon. Although God spoke these words to Ezekiel, allegories can play out in dreams and visions.

Almighty One: a name for Jesus as seen in Revelation 1:8, "I am the Alpha and the Omega, the Beginning and the End," says the Lord, "who is and who was and who is to come, the Almighty."

Alpha: a name for Jesus as seen in Revelation 1:8, "I am the Alpha and the Omega, the Beginning and the End," says the Lord, "who is and who was and who is to come, the Almighty."

Alternate Reality: the spirit world that parallels the natural world; the unseen realm that is as real as the seen realm; The spirit world we do not see is more real than the physical world we do see. To better understand this, we look at the *Merriam-Webster's Dictionary* definition of alternate: "arranged one above or alongside each other." In the context of the first, second, and third heavens, there are three alternate realities. (See definitions of these three heavens in this book.)

Amazement: a feeling you get when you see something spectacular in the spirit realm. *Merriam-Webster's Dictionary* defines amazement as, "a feeling of astonishment." And the same dictionary defines astonished as "feeling or showing great surprise or wonder."

Amazement or astonishment can manifest during epic visions or after waking from an epic dream. *The International Bible Encyclopedia* defines astonished as, "the state of being surprised, startled, stunned by some exceptional wonder, some overwhelming event or miracle." Ezekiel was astonished by what he saw in Ezekiel 8:1-4:

"In the sixth year, in the sixth month and the fifth day, while I was sitting at home meeting with the leaders of Judah, it happened that the hand of my Master, God, gripped me. When I looked, I was astonished. What I saw looked like a man—from the waist down like fire and from the waist up like highly burnished bronze. He reached out what looked like a hand and grabbed me by the hair. The Spirit swept me high in the air and carried me in visions of God to Jerusalem, to the entrance of the north gate of the Temple's inside court where the image of the sex goddess that makes God so angry had been set up. Right before me was the Glory of the God of Israel, exactly like the vision I had seen out on the plain."

Amazing Vision: *see Great Vision*

Ambassador: a diplomat sent into the earth realm on behalf of the Kingdom of God (see 2 Corinthians 5:20); a citizen of heaven fulfilling his or her purposes in the earth realm (see Philippians 3:20)

Ambidextrous in the Spirit: the ability to see and hear, or tap into or flow in multiple gifts of the Spirit

Amethyst: a purplish precious stone John the Revelator saw on the foundations of the wall around the New Jerusalem (see Revelation 21:19-21)

Amos: a seer prophet whose name means burden-bearer. Amos was a contemporary of the prophets Hosea and Isaiah in the days of Uzziah, king of Judah. Unlike many other prophets, he was not the son of a prophet or trained in the prophetic (see Amos 7:14). God called him while he was tending to flocks. In Amos 7:2, we see the ruler of his day did not welcome him: "Then Amaziah said to Amos: 'Go, you seer! Flee to the land of Judah. There eat bread, and there prophesy.'"

Amos Anointing: as explained in the book *Seer Activations*, Amos means burden-bearer. The Amos anointing is a seer anointing for intercession, or bearing the burdens of the Lord.

Ancestor Worship: a form of worship in which observers pray and make offerings to the dead

Ancestral Curses: *see Generational Curses*

Ancestral Spirits: spirits of the dead from past generations; Communication with ancestral spirits is necromancy, a form of divination

Ancient Nation: a nation from times past that either does not exist or has been renamed or reconstituted (see Jeremiah 5:15)

Ancient of Days: another name for God (see Daniel 7:9)

Ancient Paths: perpetual paths that have long existed (see Jeremiah 18:15)

Ancient Serpent: another name for Satan (see Revelation 12:9)

Ancient Times: the earliest time period; the beginning (see Isaiah 37:26)

Ancient World: a time that goes back as far as the days of Noah (see 2 Peter 2:5)

Angel: from the Greek word *aggelos*, and the Hebrew word *malak*, an angel is a messenger. Both words are masculine nouns that mean "a messenger, generally a (supernatural) messenger from God, an angel, conveying news or behests from God to men," according to *Strong's Concordance*

Angel Army: a host of angels in war array (see 2 Kings 7:17-20)

Angel of Light: a false angel; 2 Corinthians 11:14 warns us, "For even Satan disguises himself as an angel of light."

We know Satan is a fallen angel. We know he's crafty. We know he sets out to deceive. Seers can be deceived by false angels. The Greek word for disguise in this verse is *metaschematizo*. According to *The KJV New Testament Greek Lexicon*, it means "to change the figure of, to transform." Sometimes what one sees in the spirit is not as it appears. Beware angels of light.

Angel of the Bottomless Pit: also known as Apollyon or Abaddon (see Revelation 9:11), a dark angel on assignment who battles Michael and his angels (see Revelation 12:7-9)

Angel Worship: the veneration of angelic beings; a heresy that has infiltrated the church (see Colossians 2:18; Revelation 22:8-9)

Angelic Dimension: a dimension in the spirit in which one sees, encounters or engages with angels; (See *The Seer Dimensions* book for more on seer dimensions.)

Angelic Encounter: a supernatural experience in which one sees or has communication with an angel; Angels typically come with messages and point you to Jesus. We do not worship angels.

Angelic Hosts: the heavenly hosts on assignment to praise God day and night, and carry out many other functions according to the Word of God (see 1 Kings 22:19; Psalm 103:21)

Angels of Announcement: angels on assignment to release prophetic announcements; Angels announced the birth of John the Baptist and Jesus (see Matthew 1:20-21; Luke 1:11-13).

Angels of Deliverance: angels on assignment to deliver us from dangerous situations (see Acts 5:19; Acts 12:7-11)

Angels of Destruction: angels on assignment for destructive purposes (see Genesis 19:13; 2 Samuel 24:16; 2 Kings 19:35, etc.)

Angels of Direction: angels on assignment to help direct people (see Genesis 24:1-7; Acts 8:26)

Angels of Fire: angels who minister the fire of God to prepare and empower believers for the work of the ministry (see Psalm 104:4; Hebrews 1:7; Acts 2:3)

Angels of His Presence: angelic messengers that behold the face of God. Isaiah 63:9 speaks of the angels of His Presence: "In all their affliction He was afflicted, and the Angel of His Presence saved them; In His love and in His pity He redeemed them; And He bore them and carried them all the days of old." God saved Israel with the Angel of His Presence.

Angels of Interpretation: angels with the assignment to help interpret God-given dreams (see Daniel 7:16; Daniel 10:5)

Angels of Judgment: angels on assignment in the end-times to execute judgment (see Revelation 7:1; Revelation 8:2)

Angels of Promise: angels on assignment to deliver or remind us of the promises of God (see Genesis 16:6-10)

Angels of Provision: angels on assignment to bring the Lord's provision (see Genesis 21:15-19; 1 Kings 19:5-6)

Angels of Rebuke: angels on assignment with a word of rebuke to correct people on their path (see Numbers 22:22-23)

Angels of Revelation: angels on assignment to bring revelation to His people (see Acts 8:26-27; Acts 27:23-24; Daniel 9:21-22)

Angels of the Seven Churches: angels on assignment over the various churches in the Book of Revelation (see Revelation 1:20; Revelation 2:1, 8, 12, 18; Revelation 3:1, 7, 14)

Angels of Transition: angels that help believers transition to the next place God is taking them. The Holy Spirit leads and guides us, but ministering spirits can minister to believers in times of transition, even into heaven (see Luke 16:22).

Angels of Warning: angels on assignment to warn us of situations and circumstances we need to avoid and even show us the way of escape (see Genesis 19:1-10)

Anna: a prophetess in the Bible who gave her life over to prayer and fasting in the temple (see Luke 2:36-38)

Anointed Cherub: a description of Lucifer before his insurrection and fall (see Ezekiel 28:1-6)

Anointing: the power of the Holy Spirit (see 1 John 2:27)

Antichrist: the adversary of Jesus (see 1 John 2:18)

Antichrist Spirits: a spirit that works to kill the anointing (see 1 John 2:22)

Apocalyptic: relating to the end times

Apocalyptic Dreams: dreams typically revealing acts in the end times

Apocalyptic Numbers: numbers typically related to the end times, such as 666

Apocalyptic Vision: visions typically revealing acts in the end times; Daniel and John the revelator both had apocalyptic visions. Apocalyptic means, "of, relating to, or resembling an apocalypse; apocalyptic events; forecasting the ultimate destiny of the world: prophetic apocalyptic warnings; foreboding imminent disaster or final doom: terrible; apocalyptic signs of the coming end-times; wildly unrestrained: grandiose; ultimately decisive: climactic," according to *Merriam-Webster's Dictionary*.

Apocrypha Writing: according to *Baker's Evangelical Dictionary of Biblical Theology*, "*Apocrypha* comes from the Greek word *apokrypha*, which means 'things that are hidden, secret.' 'The Apocrypha' refers to two collections of ancient Jewish and Christian writings that have certain affinities with the various books of the Old Testament and New Testament but were not canonized by Christians as a whole: the Old Testament Apocrypha, which is still viewed as canonical by some Christians, and the New Testament Apocrypha, which is not."

Some of these books are The Book of Enoch, the 1 and 2 Maccabees, 1 and 2 Esdras, Third Corinthians, Letter to the Laodiceans, Tobit, Prayer of Manasseh, Sirach, Judith, and Rest of Esther. Some other "gospels" are said to be heretical, but some of the Apocrypha writings merely contain eye-witness accounts or experiences. These are not on par with the Bible.

Apokalupsis: a Greek word translated in the New Testament as "revealed, revealing, and revelation." According to *The NAS New Testament Greek Lexicon*, the word for revelation means "laying bare, making naked; a disclosure of truth, instruction; concerning things before unknown; used of events by which things or states or persons hitherto withdrawn from view are made visible to all; manifestation, appearance."

Apollyon: *see Abbadon*

Apostolic Movement: a movement that saw the restoration of apostles to the Body of Christ; also called the New Apostolic Reformation by the late C. Peter Wagner

Apparition: a ghostish image; while there are genuine apparitions, typically when you hear this term it relates to a false or lying vision in the Catholic church

Appearance: a word seers use in the pages of Scripture to describe what something looked like (see Ezekiel 1:5; Ezekiel 1:13); a visual manifestation of something or someone in the spirit realm, such as Moses and Elijah at the Mount of Transfiguration (see Matthew 17:1-8)

Application: how to apply the revelation one receives in the spirit; Application is putting one's revelation to use in a practical way to forward God's will on the earth. Learn more about this in the *School of the Seers* at www.schoolofthespirit.tv.

Appoint: to set in place officially; God's appointment of a person into a duty, role or function in His Kingdom (see Ephesians 4:11)

Appointed Time: a time specified by God for something to occur; God's set time; God's perfect time

Archangels: a prince of angels in the hierarchy of angels (see Colossians 1:15-18; 1 Thessalonians 4:16; Jude 9)

Arguments: in reference to 2 Corinthians 10:5, seers must cast down enemy arguments in their minds that could skew their prophetic revelation or dampen their confidence to share what is seen at the appropriate time and with the appropriate people

Armageddon: the final battle between good and evil—between Jesus and His angels and Satan and his demons—before the Second Coming of Christ (see Revelation 19)

Armor of God: divine weaponry with which God equips every believer; Ephesians 6:14-17 outlines the whole armor of God: "Stand therefore, having girded your waist with truth, having put on the breastplate of righteousness, and having shod your feet with the preparation of the gospel of peace; above all, taking the shield of faith with which you will be able to quench all the fiery darts of the wicked one. And take the helmet of salvation, and the sword of the Spirit, which is the word of God."

Arrogant Eyes: eyes that exalt oneself; proud eyes; a condition of the heart that sullies a seer's vision; one of the seven abominations listed in Proverbs 6:16-19

Asaph: a seer in the Bible whose name means "one who gathers together;" 2 Chronicles 29:30 describes Asaph as both a seer and a skilled musician in King David's time. As a psalmist, he wrote Psalm 50 and Psalm 73-83. Asaph was part of the original tabernacle of David.

Asaph Anointing: a seer anointing for creativity, including musical expression and writing; Kim Clement had an Asaph anointing. Ask the Lord for an Asaph anointing if God has also given you musical gifts.

Ascend: the act of going up to the second or third heaven. Elijah ascended to heaven (see 2 Kings 2:1). Jesus ascended to heaven (see Psalm 68:18). Psalm 139:8, "If I ascend into heaven, You are there; If I make my bed in hell, behold, You are there." Also, to rise, climb or go up in the spirit realm; angels ascended and descended on Jacob's Ladder (see Genesis 28).

Ashtoreth: a goddess Jezebel served; Ashtoreth is also known as the Queen of Heaven in Jeremiah 44:25; Ashtoreth, a seducing goddess of war, was the God of the Canaanites as well as the moon goddess of the Phoenicians. Other names for Ashtoreth are Astarte or Ishtar, variations of the same false god served by various people groups.

Assignment: a seer's God-given task or mission, which could include praying, watching, or reporting; an office, post, mission, or task to which the Lord assigns a seer; Seers have various assignments, including intercession, watching, equipping, etc., and those assignments can change in different seasons depending on what God wants to demonstrate or reveal in the earth.

Astonished at the Vision: a vision that astonishes you and is difficult to understand, often requiring angelic assistance to interpret; After seeing an end-times vision and having an encounter with an angel, Daniel wrote, "And I, Daniel, fainted and was sick for days; afterward I arose and went about the king's business. I was astonished by the vision, but no one understood it" (Daniel 8:27).

Astral Projection: unlike God transporting a person in the spirit like He did Philip the evangelist (see Acts 8:26-40), astral projection is the domain of the supernatural realm's dark side; *Merriam-Webster's Dictionary* defines an astral project as, "the ability of a person's spirit to travel to distant places." Unlike Philip's experience, astral projection is an at-will out-of-body experience.

Astrology: in Bible terms, astrology was akin to divination; *Merriam-Webster's Dictionary* defines astrology as "the divination of the supposed influences of the stars and planets on human affairs and terrestrial events by their positions and aspects."

Seers may be tempted in many areas of divination, including astrology, but the Bible speaks against it. Isaiah 47:13-14 reads, "You are wearied in the multitude of your counsels; Let now the astrologers, the stargazers, and the monthly prognosticators stand up and save you from what shall come upon you. Behold, they shall be as stubble, the fire shall burn them; They shall not deliver themselves from the power of the flame; It shall not be a coal to be warmed by, nor a fire to sit before!"

Athaliah: The Old Testament Queen Jezebel's daughter. According to *Smith's Bible Dictionary*, the name Athaliah means "afflicted of the Lord," and *Easton's Bible Dictionary* defines the name as "whom God afflicts."

Athaliah came from the royal line of Omri, the sixth king of Israel. With parents who sought political alliances to advance their kingdom, Athaliah was given in marriage to Jehoram, the eldest son of Judah's King Jehoshaphat (see 2 Kings 8:18). Athaliah murdered her own grandchildren to gain power (see 2 Chronicles 22:11), outdoing the evil of her wicked mother. (Find an intensive on the wicked spirit of Athaliah at www.schoolofthespirit.tv, as well as the book, *Jezebel's Revenge*.)

Attentive: paying close attention to the things of the spirit; keeping your spiritual eyes open to see what God is showing you

Audible Voice of God: as opposed to the still small voice you hear internally; the audible voice of God is something you hear from the outside; Adam and Eve heard the audible voice of God in the Garden of Eden (see Genesis 3:8-10). God spoke to Moses face to face (see Numbers 12:6-8). When Jesus was baptized, a voice came out of heaven and spoke audibly (see Matthew 3:16-17). When Paul was on the Road to Damascus, he heard the audible voice of God (see Acts 9).

Audiovisual: the combination of audible and visual revelation; a vision accompanied by revelatory sounds or messages

Author and Perfecter of our Faith: another name for Jesus seen in Hebrews 12:2, "Looking unto Jesus, the author and finisher of our faith, who for the joy that was set before Him endured the cross, despising the shame, and has sat down at the right hand of the throne of God."

Authority: beyond the authority we have as believers, seers have different levels of authority or rank; For example, a newly born-again believer with a seer gift has a different level of authority in the spirit than one who has been pursuing the Lord and walking in his office for decades.

A good example of this is how the Israelites recognized Jesus was walking in a greater authority than other teachers of His day. Mark 1:22 notes, "And they were astonished at His teaching, for He taught them as one having authority, and not as the scribes."

Awe: the feeling or emotion when one sees the Lord in a dream or vision, encounter or out of body experience. The International Standard Bible Encyclopedia defines awe as "Fear mingled with reverence and wonder, a state of mind inspired by something terrible or sublime... This is the characteristic attitude of the pious soul toward God in the Scriptures, especially in the Old Testament. It arises from a consciousness of the infinite power, sublimity and holiness of God, which fills the mind with the 'fear of the Lord,' and a dread of violating His law."

B

Baal: god of prophetic divination; This spirit leads people into idolatry today just like it led the Israelites into idolatry when Moses was up on the mountain. Prophets (including seers) of Baal will use divination to tap into the idolatry in your own heart and prophesy words that confirm what you really want to hear.

Baal Prophets: prophets who serve Baal; prophets influenced by the spirit of Baal

Back Door: an illegal access point to seeing in the spirit; Backdoor access is an unauthorized method for entering seer realms, such as choosing by your will to check in on someone in the spirit, eavesdrop on conversations, or otherwise cooperate with familiar spirits to see something the Holy Spirit is not trying to show you.

Balaam: a prophet in Numbers 22 who was lured by his own greed; Jewish history calls him a seer. King Balaak wanted to hire Balaam to curse Israel. In a vision, God told him not to do it. Balaam denied the king's offer more than once but nevertheless kept asking God if he could go with the king's men. Jehovah eventually let him follow his own course. It's critical that seers are submitted to the Lord's will and not greedy gain.

Balaam's Donkey: a wayward prophet's donkey who saw in the spirit what the prophet himself did not see; God will use the foolish things of the world to confound the wise (see 1 Corinthians 1:27). This is a warning to seers, whose eyes can be blinded by sin to things that others see clearly. Numbers 22:21-23 explains: "Balaam got up in the morning, saddled his donkey and went with the Moabite officials. But God was very angry when he went, and the angel of the Lord stood in the road to oppose him. Balaam was riding on his donkey, and his two servants were with him. When the donkey saw the angel of the Lord standing in the road with a drawn sword in his hand, it turned off the road into a field. Balaam beat it to get it back on the road."

Baptism in the Holy Spirit: an experience in which Jesus, the Baptizer, immerses a believer in the Holy Spirit to empower them to live a holy life and serve His Kingdom; We see mention of baptism in, with or by the Spirit seven times in Scripture: Matthew 3:11, Mark 1:8, Luke 3:16, John 1:33, Acts 1:5, Acts 1:11, Acts 1:16, 1 Corinthians 12:3. A believer doesn't have to be baptized in the Holy Spirit to see in the spirit, but Holy Spirit baptism makes one more aware and more open to spirit realms.

Baptism of Fire: the church is torn on this meaning; Many believe this is a baptism reserved for the rebellious and unrepentant. In Matthew 3:11 Jesus said, "I indeed baptize you with water unto repentance, but He who is coming after me is mightier than I, whose sandals I am not worthy to carry. He will baptize you with the Holy Spirit and fire."

The Greek word for fire in that verse is "pyro," which means "fire, the heat of the sun, lightning," according to *Strong's Concordance*. Figuratively, the concordance reports, it means strife, trials, and the eternal fire.

However, *Ellicott's Bible Commentary for English Readers* says: "As heard and understood at the time, the baptism with the Holy Ghost would imply that the souls thus baptized would be plunged, as it were, in that creative and informing Spirit which was the source of life and holiness and wisdom. The baptism 'with fire' would convey, in its turn, the thought of a power at once destroying evil and purifying good; not, in any case, without the suffering that attends the contact of the sinner's soul with the 'consuming fire' of the holiness of God, yet for those who had received the earlier baptism, and what it was meant to convey, consuming only what was evil, and leaving that which was precious brighter than before. The appearance of the "tongues like as of fire" that accompanied the gift of the Spirit on the day of Pentecost was an outward visible sign, an extension of the symbolism, rather than the actual fulfilment of the promise."

Pulpit Commentary echoes: "It has been questioned, indeed, whether 'fire' here refers to the purification of the godly who truly accept the baptism of the Spirit, or to the destruction of the wicked, as in verses 10, 12. But the thought is one. The Divine presence will in fact, as is recognized by Isaiah (see Isaiah 33:14; Isaiah 31:9), be twofold in its working, according as it is yielded to or the reverse. It burns away sin out of the godly, and it consumes the ungodly if they cleave to their sin."

Bar-Jesus: *see Elymas*

Bear Witness: to know in your spirit that something is true, even if you don't see it with your physical eyes; Your spirit man can bear witness to even obscure things you see with your spiritual eyes. Romans 8:16 reveals the act of bearing witness in your spirit by the Holy Spirit to something your physical eyes can't see: "The Spirit Himself bears witness with our spirit that we are children of God."

Beasts: symbolic representations of end-times drama. Daniel had a vision of the four beasts (see Daniel 7); In Ezekiel 8:10, the prophet saw abominable beasts.

Beelzebub: lord of the flies; another name for Satan. Mark 3:22 reads, "And the scribes who came down from Jerusalem said, 'He has Beelzebub,' and, 'By the ruler of the demons He casts out demons.'"

Before the Time: ahead of God's predestined time; Matthew 8:29, "And suddenly they cried out, saying, "What have we to do with You, Jesus, You Son of God? Have You come here to torment us before the time?"

Beginning of Knowledge: knowledge opens up to seers when they embrace the spirit of the fear of the Lord; Proverbs 1:7 assures us the fear of the Lord is the beginning of knowledge. Seers must cultivate a fear of the Lord to keep their eyes pure and open to what the Holy Spirit wants to show them.

Behemoth: a water spirit, a principality that enthrones itself over regions to forward ideologies; also called a hippopotamus in the Bible, a behemoth spirit crosses land and sea and builds systems that oppress people across two of the three strongholds in creation; These are widespread strongholds, like Communism or Islam, that affect the masses.

The KJV Old Testament Hebrew Lexicon defines behemoth, which comes from the word *b@hemowth,* this way: "perhaps an extinct dinosaur; a Diplodocus or Brachiosaurus, exact meaning unknown. Some translate as an elephant or a hippopotamus, but from the description in Job 40:15-24, this is patently absurd." Read more about this in *The Spiritual Warrior's Guide to Defeating Water Spirits.*

Behold: "to perceive through sight or apprehension" or "to gaze upon, observe," according to *Merriam-Webster's Dictionary;* Apprehension speaks of the power to perceive or comprehend, and that power comes from God. You can only behold what God opens your eyes to see, but once you see it, you should press in to behold it.

Beholding is not a quick glimpse. Beholding is a gaze. *Merriam-Webster's Dictionary* defines gaze as "to fix the eyes in a steady intent look often with eagerness or studious attention" and "a fixed intent look." When David said in Psalm 27:4 that his one desire was to gaze upon the Lord, he wasn't taking a quick glimpse. He was seeing with intelligence.

But the Bible definition goes deeper. *Strong's Concordance* translates *chazah*, the Hebrew word for "behold," as: "envisioned in visions, gaze, look, prophesy, saw, see, seeing, seen, sees." This implies that we are to keep on looking.

Brown-Driver-Briggs defines gaze as "to see, see as a seer in the ecstatic state, accusative of the vision seen, with the intelligence." This implies that when we behold a thing, we gain insight and intelligence.

The Greek word for behold is *ide*. It carries a more forceful command to see. According to *Strong's Concordance*, it means, literally, "be sure to see" in the sense of "Don't miss this! It is an observable, objective fact!" When God shows you a spiritual truth in the seer dimensions, He wants you to be sure to see it.

Belial: another name for Satan (see 2 Corinthians 6:15)

Belshazzar: a king in the days of Daniel the prophet who used the temple vessels to drink wine and party when he was suddenly confronted with a handwriting on the wall;

In this instance, God let a wicked king see into the spirit. Daniel 5:6-7 explains the king's reaction: "Then the king's countenance changed, and his thoughts troubled him, so that the joints of his hips were loosened and his knees knocked against each other. The king cried aloud to bring in the astrologers, the Chaldeans, and the soothsayers."

Bending Light: light refraction at the hands of angels; Although light refraction can be a natural occurrence that creates a mirage, angels bend light beams due to the speed at which they travel. Angels travel faster than the speed of light, which is one reason these ministering spirits sometimes appear as light.

Scientifically speaking, light refraction is "deflection from a straight path undergone by a light ray or energy wave in passing obliquely from one medium (such as air) into another (such as glass) in which its velocity is different," according to *Merriam-Webster's Dictionary*.

Beryl: a hard, light blue-yellowish-green precious stone John the Revelator saw on the foundations of the wall around the New Jerusalem (see Revelation 21:19-21)

Beware: a command in Scripture to be on one's guard; a warning to be watchful of demon powers who seek to steal, kill, and destroy (see 1 Peter 5:8); a warning to test spirits that seek to deceive you (see 1 Thessalonians 5:21); a warning about false prophets and seers (see Matthew 7:15-20)

Bewitch: the operation of an evil influence that has injury in mind; an operation of false seers. Paul wrote to the church at Galatia: "O foolish Galatians! Who has bewitched you that you should not obey the truth, before whose eyes Jesus Christ was clearly portrayed among you as crucified?" (Galatians 3:1-2).

The Greek word for bewitched in this verse is *baskaino*. According to *The KJV New Testament Greek Lexicon*, it means "to charm, to bewitch, to bring evil on one by feigning praise or an evil eye." The core of this is witchcraft that produces fascination and deals in the realm of perversion.

Biblical: in line with the teachings of the Bible, the character of God and the ways of God; We know all of Christ's acts could not be recorded in the Bible.

John 21:25 tells us, "There are also many other things which Jesus did. Were every one of them to be written, I suppose that not even the world itself could contain the books that would be written. Amen."

Therefore, one may see things in the spirit that people in the Bible did not see. One may encounter things in the spirit that we do not see recorded in the Bible.

Biblically Curious: a desire to search out the scriptures on topics by the leading of the Holy Spirit; a hunger to learn what the Bible says and what God is showing you; spiritually inquisitive

Bind: to tie up; to put in bondage; to forbid; In Matthew 18:18, Jesus said, "Assuredly, I say to you, whatever you bind on earth will be bound in heaven, and whatever you loose on earth will be loosed in heaven."

Birthing: bringing forth, to give birth to something God has placed in you; the beginning of a thing; travail; the entrance of a new thing God is doing in your life

Black Art: *see Black Magic*

Blind and bind: a spiritual warfare strategy to use against monitoring spirits; *also see Monitoring Spirits*

Blinders: satanic devices used to keep the seer's eye from seeing or his mind from understanding what he has seen; demonic obstruction that aims to limit a seer's discernment into a situation; the deception that covers the minds of the lost

Blind Spot: used to scribe when a seer's vision is obstructed, either by personal bias, deception, or demonic forces; a lack of revelation that hinders the seer gift

Blow the Trumpet: to make a warning; to tell the Body of Christ about impending danger so the saints can drop to their knees and lift up their voices in intercession; Blow the trumpet can also speak of warning people of their sins. Isaiah 58:1 says, "Cry aloud, spare not; Lift up your voice like a trumpet; Tell My people their transgression, and the house of Jacob their sins."

When Scripture says to "blow the trumpet in Zion" (see Joel 2:1), it is speaking in direct reference to the Day of the Lord, or Judgment Day. In fact, we see many references to trumpets in relation to the Second Coming of Christ in Scripture. 1 Corinthians 15:52 speaks of "the last trumpet." 1 Thessalonians 4:13-18 speaks of the Lord descending from heaven with the sound of a trumpet of God.

The blowing of trumpets in the Bible was also used in praising God and announcing new moon and feasts, but the most common connotation is a warning.

Blur: an indistinguishable form you see in the spirit; an angel or demon that moves so fast in the spirit that you can't make out the finer details of its being

Book of Adam: also called Books of Adam, non-canonical books that recount events in the lives of Adam and Eve

Book of Christ: another name for the Bible

Book of Chronicles: two books in the Bible—1 Chronicles and 2 Chronicles—most likely written during the time of Ezra or Nehemiah while the Jews were in exile; The books deal a lot with genealogies. There is some repeated material from 1 and 2 Samuel and 1 and 2 Kings, but Chronicles takes a look at these events after they occurred while the books of Samuel and Kings were written while history was unfolding.

Book of Enoch: a book reportedly written by the biblical prophet Enoch. This is termed an Apocrypha writing. Along with Elijah, Enoch was one of only two people who were taken up to heaven without dying. Genesis 5:24 tells us "And Enoch walked with God; and he was not, for God took him."

Jude quotes from the Book of Enoch in verses 14-15, "Now Enoch, the seventh from Adam, prophesied about these men also, saying, 'Behold, the Lord comes with ten thousands of His saints, to execute judgment on all, to convict all who are ungodly among them of all their ungodly deeds which they have committed in an ungodly way, and of all the harsh things which ungodly sinners have spoken against Him.'"

Book of Gad the Seer: a book Gad the Seer wrote. 1 Chronicles 29:29 tells us of this book: "Now the acts of King David, first and last, indeed they are written in the book … of Gad the seer…" Biblefacts Ministries publishes the *Ancient Book of Gad the Seer* and describes it this way:

"Written by Gad, seer of King David, about 1000 BC, this book of prophecy is recommended reading by the Bible, but was never included in the Canon. It was thought to have been lost over three millennia ago. The books of Gad, Nathan, Ahijah, Shemaiah and Iddo are referred to as 'The Lost Five.'"

The description continues, "This long-lost book includes two revealing sermons given by King David. We have a prophecy that outlines the end times beginning with the Rapture, the seven-year tribulation and the establishment of Christ's millennial reign. More intriguing than that, it actually reveals who Mystery Babylon is and how it tries to destroy the Jews though a union with Islam, both groups having different replacement theology religions. There are also two discussions on how the Law of Moses views Gentiles. Do they keep the whole Law or not?"

Book of Jashar: a book written by Jashar. Joshua 10:13 tells us of this book: "Is this not written in the Book of Jasher? So the sun stood still in the midst of heaven, and did not hasten to go down for about a whole day." *The Encyclopedia of the Bible* writes:

"An ancient writing, no longer extant, mentioned in Joshua 10:13 and 2 Samuel 1:18. Some scholars, by transposing two Hebrew letters, find a possible third reference to the work in the LXX (1 Kings 8:12, 53). The LXX omits the reference to the work in Joshua 10:13.

"On the basis of the quotations in the OT, it has been inferred by some scholars that the book was poetical in nature, which contained songs of a national character. The references in the OT to the book are made in such a way as to imply that it was well known and respected, and consequently other references, though not positively identified, could be present in the OT.

The origin of the book is a matter of speculation, and it is generally believed that it was the result of a gradual compilation of material. On the basis of the Biblical references, it appears that it was a written collection, not oral, that was begun in the early period of Israel's history. As time went on, it was expanded, and at the time of the institution of the monarchy it probably became a part, and perhaps was the beginning, of the literary archives that formed the official records of the period of the monarchy.

"The uncertain and mysterious character of the missing Book of Jashar has led to attempts to reproduce, imitate, or falsify it. One of the last compositions of the haggadic lit. of Judaism, called the 'Book of Jashar,' is a falsification of the missing book in an attempt to reproduce it. It is written in good Heb. and has to do with the era from Adam to Judges. The greater part of this work is concerned with pre-Mosaic material. Much of the material is invention, interpolated between Biblical texts, in the author's desire to reconstruct the original Book of Jashar. Many legends are added to the Biblical narrative. The account of Abraham is given in elaborate detail, including stories of his two journeys to see his son Ishmael, and of an apparition of a star. It contains a detailed explanation of the murder of Abel by Cain.

"It is believed by some scholars that this attempt to reconstruct the OT Book of Jashar originated in southern Italy. The author was familiar with Italian place names. The Arab names in the book are due to the strong influence of Arab culture on southern Italy."

Book of Life: also called the Book of the Living, five Scriptures speak of this book: Philippians 4:3, Revelation 3:5, Revelation 13:8, Revelation 17:18, and Psalm 69:28

Philippians 4:3, "And I urge you also, true companion, help these women who labored with me in the gospel, with Clement also, and the rest of my fellow workers, whose names are in the Book of Life."

Revelation 3:5, "He who overcomes shall be clothed in white garments, and I will not blot out his name from the Book of Life; but I will confess his name before My Father and before His angels."

Revelation 13:8, "All who dwell on the earth will worship him, whose names have not been written in the Book of Life of the Lamb slain from the foundation of the world."

Revelation 17:18, "And the woman whom you saw is that great city which reigns over the kings of the earth."

Psalm 69:28 tells us of this book, "Let them be blotted out of the book of the living, and not be written with the righteous."

Book of Memorable Acts: another name for the Book of Chronicles (see Esther 6:1)

Book of Nathan the Prophet: a book written by Nathan the prophet; 1 Chronicles 29:29 tells us of this book: "Now the acts of King David, first and last, indeed they are written ... in the book of Nathan the prophet..." You can find supposed renditions of this book at online bookstores. This book is not on par with Scripture

Book of Records of Your Fathers: a book of records; Ezra 4:15 tells us of this book: "that search may be made in the book of the records of your fathers. And you will find in the book of the records and know that this city is a rebellious city, harmful to kings and provinces, and that they have incited sedition within the city in former times, for which cause this city was destroyed."

Book of Remembrance: a book God Himself writes in; Malachi 3:16 tells us of this book: "Then those who feared the Lord spoke to one another, and the Lord listened and heard them; So a book of remembrance was written before Him for those who fear the Lord and who meditate on His name."

Book of Samuel the Seer: books attributed to the authorship of Samuel the seer; 1 Chronicles 29:29 tells us of this book, 1 Chronicles 29:29 tells us of this book: "Now the acts of King David, first and last, indeed they are written in the book of Samuel the seer, in the book of Nathan the prophet, and in the book of Gad the seer..."

Book of Someone's Life: the book God has written about a person's life; Psalm 139:16 says, "You saw me before I was born. Every day of my life was recorded in your book. Every moment was laid out before a single day had passed." God has written the days of every person in a book. God can allow seers to look into the pages of the book of someone's life to minister life to them.

Book of the Acts of Solomon: a book about the acts of Solomon; 1 Kings 11:41 tells us about the existence of this book: "Now the rest of the acts of Solomon, all that he did, and his wisdom, are they not written in the book of the acts of Solomon?" *The Geneva Bible* editors suggest this book was lost during the exile in Babylon. However, you can purchase it today. This book is not on par with Scripture, but can be taken as more historical.

Book of the Covenant: also called the Covenant Code, Exodus 24:7 tells us of this book: "Then he took the Book of the Covenant and read in the hearing of the people. And they said, 'All that the Lord has said we will do, and be obedient.'" This book officially follows the Ten Commandments and spans Exodus chapters 20-23.

Book of the Genealogy of Christ: Matthew 1. Matthew 1:1 reads, "The book of the genealogy of Jesus Christ, the Son of David, the Son of Abraham."

Book of the Generations of Adam: Genesis 5. Genesis 5:1 reads, "This is the book of the genealogy of Adam. In the day that God created man, He made him in the likeness of God."

Book of the Law: the Pentateuch—the first five books of the Bible, Genesis, Exodus, Leviticus, Numbers, and Deuteronomy—written by Moses.

Deuteronomy 29:21 tells us of this book: "And the Lord would separate him from all the tribes of Israel for adversity, according to all the curses of the covenant that are written in this Book of the Law…"

Joshua 1:8 also speaks of this book: "This Book of the Law shall not depart from your mouth, but you shall meditate in it day and night, that you may observe to do according to all that is written in it. For then you will make your way prosperous, and then you will have good success."

Book of the Wars of the Lord: a book containing songs of victory the Israelites sang after winning battles; Numbers 21:14 tells us of this book: "Therefore it is said in the Book of the Wars of the Lord: 'Waheb in Suphah, the brooks of the Arnon…"

Book that is Sealed: books that cannot be opened; Three Scripture passages speak of books that are sealed:

Isaiah 29:11 reads, "The whole vision has become to you like the words of a book that is sealed, which men deliver to one who is literate, saying, 'Read this, please.' And he says, 'I cannot, for it is sealed.'"

Daniel 12:14 reads, "But you, Daniel, shut up the words, and seal the book until the time of the end; many shall run to and fro, and knowledge shall increase."

Revelation 5:9 reads, "And they sang a new song, saying: 'You are worthy to take the scroll, and to open its seals; For You were slain, and have redeemed us to God by Your blood out of every tribe and tongue and people and nation…"

Bottomless Pit: the realm of the dead, which is mentioned in the Book of Revelation four times (see Revelation 9:1; Revelation 11:7; Revelation 17:8; Revelation 20:1); another word for the bottomless pit is abyss, it's a pit with immeasurable depth.

An angel from heaven will hold the key to the bottomless pit, while there is a king over the abyss named *Abaddon* in Hebrew and *Apollyon* in Greek. The bottomless pit is the home of the beast who makes war against the two witnesses. Satan will be bound there during the Millennial Kingdom.

Breach in the Spirit: a violation of spiritual dimensions, either by sin, illegal operations of the seer or by enemy maneuvers (regardless of the source); Breaches open gaps in which the enemy can operate. This is why God looks for an intercessor to stand in the gap (see Ezekiel 22:30) and for repairers of the breach.

Isaiah 58:12 reads, "Those from among you shall build the old waste places; You shall raise up the foundations of many generations; And you shall be called the Repairer of the Breach, The Restorer of Streets to Dwell In." This verse refers to the Lord Himself as the Repairer, but God can call seer-intercessors to work with Him to repair breaches in the spirit."

Proverbs 15:4 (KJV), "A wholesome tongue is a tree of life: but perverseness therein is a breach in the spirit." The tongue is not the only means of a breach. Eyes can breach spiritual protocols. In the context of the seer, this is called illegal access or moving through back doors in the spirit.

The Hebrew word breach in Proverbs 15:4 is *sheber*. It means breaking, fracture, crushing, crash, ruin, shattering. When a seer breaches spiritual dimensions, he is breaking in or crashing in without an invitation of the Lord. He is shattering spiritual protocols and opening himself up for deception.

Bread from Heaven: daily revelation from the throne room of God. Exodus 16:4 speaks of the bread of heaven: "Then the Lord said to Moses, "Behold, I will rain bread from heaven for you. And the people shall go out and gather a certain quota every day, that I may test them, whether they will walk in My law or not." Bread from Heaven is God's daily provision. Jesus taught the disciples to pray, "Give us this day our daily bread" (Matthew 6:11).

In Matthew 4:4, Jesus brings it home to the seer, saying, "It is written, 'Man shall not live by bread alone, but by every word that proceeds from the mouth of God.'" Seers have to show up to the heavenly food line to receive their daily bread, like manna falling from heaven.

This is the John 4:32, "meat that you know not of." Meat often symbolizes revelation in the seer dimensions. God will give the seer a complete meal—a heavenly sandwich that will satisfy your hunger—as the seer seeks His face.

Bread of Adversity: situations the Lord uses to sanctify us, combat pride in us, and prepare us as a vessel to help others; Isaiah 30:20 reads," And though the Lord gives you the bread of adversity and the water of affliction, yet your teachers will not be moved into a corner anymore, but your eyes shall see your teachers."

Bread of Life: another name for Jesus; in seer dimensions, you may see the bread of life as a symbol for Jesus; Jesus said, "I am the bread of life. He who comes to Me shall never hunger, and he who believes in Me shall never thirst" (see John 6:35).

Bread of the Presence: also called showbread (see Exodus 25:30) or holy bread (see 1 Samuel 1:24); The Bread of the Presence is the bread that was always present on a table in the temple. The Bible requires the bread to be constantly in the presence of God. David ate the showbread (see Matthew 12:4).

Break the Seal: also see loose the seal, to break open the seal that contains visions of the end times. Only Jesus can break the seal. Seers who claim they have broken the seal are in deception. Revelation 5:1-5 reads:

"And I saw in the right hand of Him who sat on the throne a scroll written inside and on the back, sealed with seven seals. Then I saw a strong angel proclaiming with a loud voice, 'Who is worthy to open the scroll and to loose its seals?' And no one in heaven or on the earth or under the earth was able to open the scroll, or to look at it. So I wept much, because no one was found worthy to open and read the scroll, or to look at it. But one of the elders said to me, 'Do not weep. Behold, the Lion of the tribe of Judah, the Root of David, has prevailed to open the scroll and to loose its seven seals.'"

Breaker Anointing: an anointing to break through opposition to God's will in a seer's personal life, or corporately. The concept of the breaker anointing comes from Micah 2:13, "The breaker is come up before them: they have broken up, and have passed through the gate, and are gone out by it: and their king shall pass before them, and the Lord on the head of them."

The Breaker is the Lord Jesus Christ. Isaiah 10:27 offers more understanding: "It shall come to pass in that day that his burden will be taken away from your shoulder, and his yoke from your neck, and the yoke will be destroyed because of the anointing oil."

And again Isaiah 61:1, "The Spirit of the Lord God is upon Me, because the Lord has anointed Me to preach good tidings to the poor; He has sent Me to heal the brokenhearted, to proclaim liberty to the captives, and the opening of the prison to those who are bound."

Breath of the Almighty: another name for the Holy Spirit; Job 33:4 reads, "The Spirit of God has made me, and the breath of the Almighty gives me life."

Bridegroom: another name for Jesus, as seen in Matthew 9:15: "And Jesus said to them, 'Can the friends of the bridegroom mourn as long as the bridegroom is with them? But the days will come when the bridegroom will be taken away from them, and then they will fast.'"

Brightness: a visual indication of the presence of the Lord; Psalm 18:12 says, "From the brightness before Him, His thick clouds passed with hailstones and coals of fire." And Isaiah 60:19 speaks of the brightness of His rising. Habakkuk 3:4 says, "His brightness was like the light; He had rays flashing from His hand, And there His power was hidden."

Ezekiel 1:27 goes deeper into this concept: "Also from the appearance of His waist and upward I saw, as it were, the color of amber with the appearance of fire all around within it; and from the appearance of His waist and downward I saw, as it were, the appearance of fire with brightness all around."

2 Thessalonians 2:8 speaks of "the brightness of His coming." And Hebrews 1:3 says, "who being the brightness of His glory and the express image of His person, and upholding all things by the word of His power, when He had by Himself purged our sins, sat down at the right hand of the Majesty on high."

Bronze Heaven: also called a brass heaven or a hard heaven, a bronze heaven is a heaven that is hard; Bronze is a hard metal. For frame of reference, it's harder than both copper and iron.

When you find bronze, brass, or copper heavens—when it feels like a hard heaven and your prayers don't seem to be working—you'll often find Behemoth's systems are prevailing. Bronze heavens are part of the curse of the law. Deuteronomy 28:23 reads "And your heavens which are over your head shall be bronze, and the earth which is under you shall be iron."

Bronze is a mixture of metals—not pure like gold or silver. According to *Sciencing.com*, "It is extremely strong and resistant to atmospheric corrosion. It has been used since prehistoric times to forge tools, weapons, statues and ornaments."

Burden: typically used to describe a prayer burden

C

Calamity: seers may see calamity through dreams and visions; Jeremiah and others warned repeatedly of calamity, also called a disaster. The purpose of God showing a seer calamity is to pray and warn the people of what the enemy is planning in the unseen realm so as to avert it.

Camp: describing a company or tribe of seers: different camps have different distinguishing factors, either by denomination or culture or by the flow of their revelation, etc.; The danger often found in camps is that its members camp out on a revelation and may not pursue seer diversity.

Canopy: the protective covering of God Himself that spreads out over a person or a congregation; this canopy can take on different forms, and hence different colors; You may see a canopy of love or a canopy of angels, etc. The canopy forms a shelter.

Two scriptures speak of this canopy. Job 36:29 reads, "Indeed, can anyone understand the spreading of clouds, The thunder from His canopy?" and Psalm 18:11 reads, "He made darkness His secret place; His canopy around Him was dark waters *and* thick clouds of the skies."

Carnal Mind: an enemy to the seer, the carnal mind can blind or dramatically reduce spiritual vision; Romans 8:6 says, "For to be carnally minded is death, but to be spiritually minded is life and peace."

Cave: a hiding place for seers and prophets who fear persecution; If Jezebel can't kill a seer's anointing through perversion or hinder their operations with spiritual warfare, she will tempt the seer to hide in a cave.

Consider this reality in 1 Kings 18:4, "For so it was, while Jezebel massacred the prophets of the Lord, that Obadiah had taken one hundred prophets and hidden them, fifty to a cave, and had fed them with bread and water."

Ceiling: the height of a seer's gift; a growth plateau seers reach; an invisible barrier through which the seer must break to get to the next level

Celestial: relating to the second or third heavens; 1 Corinthians 15:40, "There are also celestial bodies and terrestrial bodies; but the glory of the celestial is one, and the glory of the terrestrial is another."

The Greek word for celestial in this verse is *epouranios*. According to *The KJV New Testament Greek Lexicon*, it means, "existing in heaven, things that take place in heaven, the heavenly regions, heaven itself, the abode of God and angels, the lower heavens, of the stars, the heavens, of the clouds, the heavenly temple or sanctuary, of heavenly origin or nature."

Celestial bodies are referring to spiritual beings, including angels. Some debatably include the planets and the stars as celestial bodies, but the host of heaven—angels—are definitely in this classification.

Certain Time: *see Kairos Time*

Chalcedony: a translucent quartz precious stone John the Revelator saw on the foundations of the wall around the New Jerusalem (see Revelation 21:19-21)

Chamber: a room in the courts of heaven; Seers and seeing people may see into the courts of heaven, hearing accusations of the enemy for the purpose of legislating in prayer.

Channel: a backdoor in the spirit of which seers should beware: a demonic portal through which information can be transmitted by familiar spirits; Channelers—those who see into the spirit realm how dead relatives are doing, and send back messages—are forbidden in the Bible.

Seers who do not go through the door of Jesus could be deceived and channel through a familiar spirit. God forbids this. Leviticus 19:31, "Give no regard to mediums and familiar spirits; do not seek after them, to be defiled by them: I am the Lord your God."

Charismatic Movement: a Christian renewal movement birthed in the 1970s that emphasized the gifts of the Holy Spirit, with a focus on the presence and power of God

Charm: an incantation or spell. Seers can at times see spells—or the effects of spells—in the spirit; Seers may discern witchcraft or the practitioners of witchcraft. Deuteronomy 8:9-12 speaks against charmers and charms.

Chattering Spirits: *see Peeping Spirits*

Check in Your Spirit: a caution or lack of peace in your inner man; an internal knowing that you should or should not do or say something

Cherubim: angelic beings (see Exodus 25:20); Cherubim expelled Adam and Eve from the Garden of Eden (see Genesis. 3:24). Cherubim sits to the right and left of God's throne, seen as an image above the Ark of the Covenant.

Chew on a dream: to meditate on a prophetic dream, pondering its meaning

Chief Cornerstone: another name for Jesus, as seen in Psalm 118:22: "The stone which the builders rejected has become the chief cornerstone."

Children's Bread: deliverance for believers; In Matthew 15:26 when a Samaritan was seeking deliverance for her daughter, Jesus said, "It is not good to take the children's bread and throw it to the little dogs."

Chirping Spirits: *see Peeping Spirits*

Chozeh: a third word used for prophet in the Old Testament, which we find in 2 Samuel, 2 Kings, 1 and 2 Chronicles, Isiah, Amos, and Micah is *chozeh*; According to *The NAS Old Testament Hebrew Lexicon*, it also means "seer." The word *chozeh* occurs 22 times in the Hebrew Old Testament; on 11

of these occasions, it is linked with people to whom God had given a prophetic ministry.

Chozeh prophets are also seers, but it's a different type of seeing. According to *Strong's Concordance*, *chozeh* is an active participle of the Hebrew word *chazah*, which means "beholder of a vision." This word occurs 46 times in the Old Testament.

The NAS Old Testament Hebrew Lexicon defines *chazah* as "to perceive, look, behold, prophesy, provide; to see as a seer in the ecstatic state; with intelligence."

David's seer Gad was this type of prophet (see 1 Chronicles 21:9). Often, the *chazah* prophet sees and hears from God at the same time, as the ancient Aramaic meaning of *chazah* is "the hearing eye" or "the seeing ear."

Chronicle: a written report of what a seer sees in the spirit or dreamt for the purpose of preserving the revelation either to share with others accurately and/or for further meditation to unlock additional revelation

Chronicler: one who chronicles

Chrysolite: a greenish stone John the Revelator saw on the foundations of the wall around the New Jerusalem (see Revelation 21:19-21)

Chrysoprase: an apple-greenish colored precious stone John the Revelator saw on the foundations of the wall around the New Jerusalem (see Revelation 21:19-21)

Closed Vision: *see Inner Vision*

Closet: a place of prayer

Closeup: a vision in the seer dimensions where the focus seems zoomed in; Think about a lens on a camera that can see far beyond what the naked eye alone could view—and see it in minute detail.

Cloud: often representing the presence of God: seers may see glory clouds, the cloud of witnesses; Daniel saw the clouds of heaven in Daniel 3:17: "I was watching in the night visions, and behold, One like the Son of Man, coming with the clouds of heaven! He came to the Ancient of Days, and they brought Him near before Him."

John saw a white cloud: "Then I looked, and behold, a white cloud, and on the cloud sat One like the Son of Man, having on His head a golden crown, and in His hand a sharp sickle" (Revelation 14:14). Thick clouds veil the Lord (see Job 22:14). Clouds can also be demonic, including dark clouds.

Cloud of Witnesses: people who have passed into glory who are in heaven with the Lord; Hebrews 12:1 says, "We are encompassed with such a great cloud of witnesses…" There's been much debate about who these witnesses are, but the general belief is that they are members of the Hebrews 11 "Hall of Faith" and others who walked with the Lord.

Barnes' Notes on the Bible reads, "The phrase, 'a cloud of witnesses,' means many witnesses, or a number so great that they seem to be a cloud." These witnesses are those who went before us who bore witness to the truth.

Cloudy in the Spirit: conditions in which it is difficult to see clearly in the spirit; hard to get an accurate picture of what is happening

Come Up Here: a Holy Spirit invitation to ascend in order to receive visual revelation or encounter the Lord or His angels (see Revelation 4:1)

Comforter: another name for the Holy Spirit

Commission: typically known as an ordination, commissioning is the laying on of hands by elders to charge one to fulfill his or her ministry duties in the grace of God;

Jehu was anointed with oil and commissioned as king with an assignment to take down Jezebel (see 2 Kings 9:2). Elijah commissioned Elisha to follow in his footsteps by throwing his mantle upon him.

Paul commissioned Timothy by the laying of hands, as referenced in 2 Timothy 1:6, "Therefore I remind you to stir up the gift of God which is in you through the laying on of my hands. For God has not given us a spirit of fear, but of power and of love and of a sound mind."

In 1 Timothy 1:18-19, we see Paul reminding his son of the commissioning: "This charge I commit to you, son Timothy, according to the prophecies previously made concerning you, that by them you may wage the good warfare, having faith and a good conscience, which some having rejected, concerning the faith have suffered shipwreck…"

Company of Prophets: a group, family, nest, hub or school of prophets or seers; a fellowship or network of prophetic people; a camp within the prophetic movement

Company of Seers: *see Company of Prophets*

Concealed: something hidden from view, either by the enemy or by God; The enemy hides in shadows and can be difficult to distinguish, which is why we have to ask God to break in with light. But God can also conceal things from us.

The Lord hid the reality that the Shunammite woman's son died from Elisha. He had prophesied her pregnancy and it came to pass, but some years later the boy was injured in the field working with his father. When he died, she laid him on Elisha's bed in the prophet's quarters they had prepared for him and went to see the man of God.

"Now when she came to the man of God at the hill, she caught him by the feet, but Gehazi came near to push her away. But the man of God said, 'Let her alone; for her soul is in deep distress, and the Lord has hidden it from me, and has not told me'" (2 Kings 4:27).

Conclusion of the Matter: the takeaway or action steps one should understand based on the interpretation of the dream or vision; Ecclesiastes 12:13 reads, "Let us hear the conclusion of the whole matter: Fear God and keep His commandments, for this is man's all."

Conditional Dreams: dreams that show what God wants to do, but are conditional on people acting on the dream

Conditional Visions: visions that show what God wants to do, but are conditional on people acting on the vision

Confirmation: information or revelation that further establishes or coincides with other information or revelation; God-given evidence or proof that your revelation came from him; by the mouth of two or three witnesses confirmation is established (see 2 Corinthians 3:1)

Confirming Dreams: dreams that confirm a circumstance the Lord has been speaking to you or someone else about; dreams that confirm what you already know to be true; dreams that confirm prophetic words; dreams that confirm visions; dreams that confirm other dreams

Confirming Visions: visions that confirm a circumstance the Lord has been speaking to you or someone else about; visions that confirm what you already know to be true; visions that confirm prophetic words; a vision that confirms a dream; a vision that confirms another vision

Conjure: a practice of false prophets and seers to summon familiar spirits to retrieve information about their victims, or intelligence from the spirit realm; This information false seers conjure up by invocation or incantation may be accurate but the source is demonic

Consecration: to pull away from something in order to draw to God. Seers must consecrate their eyes; that is to set them apart for God's use. It's critical that seers guard their eye gates so that worldly influences don't taint their spiritual vision; Romans 12:1-2 puts it this way:

I beseech you therefore, brethren, by the mercies of God, that you present your bodies a living sacrifice, holy, acceptable to God, which is your reasonable service. And do not be conformed to this world, but be transformed by the renewing of your mind, that you may prove what *is* that good and acceptable and perfect will of God.

Consider the Vision: to meditate, ponder and pray about the vision in order to find deeper meanings and applications; This was Daniel's practice.

"At the beginning of your supplications the command went out, and I have come to tell you, for you *are* greatly beloved; therefore consider the matter, and understand the vision" (Daniel 9:23).

Conspiracy: an unlawful alliance in the spirit that seeks to oppose the will of God; While there can be godly conspiracies, most conspiracies are wicked. (See Judges 9:1; 2 Samuel 15:12; 2 Kings 12:20; 2 Kings 14:19; 2 Kings 15:15 as examples.)

Consuming Fire: another name for God as seen in Deuteronomy 4:24: "For the Lord your God is a consuming fire, a jealous God."

Contemplate: to think about a spiritual truth for extended periods of time; to keep a matter in mind

Contemplation: the act of contemplating

Contemplative Prayer: If you ask 10 leaders what contemplative prayer is, you may get 10 different answers. There's no one standard definition. Let's start by understanding the word contemplative, which is related to contemplation. Contemplation is a concentration on spiritual things as a form of private devotion or a state of mystical awareness of God's being. It's an act of considering with attention, the act of regarding steadily, intention and expectation.

Contemplative prayer is an ancient Christian practice that dates all the way back to the early church and even to the life of King David. The Psalms give proof of David's contemplative prayer life. Contemplative prayer releases the

Holy Spirit's supernatural activity in our spirits as we encounter His heart. We enter into enjoyable communion with God that transforms us.

(I write more about this in my book, *The Seer Dimensions*, and teach on it in the *School of the Seers* at schoolofthespirit.tv.)

Continuing Prophetic Education: the ongoing study and outside instruction of prophets and seers; a necessary commitment to continuing to grow in the gifts and offices to which God calls prophetic people

Contracts: binding agreements between two or more parties, including demon powers; Just as in the natural realm, contracts are legally enforceable agreements, and are inked in the spirit with the words of your mouth in the form of pledges and vows. Seers may see contracts in the spirit between people and demons or false prophets that need to be broken, as well as positive covenants God is linking between people in divine connections.

Conversation: a verbal exchange that can happen between the seer and God, the seer and an angel, the seer and some other spiritual being, the seer and an elder in heaven, or the seer and a demon; a two-way exchange of information, such as when an angel brings a message and the seer asks for help understanding when the Lord asks the seer what he sees, etc.

Corruption: the fate of seers who seek platforms and paychecks (fame and fortune) instead of exclusively seeking to glorify God with their seer gift; The eyes of these seers become slaves to corruption and their prophetic revelation is tainted. This is dangerous because the seer becomes the blind leading the blind, deceiving and being deceived.

When seers consistently sow to the flesh, they reap corruption (see Galatians 6:8). Speaking of corrupted ones, 2 Peter 2:19 tells us "While they promise them liberty, they themselves are slaves of corruption; for by whom a person is overcome, by him also he is brought into bondage."

Cost: the price to pay to operate in high levels of the seer anointing. Jesus speaks of counting the costs in Luke 14:26-33:

"If anyone comes to Me and does not hate his father and mother, wife and children, brothers and sisters, yes, and his own life also, he cannot be My disciple. And whoever does not bear his cross and come after Me cannot be My disciple.

"For which of you, intending to build a tower, does not sit down first and count the cost, whether he has enough to finish it—lest, after he has laid the foundation, and is not able to finish, all who see it begin to mock him, saying, 'This man began to build and was not able to finish?'

"Or what king, going to make war against another king, does not sit down first and consider whether he is able with ten thousand to meet him who comes against him with twenty thousand? Or else, while the other is still a great way off, he sends a delegation and asks conditions of peace. So likewise, whoever of you does not forsake all that he has cannot be My disciple."

Council: an assembly or group of people the seer has access to or gathers to judge what they see in the spirit, discuss spiritual things, get advice on personal matters, or to consult on spiritual warfare challenges

Council of God: *see Secret Council of God*

Counselor: another name for the Holy Spirit (see John 14:16); another name for Jesus seen in Isaiah 9:6: "For unto us a Child is born, unto us a Son is given; And the government will be upon His shoulder. And His name will be called Wonderful, Counselor, Mighty God, Everlasting Father, Prince of Peace."

Counterfeit Anointing: the power behind lying signs and wonders (see 2 Thessalonians 2:9); 1 John 2:27 speaks of a counterfeit anointing: "As for you, the anointing you received from him remains in you, and you do not need anyone to teach you. But as his anointing teaches you about all things and as that anointing is real, not counterfeit—just as it has taught you, remain in him."

Counterfeit Spirits: an imitation of God's voice, Spirit or heavenly host; deceiving spirits that work to convince you of revelations that contradict the Word of God; deceptive spirits that mimic God's voice

Course of Time: *see Process of Time*

Courtroom of Heaven: although not a phrase used in the Bible itself, the concept of the courts of heaven is biblical. Revelation 12:10 shares, "Then I heard a loud voice saying in heaven, 'Now salvation, and strength, and the kingdom of our God, and the power of His Christ have come, for the accuser of our brethren, who accused them before our God day and night, has been cast down.'"

The idea is that God as judge presides over cases the enemy has brought against someone in heaven. The open cases are what gives him legal access to your life. When a person appears before the courts of heaven and repents, it closes the case and strips the enemy of his power in that area of their life.

Crooked Serpent: another name for Satan (see Isaiah 27:1)

Crown of Life: a reward for believers who persevere in trials. James 1:12,: "Blessed is the man who endures temptation; for when he has been approved, he will receive the crown of life which the Lord has promised to those who love Him." A seer may see the crown of life over someone who has gone home to be with the Lord to comfort those who mourn.

Crucify the Flesh: denying the desires of the flesh: Paul wrote, "And those who are Christ's have crucified the flesh with its passions and desires" (see Galatians 5:24).

One of the seer's goal should be to walk in the reality of Galatians 2:20, "I have been crucified with Christ; it is no longer I who live, but Christ lives in me; and the life which I now live in the flesh I live by faith in the Son of God, who loved me and gave Himself for me."

When Christ lives in us, our spiritual sight increases dramatically. When our flesh rules, our spiritual eyesight grows dimmer.

Cruel Vision: *see Grievous Vision*

Crushing: the process through which many prophets and seers go as part of God's refining process; a series of trials and tribulations that mold the seer into the image of Christ, the ultimate Seer

Consider the *Merriam-Webster's* definition of crush: "to squeeze or force by pressure so as to alter or destroy structure." When grapes go through the winepress, they are crushed to become something new.

Curse: maledictions; evil decrees against a person, place, or thing; thoughts of evil or injury upon a person; imprecatory prayers for the sake of vengeance; words of condemnation, judgment, vexation, affliction or other forms of harm;

According to *Easton's Bible Dictionary*, "Prophetical curses were sometimes pronounced by holy men (Genesis 9:25; 49:7; Deuteronomy 27:15; Joshua 6:26). Such curses are not the consequence of passion or revenge, they are predictions."

Cursed Things: also called detestable things and abominations, cursed things—or accursed things—carry curses that hinder the lives of unsuspecting people;

Deuteronomy 7:26 tells us, "Nor shall you bring an abomination into your house, lest you be doomed to destruction like it. You shall utterly detest it and utterly abhor it, for it is an accursed thing." At times, God will show seers the cursed objects in people's homes so they can cleanse their houses from evil. (Find more in the book, *Cleansing Your Home from Evil.*)

Cycle: a period of time during which events repeat themselves in the spirit or in the natural. In heaven, the seraphim cry "holy, holy, holy" in a cycle (see Isaiah 6:2-4); The Bible also speaks of time and harvest time, day and night, etc.

D

Damascus Road Experience: an encounter with God that occurs when you are moving against His will; an encounter that is dramatic, startling and leaves a major impact on your life (See Acts 9)

Daniel: a prophet of princely lineage who wrote the Book of Daniel; Daniel lived about 620–538 B.C. and was carried off to Babylon in 605 B.C. by Nebuchadnezzar. Daniel stood in one of the highest offices of the state of Babylon, even though he was in captivity. He had significant dreams and visions of the end-times, and also possessed the gift of interpreting dreams.

Dark Dreams: dreams marked by the presence of evil; Dark dreams often reveal spiritual warfare, hopeless situations, or depressing circumstances. Dark dreams can reveal the enemy's plans to attack finances, relationships, health, or other areas of a person's life. It's vital that you discern the source of these dreams and stand against the enemy's plans.

Dark Night of the Soul: a spiritual crisis of sorts, in which you don't seem to feel God's presence, hear His voice or see what He is doing in our life; Different from a wilderness experience, a dark night of the soul is a transition into a deeper union with God by faith.

Dark Sayings: sayings that are difficult to understand, except by the Spirit of God; Psalm 78:2 reads, "I will open my mouth in a parable; I will utter dark sayings of old…" and Proverbs 1:6 (KJV) reads, "To understand a proverb, and the interpretation; the words of the wise, and their dark sayings."

Dark Side: the enemy's domain; When seers or seeing people operate in illegal maneuvers to access the seer dimensions, they are not accessing heaven's revelation but second-hand information from familiar spirits. True prophets and seers operate in the light. False prophets and seers operate on the dark side, like the Witch at Endor who called up Samuel from the dead at King Saul's request (see 1 Samuel 28).

Dark Speech: *see Dark Sayings*

Dark Spirit: an invading force on assignment to steal, kill, or destroy. The seer may not be able to immediately discern what spirit it is because it's cloaked in darkness. This is where the seer has to press into listening to the voice of the Lord to get more insight. Psalm 139:12 says, "Indeed, the darkness shall not hide from You, but the night shines as the day; The darkness and the light are both alike to You."

Dark Visions: visions marked by the presence of evil; Dark visions often reveal spiritual warfare, hopeless situations, or depressing circumstances. Dark visions can reveal the enemy's plans to attack finances, relationships, health, or other areas of a person's life. It's vital that you discern the source of these dreams and stand against the enemy's plans.

Darkened Eyes: eyes that do not see. David prayed an imprecatory prayer: "Let their table become a snare before them, and their well-being a trap. Let their eyes be darkened, so that they do not see; And make their loins shake continually. Pour out Your indignation upon them, and let Your wrathful anger take hold of them" (Psalm 69:22-24). When you are dealing with monitoring spirits, one strategy is to ask God to darken their eyes.

By contrast, a seer who goes wayward can find their eyes have been darkened. The seer's spiritual sight grows dim or even dark when they operate in rebellion to God's will. Although the gifts and callings are without repentance, remember God darkened the eyes of Paul the apostle on the Road to Damascus to get his attention (see Acts 9).

Darkly: something hidden in darkness that can't be clearly recognized or easily expressed; a spirit being, either an angel, a living creature, demon or other creation, that is obscured from plain sight either by the Lord or by demon powers;

Paul wrote, "For now we see through a glass, darkly; but then face to face: now I know in part; but then shall I know even as also I am known" (1 Corinthians 13:12).

Ellicott's Bible Commentary for English Readers says, "The illustration here is from a mirror when the image appears far behind the mirror itself. If we remember the imperfect metal surfaces which formed the mirrors of those days, we can imagine how imperfect and enigmatical (the Greek word is in an enigma) would the image appear."

Darkness: the absence of God's light; a place without revelation light; a place where pestilence walks (see Psalm 91:6); the shadow of death (see Psalm 107:10); a place the enemy dwells (see Psalm 143:3)

Also relevant to the seer are Jesus' words in Matthew 6:22-23, "The lamp of the body is the eye. If therefore your eye is good, your whole body will be full of light. But if your eye is bad, your whole body will be full of darkness. If therefore the light that is in you is darkness, how great is that darkness!" The seer must guard his eyes from darkness so darkness does not affect his spiritual sight.

Dart: a weapon of the enemy you may see in the spirit; Paul mentions fiery darts of the enemy in Ephesians 6:16. You don't have to be afraid of darts in the spirit, which may be attacking you—or someone or something else. Job 41:29 assures us, "Darts are regarded as straw; He laughs at the threat of javelins." Instead, you pray against them.

Day of the Lord: also called "that day," the Day of the Lord is the Second Coming of Jesus Christ; a time of salvation and judgment; the culmination of the end of the age; 1 Thessalonians 5:1-2 reads, "But concerning the times and the seasons, brethren, you have no need that I should write to you.

For you yourselves know perfectly that the day of the Lord so comes as a thief in the night."

Day Star: another name for Satan (see Isaiah 14:12)

Daydream: a vision in one's own imagination; not to be confused with divine revelation

Deborah: a prophetess and a judge in the Book of Judges who led the Israelites into victorious battle (see Judges 4-5)

Deceive: any attempt or tactic to manipulate the truth for one's own advantage; subtly putting forth a lie or falsity that misleads someone into taking a desired action

Deceived: the state of one's mind that is under the influence or control of a lie; Eve said the serpent deceived her (see Genesis 3:13).

Deceiver: another name for Satan (see Revelation 12:9)

Deceptive Visions: visions conjured up in man's imagination to lead people astray; Lamentations 2:14 warns us, "Your prophets have seen for you false and deceptive visions; They have not uncovered your iniquity, to bring back your captives, but have envisioned for you false prophecies and delusions."

Decree: words that carry the force of God's law to cut off the enemy's plans and/or to establish His will in the earth as it is in heaven; Sometimes the Lord will have a seer decree what he sees.

Deep Darkness: the deepest blackness such as occurs in the middle of the night, where nothing is visible; a darkness that brings obscurity to your vision; hindered visibility as by heavy, dark clouds

Deep Sleep: a state of sleep when God escorts you into a seer dimension, and you may or may not remember the entire encounter; Job 4:13 reveals, "In disquieting thoughts from the visions of the night, when deep sleep falls on men."

Deep Things of God: the depths of God; the deeper truths of God; revelations below the surface that can only be brought forth by the Spirit of God. Paul said in 1 Corinthians 2:10, "But God has revealed them to us through His Spirit. For the Spirit searches all things, yes, the deep things of God."

Defect in the Eye: a spiritual problem, such as a bias or sin, in the seer's eye that skews his vision; Leviticus 20:4 reveals, "And if the people of the land should in any way hide their eyes from the man, when he gives some of his descendants to Molech, and they do not kill him."

Degree: the temperature in the spirit; a rank or position; the extent or measure of a thing; Seers can sometimes see temperatures of churches or atmospheres, people's ranks, or the degree to which something is damaged.

Deliberation: the process of pondering and/or discussing the interpretation and application of a seer revelation with other seers and prophets who help judge the dream, vision, or encounter

Delilah Spirit: a nemesis of seers; a woman in Judges that seduced Samson and delivered him to the enemy to gouge out his eyes

Deliverance: freedom from demonic powers that have infiltrated the souls of people and developed strongholds in minds or brought disease to bodies; God's rescue from enemy attack; Seers can often see the demons oppressing people, which is helpful in the process of casting them out.

Deliverer: another name for Jesus seen in 1 Thessalonians 1:10: "and to wait for His Son from heaven, whom He raised from the dead, even Jesus who delivers us from the wrath to come."

Delusion: *see Strong Delusion*

Demon: evil spirits roaming the earth under Satan's command (see Luke 4:35; Luke 11:15; John 10:21)

Demonic: someone or something inspired by demons

Demonic Chatter: the sound of demons conspiring in the spirit; the voice of vain imaginations launched against someone's mind

Demonic Dimension: a dimension in the spirit where a seer is aware of or sets his spiritual eyes on demon powers; second heaven encounters; (Learn more in the book, *The Seer Dimensions*.)

Demonic Dust: residue of a past attack that brings fear, discouragement, bitterness, resentment or unforgiveness into someone's soul; The seer can sometimes see demonic dust on a person as they pray.

Demonic Encounter: an encounter with demon forces

Demonic Messengers: demons who visit seers and seeing people with messages, usually with some form of deception, intimidation tactic, or threat

Demonic Wisdom: wisdom that comes from the pits of hell and sets out to lead people astray; James 3:14-15 says, "But if you have bitter envy and self-seeking in your hearts, do not boast and lie against the truth. This wisdom does not descend from above, but is earthly, sensual, demonic."

Depart From Me: words Jesus will say to false prophets, seers, deliverance ministers and miracle workers on Judgement Day; words that should inspire a fear of the Lord among seers and prophets who operate in His name and under His authority;

In Matthew 7:21-23 Jesus said, "Not everyone who says to Me, 'Lord, Lord,' shall enter the kingdom of heaven, but he who does the will of My Father in heaven. Many will say to Me in that day, 'Lord, Lord, have we not prophesied in Your name, cast out demons in Your name, and done many wonders in Your name?' And then I will declare to them, 'I never knew you; depart from Me, you who practice lawlessness!'"

Descend: to come back from heaven to earth; to go into demonic realms, including hell. Seers cannot ascend or descend at will, but only through the door of Jesus, who is the Way;

Speaking of Jesus, Ephesians 4:9-10 says, "When He ascended on high, He led captivity captive, and gave gifts to men." (Now this, "He ascended"—what does it mean but that He also first descended into the lower parts of the earth? He who descended is also the One who ascended far above all the heavens, that He might fill all things.)"

Describe: the responsibility of the seer to tell forth what he saw with as much accurate detail as possible; In Habakkuk 2:2, the Lord told the prophet, "Write the vision and make it plain on tablets, that he may run who reads it."

Desert Place: *see Wilderness*

Destiny: a predestined outcome of the Lord for your life. Although the word destiny is not used in the *King James Version of the Bible* and is used rather loosely in some other translations, the word predestined is; Seers can often see into someone's destiny; *see also Predestined*

Destroyer: another name for the devil; demons that destroy; In John 10:10, Jesus said the enemy comes to steal, kill, and destroy. Paul specifically mentions the Destroyer in 1 Corinthians 10:8-10, "Nor let us commit sexual immorality, as some of them did, and in one day twenty-three thousand fell; nor let us tempt Christ, as some of them also tempted, and were destroyed by serpents; nor complain, as some of them also complained, and were destroyed by the destroyer." (Also see Hebrews 11:8; Exodus 12:23).

Detail: an aspect of a dream, vision, or encounter; something that stands out in a prophetic revelation as a matter of emphasis; the ability to describe with precision a seer revelation

Device: a tactic of the enemy; Paul warned us not to be ignorant of the devil's devices (2 Corinthians 2:11). Clearly, God wants us to understand the enemy's devices. Some translations say "sly ways," "schemes," "designs," "intentions," and "thoughts." The word *devices* in 2 Corinthians 2:11 comes from the Greek word *noema*, according to The King James New Testament Greek Lexicon. It means a material perception, "a mental perception, thought; an evil purpose; that which thinks, the mind, thoughts or purposes."

Devil: another name for Satan (see Revelation 12:9)

Difficult Vision: *see Grievous Vision*

Dim: a condition of one's spiritual eyes in which spiritual light is not entering due to demonic oppression or sin; dullness of spirit; faint visual perception due to spiritual atmospheric conditions; the inability to perceive clearly or fully what is happening in the spirit realm

Dimension: a measure or element of the seer realm

Diminishing Dreams: a condition, usually temporary, in which the dream life gives way to other modes of godly revelation

Diminishing Visions: a condition, usually temporary, in which visionary revelation gives way to other modes of godly revelation

Diplomacy: a seer skill that helps us communicate prophetic revelation with tact, without offending the hearers or sparking hostility; Sometimes that's not possible as some will be offended by God's Word.

Diplomacy in the seer dimensions begins with the way we see God. In order to express God's heart in a matter, we need to see His heart and not just His visions or dreams. If we miss God's heart, we can miscommunicate His will and lead people astray or cause them to shut their ears to the message.

When we see well, we will share responsibly. If we see God through the lens of our bias, we will speak with prejudice. If we see God through the filter of bitterness, we will speak with judgement. If we see God through the ears of grace and mercy, we will speak the bold truth in love.

Direction: seer revelation that offers guidance on how someone or some group should think, see, or act: seer revelation that inspires or motivates someone to take godly action to accomplish His purposes

Discern: the ability to accurately test the spirits; the quality of distinguishing between something good and bad, or between something good and something better; Interestingly, *Merriam-Webster's* definition of discern is "to detect with the eyes" which shows you the importance of visual revelation both in the natural and the spirit to judge a thing. Of course, there are many ways to discern besides visual revelation.

Discerner: one who discerns angels, demons and God; one who discerns the motives of people

Discernment: *see Discern*

Discerning of Spirits: insight into the spirit world; the ability to discern or perceive a spirit or activity in the spirit realm; Discerning of spirits is more than man's wisdom or common sense or criticism. We must not only discern evil spirits but also the Holy Spirit and angels (see Acts 9:3-8; 16:16-18).

Discover: to find prophetic intelligence by looking into the spirit realm

Discretion: a heart posture that is cautious in what it does or says publicly for the sake of protecting and preserving a person's privacy or dignity, or safeguarding the plans of God; a quality connected to the discerning person; an attribute vital to the success of a seer's ministry; operating in a way that is unnoticeable, under the enemy's radar screen;

Nathan used discretion when he brought a parable to David that caused David to see and ultimately face his sin in committing adultery with Bathsheba and having her husband Uriah murdered on the frontlines of battle (see 2 Samuel 11).

Dispensation: the working out of God's plan in any given space of time; some theologians contend there were four dispensations in the Old Testament and one dispensation in the New Testament—the dispensation of grace

Distance in the Spirit: different than distance in the natural that is measured by inches or miles, distance in the spirit is a concept rooted in God's omnipresence; Since God is everywhere, there is no distance in the spirit in the sense that someone can pray for you in China and God can immediately respond in America.

By the same token, the seer can find himself in spirit travel and discover himself on the other side of the city or of the world in an instant because there's no distance in the spirit. This happened with Philip and the Ethiopian in Acts 8:38.

And both Philip and the eunuch went down into the water, and he baptized him. Now when they came up out of the water, the Spirit of the Lord caught Philip away, so that the eunuch saw him no more; and he went on his way rejoicing. But Philip was found at Azotus. And passing through, he preached in all the cities till he came to Caesarea.

(You can read more about spirit travel in the book, *The Seer Dimensions* or take the *School of the Seers* at schoolofthespirit.tv.)

Distraction: a tactic of the enemy to divert the seer's attention from what God is trying to show him in a vision or encounter

Divination: tapping into dark spiritual forces, such as familiar spirits, to see or hear information God is not revealing; There are many Scriptures forbidding divination, particularly in Leviticus and Deuteronomy. Here is one: Leviticus 19:31, "Give no regard to mediums and familiar spirits; do not seek after them, to be defiled by them: I am the Lord your God."

Divine Encounter: a purpose-driven encounter with God or angels; every encounter with God or angels has a specific purpose to forward His Kingdom in you or through you; God is a God of purpose and works everything together for the good according to His purpose (see Romans 8:28).

Divine Osmosis: a spiritual phenomenon in which the seer unconsciously receives revelation that becomes apparent at a later time; a knowing

Divine Sight: seeing a manifestation of God's presence and power on earth through natural means. Moses with the burning bush is one example

Diviner: one who practices divination

Doctrines of Demons: false doctrines creeping into the prophetic movement, such as the ability to enter the seer dimensions at will, the irrelevance of spiritual warfare; insisting God will not let any of your words fall to the ground, etc. There are many other doctrines of demons, but these are among the most common in the seer dimensions.

1 Timothy 4:1 says: "Now the Spirit expressly says that in latter times some will depart from the faith, giving heed to deceiving spirits and doctrines of demons, speaking lies in hypocrisy, having their own conscience seared with a hot iron, forbidding to marry, and commanding to abstain from foods which God created to be received with thanksgiving by those who believe and know the truth."

Domain: *see Jurisdiction*

Doom and Gloom: a prophetic forecast of judgment; dark predictions of calamity

Doorkeeper: *see Gatekeeper*

Double-tongued: a person who lacks integrity with their words; speaking out of both sides of one's mouth; making contradictory statements about the same subject

Dragon: a symbol of Satan; Revelation 12:9 offers one example of this symbolism in Scripture: "So the great dragon was cast out, that serpent of old, called the Devil and Satan, who deceives the whole world; he was cast to the earth, and his angels were cast out with him."

Dream: a storyline that takes place while you are asleep. Dreams can come from three sources: the carnal nature, the enemy, or God; (You can learn more about dreams in the book, *Decoding Your Dreams*.)

Dream Application: the way in which one applies a dream interpretation

Dream Dimension: a dimension in the spirit realm where God speaks to you in your dreams; (For more on this, get the book, *The Seer Dimensions*.)

Dream Interpretation: the meaning of a dream

Dream Language: language of the dream realm, which can include symbols, numbers, colors, animals, types, shadows, as well as personal and cultural indicators

Dream Manifestation: when a prophetic dream comes to pass

Dream Presentation: the way in which one presents a dream to others to judge, or to suggest an interpretation or application

Dream Recall: the ability to recall a prophetic dream upon waking; a time period after the initial dream when the Holy Spirit brings it to your remembrance

Dreamer: one who consistently dreams

Dry Season: a period of time when seer activity seems sparse; a time when a person, community, or church feel spiritually exhausted; a time with little revelation. Dry seasons can result from lack of fellowship with the Holy Spirit, neglect of the Word or in times of transitions

Dual Meaning: when a dream or vision has two accurate meanings

Due time: *see Kairos Time*

Dwell: a place where we linger or live; focusing one's attention on what is seen in the spirit; meditating on a dream or vision

Dysfunction: when a seer is not functioning according to godly protocols. Seer dysfunction is often an unhealthy result of poor relational alignment, ignorance of the enemy's devices, wrong motives or failing to protect the eye gates.

E

Eagle: a symbol of the prophetic ministry; Isaiah 40:31 promises, "But those who wait on the Lord shall renew their strength; They shall mount up with wings like eagles, they shall run and not be weary, they shall walk and not faint."

Early: before dawn; a strategic time to watch and pray; Jesus arose early in the morning while it was still dark to pray (see Mark 1:35). Moses arose early in the morning to build an altar to the Lord (see Exodus 24:4). David arose early in the morning to seek God's face (see Psalm 63).

Earth Realm: of or in the earth, which God created as a temporary home for mankind

East Wind: a destructive wind, the east wind has a negative connotation in the Bible; In Genesis 41:6, the east wind is associated with scorching. In Exodus 10:13 the east wind brings in the locusts, and in Exodus 14:21 the east wind turns the sea into dry land. In Ezekiel 17:10, the east wind destroys the crops. In Hosea 13:15, the east winds are associated with drought. In Isaiah 27:8, the east wind brings expelling. In Jeremiah 18:17, the east wind brings scattering.

In the Book of Psalms, we encounter the east wind in Psalm 48:7, which speaks of destruction on the sea, and in Psalm 78:26 we see the east wind blows to the heavens. Job also speaks of the east wind carrying him away (see Job 27:21), filling him (see Job 15:12), and the east wind being scattered (see Job 27:21).

When a seer sees a wind in the spirit, it's important to discern the direction and the source of the wind. Is it God-inspired or devil-breathed?

Eat the Scroll: also called "a little book" in some translations of the Bible, eating the scroll metaphorically means digesting a difficult word of the Lord; Receiving revelation can be exciting, but the gravity of seer revelation can be disturbing. We must process the revelation before sharing it.

In Ezekiel 3:1-3 we read, "Moreover He said to me, 'Son of man, eat what you find; eat this scroll, and go, speak to the house of Israel.' So I opened my mouth, and He caused me to eat that scroll. And He said to me, 'Son of man, feed your belly, and fill your stomach with this scroll that I give you.' So I ate, and it was in my mouth like honey in sweetness."

And in Revelation 10:9-10, we read of John the Revelator's similar experience: "So I went to the angel and said to him, 'Give me the little book.' And he said to me, 'Take and eat it; and it will make your stomach bitter, but it will be as sweet as honey in your mouth.' Then I took the little book out of the angel's hand and ate it, and it was as sweet as honey in my mouth. But when I had eaten it, my stomach became bitter."

Matthew Henry's Concise Commentary reads, "Most men feel pleasure in looking into future events, and all good men like to receive a word from God. But when this book of prophecy was thoroughly digested by the apostle, the contents would be bitter; there were things so awful and terrible, such grievous persecutions of the people of God, such desolations in the earth, that the foresight and foreknowledge of them would be painful to his mind.

"Let us seek to be taught by Christ, and to obey his orders; daily meditating on his word, that it may nourish our souls; and then declaring it according to our several stations. The sweetness of such contemplations will often be mingled with bitterness, while we compare the Scriptures with the state of the world and the church, or even with that of our own hearts."

Echo: when visual or audible revelation is repeated over and again; a confirmation of what another seer has seen or heard; a copycat seer who is lifting the revelation of another seer and presenting it as his own

Echo Chamber: a phenomenon of the spirit when you can hear your words or the words of a congregation traveling through the spirit like an echo

Ecstatic Dimension: a realm in which you experience an ecstatic state; *see also Ecstatic State*; (For more, get *The Seer Dimensions* book.)

Ecstatic State: a state marked by ecstasy; We have relegated that word to a feeling of the flesh—there's even a hallucinogenic drug by this name—but ecstasy is actually a biblical concept. It's one of many mystical aspects of the prophetic. An ecstatic state is where you experience trances, are caught up in the spirit, or travel in the spirit, or experience a deep sleep brought on by the Lord. You can learn more about the ecstatic state in the book *The Seer Dimensions* or in the *School of the Seers* at schoolofthespirit.tv.

Ecstatic Vision: a vision you receive while in an ecstatic state (*see Ecstatic State*)

Edify: to build up through instruction or correction

Egenomehn ehn Pneumatic: literally, to become in the spirit; a state in which the seer receives visions by direct revelation from God; hearing from the very mouth of God. The seer must press into His presence to manifest oneness with the Spirit, which is our legal position in order to see as God sees. 1 Corinthians 16:7 says, "But he who is joined to the Lord is one spirit with Him."

Ehyeh Asher Ehyeh: a name for God that means The Eternal, All-Sufficient God, as seen in Exodus 3:14, "And God said to Moses, 'I AM WHO I AM.' And He said, 'Thus you shall say to the children of Israel, 'I AM has sent me to you.'"

Eighth Watch: the last day watch, which is from 3 pm to 6 pm; It's sometimes called the history-making watch because Jesus died on the cross at 3 pm, forever changing history. This is a time to meditate on the blood of Jesus. This is a time to come boldly before the throne of grace to find grace and obtain mercy (see Hebrews 4:16). This is the time to make intercession for healing and deliverance made possible by the shed blood of Jesus.

Ekstasis: a seer dimension in which the mind is thrown out of its normal state, often resulting in amazement, fear of the Lord and wonder; a rapt condition in which the mind is awake but undistracted by its natural surroundings in order to focus on visions in the seer dimensions; often the state of one in a trance

El Elohe Yisrael: a name of God that means "Mighty God of Israel," as seen in Genesis 33:20, "Then he erected an altar there and called it El Elohe Israel."

El Elyon: a name for God that means the "God Most High." This name for God was first used in Genesis 14:8: "And the king of Sodom, the king of Gomorrah, the king of Admah, the king of Zeboiim, and the king of Bela (that is, Zoar) went out and joined together in battle in the Valley of Siddim…"

El Emunah: a name for God that means "The Faithful God," seen in Deuteronomy 7:9, "Therefore know that the Lord your God, He is God, the faithful God who keeps covenant and mercy for a thousand generations with those who love Him and keep His commandments."

El Hakabodh: a name of God that means "God of Glory," seen in Psalm 29:3, "The voice of the Lord is over the waters; The God of glory thunders; The Lord is over many waters."

El Hayyay: a name for God that means "God of My Life," seen in Psalm 42:8, "The Lord will command His lovingkindness in the daytime, and in the night His song shall be with me—A prayer to the God of my life."

El Kanna: a name for God that means "Jealous God," seen in Exodus 20:5, "You shall not bow down to them nor serve them. For I, the Lord your God, am a jealous God, visiting the iniquity of the fathers upon the children to the third and fourth generations of those who hate Me."

El Nekamoth: a name for God that means "God That Avenges," seen in Psalm 18:47, "It is God who avenges me, and subdues the peoples under me."

El Olam: a name for God that means "Everlasting God" (see Genesis 21:33).

El Rai: a name for God that means "God Sees Me," seen in Genesis 16:13, "Then she called the name of the Lord who spoke to her, [You-Are] the-God-Who-Sees; for she said, "Have I also here seen Him who sees me?"

El Shaddai: a name for God that means "All-Sufficient One" or "Lord God Almighty." This name for God was first used in Genesis 17:1: "When Abram was ninety-nine years old, the Lord appeared to Abram and said to him, 'I am Almighty God; walk before Me and be blameless."

El Sali: a name for God that means "God, My Rock," seen in 2 Samuel 22:47, "The Lord lives! Blessed be my Rock! Let God be exalted, the Rock of my salvation!"

El Simchath Gili: a name for God that means "God My Exceeding Joy," seen in Psalm 43:4, "Then I will go to the altar of God, to God my exceeding joy; And on the harp I will praise You, O God, my God."

Eli Maelekhi: a name for God that means "God My King," seen in Psalm 68:24, "They have seen Your procession, O God, the procession of my God, my King, into the sanctuary."

Elijah: a miracle-working prophet who called for a showdown with Jezebel's false prophets at Mt. Carmel. His victory turned the hearts of Israel back to God.

Elisha: the protegee of Elijah who received a double portion of his spirit, working twice as many miracles as his spiritual father; a seer prophet who saw into the bedchambers of the Assyrian king (see 2 Kings 6:12).

Elohe Tishuathi: a name for God that means "God of My Salvation," seen in Psalm 51:14, "Deliver me from the guilt of bloodshed, O God, the God of my salvation, and my tongue shall sing aloud of Your righteousness."

Elohe Tsadeki: a name for God that means "God of My Righteousness," seen in Psalm 4:1, "Hear me when I call, O God of my righteousness!.

You have relieved me in my distress; Have mercy on me, and hear my prayer."

Elohe Yakob: a name for God that means "God of Jacob," as seen in Psalm 20:1, "May the Lord answer you in the day of trouble; May the name of the God of Jacob defend you."

Elohei Chasdi: a name for God that means "God of My Kindness, Goodness and Faithfulness," seen in Psalm 59:17, "To You, O my Strength, I will sing praises; For God is my defense, My God of mercy."

Elohei Haelohim: a name for God that means "The God of gods," seen in Deuteronomy 10:17, "For the Lord your God is God of gods and Lord of lords, the great God, mighty and awesome, who shows no partiality nor takes a bribe."

Elohei Maron: a name for God that means "God of Heights," seen in Micah 6:6, "With what shall I come before the Lord, and bow myself before the High God? Shall I come before Him with burnt offerings, with calves a year old?"

Elohei Ma'uzzi: a name for God that means "God of My Strength," seen in 2 Samuel 22:33: "God is my strength and power, and He makes my way perfect."

Elohei Mikkarov: a name for God that means "God Who is Near," seen in Jeremiah 23:23, "'Am I a God near at hand,' says the Lord, 'And not a God afar off?'"

Elohei Tehillati: a name for God that means "God of my praise," seen in Psalm 109:1, "Do not keep silent, O God of my praise!"

Elohenu Olam: a name for God that means "Our Everlasting God," seen in Psalm 48:14, "For this is God, Our God forever and ever; He will be our guide Even to death."

Elohim: a name for God that means "God" (see Genesis 1:1).

Elohim Bashamayim: a name for God that means "God in Heaven," seen in Joshua 2:11, "And as soon as we heard these things, our hearts melted; neither did there remain any more courage in anyone because of you, for the Lord your God, He is God in heaven above and on earth beneath."

Elohim Chaseddi: a name for God that means the "God of My Mercy," seen in Psalm 59:10, "My God of mercy shall come to meet me; God shall let me see my desire on my enemies."

Elohim Chayim: a name for God that means "The Living God," seen in Joshua 3:10, "And Joshua said, 'By this you shall know that the living God is among you, and that He will without fail drive out from before you the Canaanites and the Hittites and the Hivites and the Perizzites and the Girgashites and the Amorites and the Jebusites.'"

Elohim Kedoshim: a name for God that means "Holy God," seen in Joshua 24:19, "But Joshua said to the people, 'You cannot serve the Lord, for He is a holy God. He is a jealous God; He will not forgive your transgressions nor your sins.'"

Elohim Machase Lanu: a name for God that means "God Our Refuge," seen in Psalm 62:8, "Trust in Him at all times, you people; Pour out your heart before Him; God is a refuge for us. Selah."

Elohim Ozer Li: a name for God that means "God My Helper," seen in Psalm 54:4, "Behold, God is my helper; The Lord is with those who uphold my life."

Elohim Shophtim Ba-arets: a name for God that means "God That Judges the Earth," as seen in Psalm 58:11, "So that men will say, 'Surely there is a reward for the righteous; Surely He is God who judges in the earth.'"

Elohim Tsebaoth: a name for God that means "God of Hosts," seen in Psalm 80:7, "Restore us, O God of hosts; Cause Your face to shine, and we shall be saved!"

Elymas: also known as Bar-Jesus, a sorcerer who worked to block Paul and Barnabus from preaching the gospel to an authority figure in Rome; an example of a confrontation between God's power and enemy power. Acts 13:6-12 gives the important account:

"Now when they had gone through the island to Paphos, they found a certain sorcerer, a false prophet, a Jew whose name *was* Bar-Jesus, who was with the proconsul, Sergius Paulus, an intelligent man. This man called for Barnabas and Saul and sought to hear the word of God.

"But Elymas the sorcerer (for so his name is translated) withstood them, seeking to turn the proconsul away from the faith. Then Saul, who also is called Paul, filled with the Holy Spirit, looked intently at him and said, 'O full of all deceit and all fraud, you son of the devil, you enemy of all righteousness, will you not cease perverting the straight ways of the Lord? And now, indeed, the hand of the Lord is upon you, and you shall be blind, not seeing the sun for a time.'

"And immediately a dark mist fell on him, and he went around seeking someone to lead him by the hand. Then the proconsul believed, when he saw what had been done, being astonished at the teaching of the Lord."

Emerald: a green gemstone; the appearance of the rainbow around the throne of God; Revelation 4:3 reads: "And He who sat there was like a jasper and a sardius stone in appearance; and there was a rainbow around the throne, in appearance like an emerald."

Also, a stone in the breastplate of judgment worn by the Old Testament priests (see Exodus 28:17).

Also, a stone in the wall around the New Jerusalem. Revelation 21:18-20 reads, "The construction of its wall was of jasper; and the city was pure gold, like clear glass. The foundations of the wall of the city were adorned with all kinds of precious stones: the first foundation was jasper, the second sapphire, the third chalcedony, the fourth emerald, the fifth sardonyx, the sixth sardius, the seventh chrysolite, the eighth beryl, the ninth topaz, the tenth chrysoprase, the eleventh jacinth, and the twelfth amethyst."

Emmanuel: also Immanuel; a name for Jesus, which means God with us. Matthew 1:23 reads, "Behold, the virgin shall be with child, and bear a Son, and they shall call His name Immanuel," which is translated, 'God with us.'"

Enchanter: *see Sorcerer*

Enchantments: *see Secret Arts*

Encoded: a visual revelation conveyed in heaven's symbolic language, which requires interpretation

Encounter: a meeting with God, angels or demons; a confrontation with demon powers

End-Times: cataclysmic events that take place before the end of the age and Christ's Second Coming

End-Times Dreams: dreams relating to the end-times

End-Times Seer: a seer with a mandate and mission for the end-times church

End-Times Visions: visions related to the end-times

Enemy: another name for Satan (see Matthew 13:39)

Enigma: see *Dark Sayings*

Enlighten: to receive or possess spiritual insight; Ezra 9:8 speaks of God enlightening our eyes. David prays in Psalm 13:3 for God to enlighten his eyes.

Enoch: a man who walked with God and was raptured without seeing death; a man whose writings laid the foundation for the Books of Enoch. Enoch is found in Genesis 5:21, "Enoch lived sixty-five years, and begot Methuselah. After he begot Methuselah, Enoch walked with God three hundred years, and had sons and daughters. So all the days of Enoch were three hundred and sixty-five years. And Enoch walked with God; and he was not, for God took him."

Entertaining Angels: encountering angels with hospitality without knowing, at least at the time, they are angels; Abraham entertained angels in Genesis 18 when he saw three men standing nearby. He did not know they were angels, but prepared a meal for them. Hebrews 13:2 says, "Do not forget to entertain strangers, for by so doing some have unwittingly entertained angels."

Enupnion: the Greek word for a dream; This word is only used once in the Bible, found in Acts 2:17 where Peter prophesied Joel's words, "And it shall come to pass in the last days, says God, that I will pour out of My Spirit on all flesh; Your sons and your daughters shall prophesy, your young men shall see visions, your old men shall dream dreams."

Eon: an age; a long, indefinite period of time

Epic Dream: a dream that extends beyond the normal length and detail of a general dream; epic dreams have a storyline with tremendous detail and often plenty of drama

Epic Vision: a vision that extends beyond the normal length and detail of a general vision; epic visions have a storyline with tremendous detail and often plenty of drama

Epoch: a time period marked by a series of significant events

Era: *see Epoch*

Err in Vision: Isaiah 28:7 reads, "But they also have erred through wine, and through strong drink are out of the way; the priest and the prophet have erred through strong drink, they are swallowed up of wine, they are out of the way through strong drink; they err in vision, they stumble in judgment."

This is not the kind of error in the sense of misinterpreting what you see in the spirit. This is an error that causes the seer to lead people astray morally or walk-in unrepentant sin. In this case, the blind is leading the blind and they both fall into a ditch of error. It's important seers live a lifestyle of repentance so that they don't err in vision and knowingly or unknowingly lead people astray.

Error: deceit, fraud, a lie that leads people astray

Esh Oklah: a name that means "A Consuming Fire," seen in Deuteronomy 4:24, "For the Lord your God is a consuming fire, a jealous God."

Eternal: existing forever without beginning or end, typically used to describe the Alpha and Omega creator God (see Revelation 1:4).

Eternal Spirit: another name for the Holy Spirit; Hebrews 9:14 reads, "how much more shall the blood of Christ, who through the eternal Spirit offered Himself without spot to God, cleanse your conscience from dead works to serve the living God?"

Eternity: endless, infinite measures of time; forever

Eunuch: the word eunuch comes from the Hebrew word *caric*, which means "to castrate." Biblically speaking, eunuchs were often found in the households of kings, particularly to work in women's bedchambers.

Eunuchs, for example, were appointed to keep the harem of virgins for King Xerxes (see Esther 2:3). Eunuchs were permitted to work in female bedchambers because they had essentially been emasculated. We know there were eunuchs in Jezebel's household (see 2 Kings 9:32).

Modern eunuchs are often victims of the Jezebel spirit, which strips people of their power, strength and identity to transform them into spiritual servants, information seekers and spies.

Everlasting: an attribute of God; eternal; Isaiah 40:8 describes God as the Everlasting God: "Have you not known? Have you not heard? The everlasting God, the Lord, the

Creator of the ends of the earth, neither faints nor is weary. His understanding is unsearchable."

Evidence: proof that what you saw in the spirit is real, often only possible after an event in a vision or dream comes to pass or is confirmed by someone who has special knowledge

Evil Eye: an eye that is wicked, sinful, morally reprehensible or seeking to cause harm; Proverbs 28:22 reads, "A man with an evil eye hastens after riches, and does not consider that poverty will come upon him." And Jesus spoke of the evil eye in Mark 7:22." An evil eye comes from an evil heart.

Evil Heart: an immoral heart intent on wicked agendas; the heart affects the spiritual eyes so an evil heart can lead one to pursue illegal activity in the seer dimensions, such as spiritual spying.

Jesus said in Luke 6:45, "A good man out of the good treasure of his heart brings forth good; and an evil man out of the evil treasure of his heart brings forth evil. For out of the abundance of the heart his mouth speaks." (Also see Genesis 6:5; 2 Chronicles 12:14; Psalm 140:2; and Proverbs 6:18.)

Evil One: another name for Satan (see Matthew 13:19)

Evil Spirit: another name for Satan (see 1 Samuel 16:14)

Evil Time: a time of calamity; Ecclesiastes 9:12 reads, "For man also does not know his time: Like fish taken in a cruel net, like birds caught in a snare, So the sons of men are snared in an evil time, when it falls suddenly upon them."

Examine: to investigate in the spirit; to inspect something you see in the spirit closely by continuing to look upon it; to test the spirit to discern its source

Exercise: to use the seer gift; to grow the seer gift through continual training and use; to develop seer skills by practice; to walk in one's seer authority

Exhort: godly advice; a summons; a strong Spirit-inspired urging to take a course of action; Paul told Timothy, "Preach the word! Be ready in season and out of season. Convince, rebuke, exhort, with all longsuffering and teaching" (2 Timothy 4:2).

Expectation: a seer state of heart that expects the Lord to show them what they need to see in response to prayer; an attitude while waiting on the Lord to reveal visual revelation; confidence the Lord is going to reveal what needs to be seen.

Experience: knowledge and understanding the seer gains over time through the use of the gift. (*see also Encounter*)

Explaining Enigmas: a gift Daniel possessed (see Daniel 5:12)

Extrabiblical: teachings about God, His work, His will, or His Kingdom that are not found directly quoted in the pages of Scripture; teachings people claim are supported by the Bible but are not, often based on poor or erroneous interpretation of Scripture; Cults are typically based on extrabiblical teaching that twists Scripture to form some new doctrine or revelation.

Eyes But Do Not See: a reality of a foolish seer; the spiritual condition of a seer who has strayed from sound judgment and discretion in the use of their gifting. Jeremiah 5:21 says, "Hear this now, O foolish people, without understanding, who have eyes and see not, and who have ears and hear not…"

Eyeful: a vision that is awesome or breathtaking

Eye Gates: a door or gateway through which the Lord reveals revelations from the spirit realm, as well as the gateway through which the enemy can pollute a seer's spiritual vision

Seers must be careful to guard their eye gates. In Luke 11:34 Jesus said: "The eye is the lamp of the body. Therefore when your eye is good, your whole body also is full of light. But when your eye is bad, your body also is full of darkness."

Eye Witness: something you see firsthand in the spirit; evidence you present about what you see in the spirit

Eyes Darkened: a condition of the seer's eyes when they do not guard themselves from dark influences; Psalm 69:23 reads, "Let their eyes be darkened, so that they do not see; And make their loins shake continually."

Eyes Grow Dim: a state in which it is difficult to see because of compromised emotions or sinful acts. Consider the dimmer on a light; As you dim the light, it becomes more difficult to see in the natural. As darkness invades the seer's spiritual sight, it can be more difficult to see in the spirit.

In 1 Samuel 3:2, we see that Eli, Samuel's mentor, was suffering from dim eyesight in the natural. However, there was a spiritual parallel. Eli's eyes were also growing spiritually dim. We know this, in part, because the Bible tells us in those days there was no open vision (see 1 Samuel 3:1).

In Matthew 6:22-24, Jesus tell us: "The lamp of the body is the eye. If therefore your eye is good, your whole body will be full of light. But if your eye is bad, your whole body will be full of darkness. If therefore the light that is in you is darkness, how great is that darkness!"

If a seer looks upon sinful things, his spiritual eyes will grow dim. The Psalmists said more than once not to look on worthless or wicked things, and even asked for God's help to do it.

"Turn away my eyes from looking at worthless things, and revive me in Your way" (Psalm 119:37). And again, "I will set nothing wicked before my eyes; I hate the work of those who fall away; It shall not cling to me" (see Psalm 101:3).

Eyes can grow dim because of emotional issues, such as grief or trauma. Both are under the banner of afflictions. Psalm 88:9 tells us, "My eye wastes away because of affliction." Both David and Job spoke of their eyes growing dim with grief (see Psalm 6:7; Job 17:7).

Eyes of His Glory: God's glorious eyes; a manifestation of His presence as the Almighty, omniscient, omnipresent God; Isaiah 3:8, "For Jerusalem stumbled, and Judah is fallen, because their tongue and their doings are against the Lord, to provoke the eyes of His glory."

Eyes of the Lord: God's all-seeing eyes; Genesis 6:8 reads, "But Noah found grace in the eyes of the Lord." And 2 Chronicles 16:9 reads, "For the eyes of the Lord run to and fro throughout the whole earth, to show Himself strong on behalf of those whose heart is loyal to Him. In this you have done foolishly; therefore from now on you shall have wars."

Eyes of Your Heart: the eyes of your spirit; your spiritual eyes; Just as you have eyes on your face through which you see the natural world, you have eyes of your heart through which you see the spiritual world. The NIV Bible says," I pray that the eyes of your heart may be enlightened in order that you may know the hope to which he has called you, the riches of his glorious inheritance in his holy people."

Eyes of Your Spirit: *see Eyes of Your Heart*

Eyes of Your Understanding: *see Eyes of Your Heart*

Eyes That Keep Watch on the Nations: a seer who is assigned to watch over nations; Psalm 66:7, says "He rules by His power forever; His eyes observe the nations; Do not let the rebellious exalt themselves. Selah."

Eyes That Long for God's Deliverance: eyes that watch for the Deliverer to show up; Psalm 119:123, "My eyes long for Your deliverance and for the promise of Your righteousness."

Eyes That See the Great Deeds of the Lord: spoke of those who have seen the judgment of God play out; Speaking of the plagues on Egypt, their drowning in the Red Sea and other events, Deuteronomy 11:17 points us to this statement: "But your eyes have seen every great act of the Lord which He did."

Eyes to See: the ability to understand spiritual truths, which is hindered by rebellion and unbelief; Deuteronomy 29:4 reads, "Yet the Lord has not given you a heart to perceive and eyes to see and ears to hear, to this very day."

Eyes Weary for God's Word: a heart that is hungry for the Word of God; Psalm 119:82, "My eyes are weary for Your word, saying, "When will You comfort me?"

Eyesalve: the remedy for spiritual blindness; an anointing that breaks the yoke of blindness off spiritual eyes that is only found in the presence of the Lord. Revelation 3:18 reads, "I counsel you to buy from Me gold refined in the fire, that you may be rich; and white garments, that you may be clothed, *that* the shame of your nakedness may not be revealed; and anoint your eyes with eye salve, that you may see."

Ezekiel: author of the Book of Ezekiel; a priest, watchman and prophet to Israel; Ezekiel's name means "strengthened by God." Ezekiel was a seer prophet who had dramatic visions, including the Valley of Dry Bones.

Ezra: author of the Book of Ezra; a contemporary of Nehemiah during the rebuilding of the walls of Jerusalem; a priest, scholar, reformer and teacher and a leader who restored worship in Jerusalem

F

Fables: irreverent, silly myths (see 1 Timothy 4:7); *Merriam-Webster's Dictionary* defines fable as "a fictitious narrative or statement: such as a legendary story of supernatural happenings… a falsehood, lie."

Because the seer dimensions are somewhat nebulous, there are fables and myths around visions and dreams. People report things they did not see. The Bible warns in the last days people will turn away from listening to the truth and wander off into myths (see 2 Timothy 4:4).

Paul warns in Colossians 2:18, "Let no one cheat you of your reward, taking delight in false humility and worship of angels, intruding into those things which he has not seen, vainly puffed up by his fleshly mind…"

We've seen some who were exposed for writing books about visitations from heaven, for example. These are seer fables and silly myths that are irreverent.

Faces: seers may see the faces of people they know or don't know; Seers may see someone in the spirit they have never met before, only to meet them later in real life. Seers may see the outline of a face or a darkened or shrouded face and have no understanding of who you are looking at unless the Holy Spirit reveals it.

Seers may see the face of Jesus or the face of an angel in a dream, vision or encounter. Seers may see someone's face shining in the spirit after an encounter with the Lord (see Exodus 34:35). Seers may see the face of the earth from an elevated position in the spirit. The Bible has plenty to say about the face of the earth.

Seers may see a spirit pass before their face (see Job 4:15). Seers may see the face of God's throne (see Job 26:9).

Seers may see the face of a demon. Seers may see the face of beasts (Ezekiel 1:6).

Fade In: when a vision, somewhat like a movie, slowly comes into full visibility; A vision may also fade in like a polaroid picture until you can see its fullness.

Fade out: when a vision, somewhat like a movie, slowly fades out or fades away.

Faith: an element of seeing in the spirit; If you don't have faith to see in the spirit, you may miss what God is trying to show you.

Faithful and True: another name for Jesus seen in Revelation 19:11: "Now I saw heaven opened, and behold, a white horse. And He who sat on him was called Faithful and True, and in righteousness He judges and makes war."

Faithful Witness: another name for Jesus seen in Revelation 3:14: "And to the angel of the church of the Laodiceans write, 'These things says the Amen, the Faithful and True Witness, the Beginning of the creation of God…"

Fallen Angels: angels who followed Lucifer's coup and were expelled from heaven

False: anything that is not true; something deceptive; a dream or vision or encounter that is not genuine; counterfeit seer options; a seer expression that sets out to deceive, mislead or fool people

False Dream: a dream presented as true that one did not have; a dream that leads one astray because it contains lies or partial truths

False Prophecy: prophecy that is not accurate or true

False Prophet: one who sets out to deceive in the name of speaking for God

False Seer: a seer who sets out to deceive, releasing false dreams and visions

False Vision: a vision presented as truth that is fabricated; a vision that leads people astray with deceit

Falsehood: a deliberately untrue seer release; a lie. Such falsehood can stem out of a hallucination, imagination or delusion

False Vision: a vision that did not come from the Holy Spirit; Jeremiah 14:14 reveals, "And the Lord said to me, 'The prophets prophesy lies in My name. I have not sent them, commanded them, nor spoken to them; they prophesy to you a false vision, divination, a worthless thing, and the deceit of their heart.'"

Falsify: adding to or taking away from a dream or a vision with the motive of deception; to embellish or misrepresent what God reveals; to fabricate encounters

Familiar Spirits: a specific class of spirit' As its name suggests, it is characterized by familiarity. Familiar spirits offer knowledge about people, places, and things—but that knowledge comes from the dark side.

Seers who tap into familiar spirits are deceiving and being deceived, according to 2 Timothy 3:13, which reads: "But evil men and impostors will grow worse and worse, deceiving and being deceived."

This is dangerous. Leviticus 20:6 reads, "'And the person who turns to mediums and familiar spirits, to prostitute himself with them, I will set My face against that person and cut him off from his people."

Fantasy: *see Daydream*

Farther: looking beyond where you currently see to what's in the distance

Fasting: a method of mortifying the flesh to gain greater sensitivity to the spirit

Father of Lies: another name for Satan (see John 8:44)

Feeler: simply put, one who feels in the spirit realm; It's as if the feeler has a spiritual antenna—a sensory organ that you can't see—but receives information from the Holy Spirit. This spiritual antenna gives you a special sensitivity or receptiveness. The feeler gift is often tied in with the gift of discernment, which is tied in with the seer gift.

Not all seers are feelers and not all feelers are seers but both feeling and seeing are part of the realm of discerning of spirits. A seer discerns visually. A feeler discerns with feelings and sensations. In this context, feeling is like an impression but it's stronger than an impression. Most impressions are faint. Feelers have stronger impressions than your typical "check in the spirit."

Another way to put it is feelers have spiritual sensations. At times, this can manifest like with the feeling of pain in your body, which would signal someone else has pain. We've called this a manifestation of the word of knowledge, which it is, but it comes in tactile form. Feelers can be moved with strong emotion, but it's not their emotion.

(Learn more about this in the *School of the Seers* at www.schoolofthespirit.tv.)

Fellow Seer: someone in your company of seers; someone who belongs to the larger family of seers on the earth

Fervency: the spiritual temperature that remains hungry for God and the things of God

Fetters: chains or shackles with which the enemy binds someone; When the Philistines captured Samson, they put fetters on his feet (see Judges 16:21). Fetters were commonly used in the Bible to restrain people. Seers may see fetters in the spirit for the sake of delivering someone from enemy bondage.

Field of Vision: *see Visual Field*

Fifth Watch: a watch of Holy Spirit preparation that runs from 6 am to 9 am; Technically, it's the first watch of the day.

When the disciples were filled with the Holy Spirit on the Day of Pentecost, it was during the fifth watch. In Acts 2:14-16, Peter said, "Men of Judea and all who dwell in Jerusalem, let this be known to you, and heed my words. For these are not drunk, as you suppose, since it is only the third hour of the day. But this is what was spoken by the prophet Joel."

(Learn more in the book, *The Making of a Watchman.*)

Figure: an outline or shape of a person you see in the spirit without knowledge of who it is or much description about them beyond the overall shape or movements

Filled With the Spirit: the result of being baptized in the Holy Spirit; to be filled with the Spirit means to be empowered by the Spirit. Ephesians 5:18 (AMP) says, "but ever be filled and stimulated with the [Holy] Spirit."

Find: to discover something one is looking for in the seer dimensions; In the seer dimensions, seers don't always see everything readily. Often, the seer has to search it out. As the seer searches by the leading of the Holy Spirit, he will find what God is trying to show him. Jesus said seek and you will find (see Matthew 7:7).

First Heaven: the atmosphere around us; The first heaven includes the cloud, the moon, the sun, and the stars; *see also Second Heaven* and *Third Heaven*

First Watch: a watch that runs from 6 pm to 9 pm; This is the first of four night watches and serves as the foundation of the night. The first watch is a time to be still and know that He is God (see Psalm 46:10).

In Scripture, we see Isaac meditated on God in the first watch. Genesis 24:63 reads, "And Isaac went out to meditate in the field in the evening; and he lifted his eyes and looked, and there, the camels were coming." (See the book, *The Making of a Watchman,* for more.)

Fixate: *see Focus*

Flash: a quick glimpse of something in the spirit.

Flashback: as it relates to seers, a sudden, spontaneous memory of a dream or vision; This often occurs when the Holy Spirit is trying to show a seer something will soon take place or is urging the seer to press into a dream or vision for more meaning of the revelation.

Flashings: *See Secret Arts*

Flattering Divination: false prophetic utterance and smooth sayings that flatter the hearers in order to gain popularity or prosperity; Examples of flattery in the seer dimensions include: prophesying from a motive of self-interest; to praise someone excessively in order to draw them to yourself; to seduce by offering false encouragement. The ultimate goal of flattery is control. Ezekiel 12:24, "For there shall be no more any vain vision nor flattering divination within the house of Israel."

Fleece: taking some action or waiting on some event as a sign to confirm God's will; Gideon put out a fleece of wool twice to determine if God was speaking to Him, which is where we get the modern term "fleece." In our practice, we are not drawing lots but looking for outward signs of confirmation. Judges 6:36-39 reads:

"So Gideon said to God, 'If You will save Israel by my hand as You have said—look, I shall put a fleece of wool on the threshing floor; if there is dew on the fleece only, and it is dry on all the ground, then I shall know that You will save Israel by my hand, as You have said.'.

"And it was so. When he rose early the next morning and squeezed the fleece together, he wrung the dew out of the fleece, a bowlful of water. Then Gideon said to God, 'Do not be angry with me, but let me speak just once more: Let me test, I pray, just once more with the fleece; let it now be dry only on the fleece, but on all the ground let there be dew.'"

In the Old Testament, people put out fleeces but in the New Testament God speaks to us through His Son (see

Hebrews 1:2). There's only one time in the New Testament we see believers putting out a fleece, of sorts, and it was before they were filled with the Holy Spirit. We see the apostles cast lots in Acts 1:26 to determine who would take Judas' place in the apostolic ministry Jesus commissioned.

Fleece the Sheep: to charge undue monies or to overcharge people for kingdom goods; to charge a fee for personal prophecy

Fleshly Mind: a carnal mind; Seers must take caution not to tap into a fleshly mind; Consider Paul's warning in Colossians 2:18-19, "Let no one cheat you of your reward, taking delight in false humility and worship of angels, intruding into those things which he has not seen, vainly puffed up by his fleshly mind, and not holding fast to the Head, from whom all the body, nourished and knit together by joints and ligaments, grows with the increase that is from God."

Paul warns we can be "vainly puffed up by a fleshly mind." The AMPC translation expounds on this: "vainly puffed up by his sensuous notions and inflated by his unspiritual thoughts and fleshly conceit."

Flies: a manifestation of a monitoring spirit (see *Monitoring Spirits*)

Flint: a hard dark quartz that makes a spark when steel strikes it; flints were also used as knives in Bible days. God sets some seers' faces like flint so that when persecution comes, they are more on fire to speak His Word;

God told Ezekiel, "Like adamant stone, harder than flint, I have made your forehead; do not be afraid of them, nor be dismayed at their looks, though they are a rebellious house" (Ezekiel 3:9). Isaiah said, "For the Lord God will help me; therefore shall I not be confounded: therefore have I set my face like a flint, and I know that I shall not be ashamed" (Isaiah 50:7, ESV).

Flow: the manifestation of the Holy Spirit moving in the seer's ministry; John 7:38-40, Jesus said, "'He who believes in Me, as the Scripture has said, out of his heart will flow rivers of living water.' But this He spoke concerning the Spirit, whom those believing in Him would receive; for the Holy Spirit was not yet given, because Jesus was not yet glorified."

Flying: a sensation you may feel during an encounter with God or something you may experience as part of a dream

Flying Scroll: a unique visual revelation in Zechariah's prophetic ministry, which illustrates some of the stranger things a seer may experience; Zechariah 5:1-2, "Then I turned and raised my eyes, and saw there a flying scroll. And he said to me, 'What do you see?' So I answered, 'I see a flying scroll. Its length is twenty cubits and its width ten cubits.'"

Foe: an enemy in the spirit; Psalm 27:2 reads, "When the wicked came against me to eat up my flesh, my enemies and foes, they stumbled and fell."

Forbid: to disallow something in the spirit; In Matthew 18:18 (NLT), Jesus said, "I tell you the truth, whatever you forbid on earth will be forbidden in heaven, and whatever you permit on earth will be permitted in heaven."

Force: a demon power or the power of God you sense in the spirit, coming at you, coming against you, or as in the case of the Holy Spirit, moving on you, through you, or around you

Forecast: a report of the spiritual climate or atmosphere shift

Foreknow: to obtain knowledge beforehand by divine revelation

Foreknowledge: knowledge obtained before something happens; knowledge God reveals by His Spirit before an event occurs; a prophetic prediction; God has foreknowledge of everything and can share with you what you need to see

Foreordained: destined; determined by God ahead of time; some things you see in the spirit can't be changed because they are foreordained, but most things can be shifted through prayer and action

Forerunner: one who paved the way for future generations; Bob Jones, John Paul Jackson, and Paul Cain are among forerunners in the modern-day seer movement.

Foresee: to see something before it happens

Forerunner Angels: angels on assignment to go before us to make a way for us (see Exodus 23:23)

Foreshadow: a vision that offers a glimpse into the future; a vision that includes a warning of a future event for the purpose of prayer

Foretell: prophetically predicting the future

Forewarn: to release a warning based on what you see in the spirit

Forked-tongue: a tongue that sets out to deceive; a snake, which is representative of Satan, has a forked tongue and Satan is the father of lies (see John 8:44)

Form: the shape of something you see in the spirit; the appearance of something you see in the spirit; Job 4:16, "It stood still, But I could not discern its appearance. A form was before my eyes; There was silence; Then I heard a voice saying…"

Former Times: historical times; Ezra 4:15 reveals a request of the king, "that search may be made in the book of the records of your fathers. And you will find in the book of the records and know that this city is a rebellious city, harmful to kings and provinces, and that they have incited sedition within the city in former times, for which cause this city was destroyed."

Forthtell: re-prophesying a prophecy or an inspiration to tell forth the written Word of God as a now word, thereby making it prophetic; telling forth the Word of God

Four-Dimensional: in the earth realm, we see in three dimensions but the fourth dimension is not seen by the naked eye; When you see into the spirit realm, you are seeing into the fourth dimension.

Four Living Creatures: *see Living Creatures*

Fourth Dimension: a supernatural dimension beyond the physical senses

Fourth Watch: also called the morning watch, the fourth watch is from 3 am to 6 am; The morning watch is the last watch of the night. Exodus 14:24 speaks of the morning watch, "Now it came to pass, in the morning watch, that the Lord looked down upon the army of the Egyptians through the pillar of fire and cloud, and He troubled the army of the Egyptians."

Fragments: pieces or parts that you remember in a dream or a vision; If you meditate on those fragments, it's like pulling a string on a shirt that unravels the rest of the shirt. The fragment can unravel the dream or vision.

Fragrance of His Knowledge: the smell of God's presence; 2 Corinthians 2:14, "Now thanks be to God who always leads us in triumph in Christ, and through us diffuses the fragrance of His knowledge in every place."

Frame: the outline of something you see in the spirit; the structure of what you see in the spirit; A seer may not see the details of a person, but may see their frame so they can determine how large someone is, whether they are male female, a child or grown.

Frankincense: a common smell in the spirit associated with the presence of the Lord; a resin used in perfumes; one of the three gifts the Three Wise Men presented to baby Jesus in the manger (see Matthew 2:11)

Fraud: a deceitful seer; an imposter; a false seer

Frequency: a realm in the spirit where activity is taking place; patterns in the spirit; Seers can tune into divine frequencies or demonic frequencies like one would tune into a radio station. At times, the enemy tries to bring static to divine frequencies in the spirit. The seer must learn to wage war to break interruptions.

Fruits: a means of judging false prophets (see Matthew 7:15-16); the works and deeds of the prophet; the results of the prophet's life and ministry

Fulfilled: when visual revelation comes to pass; Luke 24:44, Jesus said, "These are the words which I spoke to you while I was still with you, that all things must be fulfilled which were written in the Law of Moses and the Prophets and the Psalms concerning Me."

Fulfillment of the Vision: the manifestation or realization of a spiritual vision; Daniel 11:14 reads, "Now in those times many shall rise up against the king of the South. Also, violent men of your people shall exalt themselves in fulfillment of the vision, but they shall fall."

Fullness of Time: the time at which God's plans are fulfilled; Ephesians 1:10 reads, "that in the dispensation of the fullness of the times He might gather together in one all things in Christ, both which are in heaven and which are on earth—in Him."

Fully Awake: when they were fully awake they saw the glory (see Matthew 17:1-8)

Furnace of Affliction: a place of testing and fiery trials; severe afflictions difficult to bear that burn away impurities in our hearts and things that hinder love; Isaiah 48:10, says "Behold, I have refined you, but not as silver; I have tested you in the furnace of affliction."

Futile Vision: *see False Vision*; Ezekiel 13:7 reads, "Have you not seen a futile vision, and have you not spoken false divination? You say, 'The Lord says,' but I have not spoken."

Future: a period of time that has yet to happen; God knows the future from the beginning (see Isaiah 46:10) and can reveal information to seers as He wills.

G

Gabriel: a messenger angel who makes significant prophetic announcements

Gad: a seer whose name means "fortune;" The Gadites were known in the Bible as "mighty men of valor, men trained for battle, who could handle shield and spear, whose faces were like the faces of lions, and were as swift as gazelles on the mountains" (1 Chronicles 2:8). Gad the seer was a prophet in the days of David and was a trusted voice in the king's life. He was known as "the king's seer" (see 2 Samuel 24:11).

Gad Anointing: a seer anointing bent toward spiritual warfare purposes

Gainsayer: one who opposes the revelation of a true seer, declaring it to be invalid; one who convinces those people that God does not speak through prophets today; Titus 1:9 (KJV), "Holding fast the faithful word as he hath been taught, that he may be able by sound doctrine both to exhort and to convince the gainsayers."

Gall of Bitterness: also called the poison of bitterness; an intense animosity that defiles the seer; a harsh, cynical spirit that sees the world through disappointment and pain; This disposition infiltrates the seer's eyes and hinders his perspective in the spirit. A bitter seer is more likely to be bent toward seeing demons everywhere, or have false demon-inspired visions he thinks are from the Lord.

In Acts 8 we see Simon the Sorcerer got saved, but he didn't get healed from bitterness and acted on this bitter envying. Peter rebuked him:

"And when Simon saw that through the laying on of the apostles' hands the Holy Spirit was given, he offered them money, saying, 'Give me this power also, that anyone on whom I lay hands may receive the Holy Spirit.'.

"But Peter said to him, 'Your money perish with you, because you thought that the gift of God could be purchased with money! You have neither part nor portion in this matter, for your heart is not right in the sight of God. Repent therefore of this your wickedness, and pray God if perhaps the thought of your heart may be forgiven you. For I see that you are poisoned by bitterness and bound by iniquity.'"

John Gill's Exposition of the Bible says of this verse, "Alluding to (Deuteronomy 29:18; 32:32) with which compare (Hebrews 12:15) and signifying, that he was in a state of nature and unregeneracy; under the power and dominion of covetousness, ambition, and hypocrisy; and in a way pernicious to himself, infectious to others, and ungrateful to God, and to good men; and that instead of the root of the matter, the truth of grace being in him, there was nothing in him but the bitter root of sin; which bore gall and wormwood, and everything that was nauseous and disagreeable."

Gap: a breach or broken down wall in the spirit that allows enemy access and requires intercession to close

Often, seers can see the gaps in the spirit and have a responsibility to stand in the gap with intercession to rebuild that wall and shut out the enemy. God told the prophet, "So I sought for a man among them who would make a wall, and stand in the gap before Me on behalf of the land, that I should not destroy it; but I found no one" (Ezekiel 22:30).

Gatekeeper: a type of intercessor; one who guards the gate or one who controls access; one who stands between the enemy and God's people to forbid access or between God and His people to plead for them

Gates: doors or portals into the spirit realm; places in cities or nations symbolic of the entrance of angels or demons

Gateways: *see Gates*

Gaze: to steadily keep your eyes on what you see in the spirit; to look upon the Lord intently; In order to gain the most detail of what God is revealing in the spirit, seers should fix their eyes on what God is showing them.

David wrote in Psalm 27:4, "One thing I have desired of the Lord, that will I seek: That I may dwell in the house of the Lord all the days of my life, to behold the beauty of the Lord, and to inquire in His temple."

Chazah, the Hebrew word for behold in this verse, is also translated gaze. *Chazah* in Hebrew means to see, perceive, look, behold, prophesy, provide; to see, behold; to see as a seer in the ecstatic state; to see, perceive; to see (by experience), according to *The KJV Old Testament Hebrew Lexicon*.

Generation: a people group living in the same period of history; a period of time that can range from 40, 70, or 100 years in Bible terms

Generational Blessings: a blessing that is passed down from one generation to another; Deuteronomy 7:9 reads, "Therefore know that the Lord your God, He is God, the faithful God who keeps covenant and mercy for a thousand generations with those who love Him and keep His commandments."

Generational Curses: a curse that is passed down from one generation to another based on sin or iniquities. Exodus 20:5 reads, "You shall not bow down to them nor serve them. For I, the Lord your God, am a jealous God, visiting the iniquity of the fathers upon the children to the third and fourth generations of those who hate Me." (See also Numbers 14:18; Exodus 34:6-7).

Generational Prophecies: prophecies that speak into someone's future generation; God told Abraham, "And I will make your descendants multiply as the stars of heaven; I will give to your descendants all these lands; and in your seed all the nations of the earth shall be blessed" (Genesis 26:4).

Generous Spirit: another name for the Holy Spirit; Psalm 51:2 says, "Restore to me the joy of Your salvation, and uphold me by Your generous Spirit."

Ghost: a demon; a spirit other than the Spirit of God, an angel or a spirit creature in the Kingdom of Light; In Mark 6:49, the disciples could not discern what spirit was walking on the water and mistook the Lord for another spirit: "And when they saw Him walking on the sea, they supposed it was a ghost, and cried out."

Gift: a divine grace God imparts freely according to His will; Paul told the church at Rome, "For I long to see you, that I may impart to you some spiritual gift, so that you may be established…"

Regarding the five-fold ministry of apostles, prophets, evangelists, pastors, and teachers, Paul wrote: "But to each one of us grace was given according to the measure of Christ's gift. Therefore He says: 'When He ascended on high, He led captivity captive, and gave gifts to men'" (Ephesians 4:7-8).

Gift of Interpreting Dreams: the divine ability to interpret dreams; Daniel and Joseph are the two people in Scripture who had this supernatural ability.

Gift of Prophecy: one of the nine gifts of the Holy Spirit mentioned in 1 Corinthians 14, for the purpose of edification, exhortation and comfort

Glimpse: to get a fleeting look at something in the spirit

Glitter: *see Gold Dust*

Glory: the weighty, almost tangible presence of God; the splendor of God

Glory Cloud: a visual manifestation of God's glory and presence; Exodus 13:21 recounts, "The Lord went before them by day in a pillar of cloud to lead them along the way, and by night in a pillar of fire, to give them light, so that they might travel by day and by night."

And in Exodus 16:10, "Now it came to pass, as Aaron spoke to the whole congregation of the children of Israel, that they looked toward the wilderness, and behold, the glory of the Lord appeared in the cloud."

When we think of Ezekiel, we're quick to point to the "blood on your hands" verses, but the watchman prophet was as much a glory watcher as a sin watcher. If you have the ability to see the sin and the demons, you have the ability to see the King of Glory and His angels. As a matter of fact, before Ezekiel was anointed as the "blood on your hands" watchman, he saw visions of God.

In Ezekiel 1, the vision starts with a whirlwind coming out of the north. He saw four living creatures, each with the likeness of the man, each with four faces and four wings. What a sight! He goes into great detail about the four living creatures and what they did before going on to describe the vision of the wheel within a wheel, with rims full of eyes. It's a dramatic vision that should inspire watchmen and seers. Finally, in Ezekiel 1:26-28 (AMPC):

"And above the firmament that was over their heads was the likeness of a throne in appearance like a sapphire stone, and seated above the likeness of a throne was a likeness with the appearance of a Man.

"From what had the appearance of His waist upward, I saw a lustre as it were glowing metal with the appearance of fire enclosed round about within it; and from the appearance of His waist downward, I saw as it were the appearance of fire, and there was brightness [of a halo] round about Him.

"Like the appearance of the bow that is in the cloud on the day of rain, so was the appearance of the brightness round about. This was the appearance of the likeness of the glory of the Lord. And when I saw it, I fell upon my face and I heard a voice of One speaking."

Glory of the Lord: the manifestation of God's presence

Gnosticism: originating in the first century A.D., Gnosticism is a collection of religious ideologies and practices that emphasizes personal experience over biblical teachings; a heresy based on man's knowledge (gnostic means knowledge); a belief that contends there is a mysterious knowledge and secrets that are only opened to those with special understanding

Go'el: a name for God that means Kinsman Redeemer, as seen in Exodus 15:13, "You in Your mercy have led forth the people whom You have redeemed; You have guided them in Your strength to Your holy habitation."

God of this World: another name for Satan (see John 12:31)

Godhead: the Father, Son, and Holy Spirit

Godward: moving toward God; looking toward God

Gold Dust: a manifestation of the glory of God; a dust that appears to be particles of gold; Job 28:6 speaks of gold dust and Psalm 68:13 speaks of shimmering gold.

Good Shepherd: another name for Jesus found in John 10:11: "I am the good shepherd. The good shepherd gives His life for the sheep."

Good Spirit: another name for the Holy Spirit; Nehemiah 9:20 reads, "You also gave Your good Spirit to instruct them, and did not withhold Your manna from their mouth, and gave them water for their thirst."

Govern: to exercise Christ's authority over a situation; to bring Kingdom influence into circumstances

Government of God: God's rule, dominion and government of the universe; a group of elders that governs a congregation, denomination or network; Apostles, prophets, and teachers make up the government of God on the earth (see 1 Corinthians 12:8)

Isaiah 9:7 reads, "Of the increase of His government and peace there will be no end, upon the throne of David and over His kingdom, to order it and establish it with judgment and justice From that time forward, even forever. The zeal of the Lord of hosts will perform this."

Grace: the favor of God; God's ever-loving kindness; a divine empowerment to do something you could not otherwise do

Grand Vision: *see Great Vision*

Great Apostasy: *see Great Falling Away*

Great Dragon: another name for Satan (see Revelation 12:9)

Great Falling Away: a period in the end-times when masses will turn away from faith in God. 1 Timothy 2:1-3 reads, "Now, brethren, concerning the coming of our Lord Jesus Christ and our gathering together to Him, we ask you, not to be soon shaken in mind or troubled, either by spirit or by word or by letter, as if from us, as though the day of Christ had come. Let no one deceive you by any means; for that Day will not come unless the falling away comes first, and the man of sin is revealed, the son of perdition…"

Great Silence: a silence that falls in anticipation of a significant word of the Lord; Acts 21:40 reads, "So when he had given him permission, Paul stood on the stairs and motioned with his hand to the people. And when there was a great silence, he spoke to them in the Hebrew language, saying…"

Great Tribulation: the last half of a seven-year period in the end-times during which the Antichrist is revealed and there is great suffering in the earth with the trumpets, seals and bowls outlined in the Book of Revelation;

Jesus said in Matthew 24:21-22, "For then there will be great tribulation, such as has not been since the beginning of the world until this time, no, nor ever shall be. And unless those days were shortened, no flesh would be saved; but for the elect's sake those days will be shortened."

Great Vision: an intense vision; a vision that is large in magnitude; an important vision; The prophet Daniel speaks of a great vision in Daniel 10:8, "Therefore I was left alone when I saw this great vision, and no strength remained in me; for my vigor was turned to frailty in me, and I retained no strength."

Green: inexperienced in the seer dimensions

Grievous: something that causes grief, pain, or sorrow. Seers sometimes see grievous visions

Grieving the Spirit: to offend, vex, irritate, insult or make the Holy Spirit sorrowful; Ephesians 4:30 warns us, "And do not grieve the Holy Spirit of God, by whom you were sealed for the day of redemption."

Grievous Vision: a vision that is difficult to watch; a vision that grieves one's spirit and is hard on the emotions; In Isaiah 21:2 Isaiah wrote, "A distressing vision is declared to me; The treacherous dealer deals treacherously, and the plunderer plunders. Go up, O Elam! Besiege, O Media! All its sighing I have made to cease."

Groanings: the expressed sound of intense yearnings, often in prayer; Romans 8:26, "Likewise the Spirit also helps in our weaknesses. For we do not know what we should pray for as we ought, but the Spirit Himself makes intercession for us with groanings which cannot be uttered."

Guard the Anointing: to protect your seer anointing by avoiding activities that would compromise or defile it; to guard someone who is carrying an anointing from unnecessary distractions or danger; 2 Timothy 1:14 (MEV) reads, "Guard the treasure that was committed to you through the Holy Spirit who lives in us."

Guardian Angels: also called angels of protection, these ministering spirits are sent on assignment to guard and protect believers (see Matthew 18:10; Acts 12:15)

Guile: deceit; treachery; Psalm 34:13 (KJV) reads, "Keep thy tongue from evil, and thy lips from speaking guile."

H

Habakkuk: a minor prophet who authored the Bible book of Habakkuk, which was penned shortly before the Babylonians seized Jerusalem in 586 B.C.; One of his most known revelations in this book is "the just shall live by faith" (see Habakkuk 2:4).

Habitation: a dwelling place; The Bible speaks repeatedly of the holy habitation of the Lord (see Exodus 15:13; Deuteronomy 26:15; Psalm 26:8). But there are also evil habitations. Isaiah 34:14 speaks of a habitation of jackals.

Hacking: *see Back Door*

Hades: also called Sheol or hell; the place or state of departed spirits; a place of punishment for the wicked; the unseen realm of the dead; When Jesus said the Gates of Hell would not prevail against the church, the Greek word for hell in that verse is *hades* (see Matthew 16:18).

Haggai: one of the twelve minor prophets and author of the Book of Haggai; a prophet who encouraged God's people to rebuild the temple

Hanani: a seer whose name means gracious; Despite the name, God sent Hanani to rebuke a king named Asa, who put him in prison. Read the account in 2 Chronicles 16:7-10:

"And at that time Hanani the seer came to Asa king of Judah, and said to him: 'Because you have relied on the king of Syria, and have not relied on the Lord your God, therefore the army of the king of Syria has escaped from your hand. Were the Ethiopians and the Lubim not a huge army with very many chariots and horsemen?.

'Yet, because you relied on the Lord, He delivered them into your hand. For the eyes of the Lord run to and fro throughout the whole earth, to show Himself strong on behalf of those whose heart is loyal to Him. In this you have done foolishly; therefore from now on you shall have wars.'.

"Then Asa was angry with the seer, and put him in prison, for he was enraged at him because of this. And Asa oppressed some of the people at that time."

Hanani also played a musical instrument after Nehemiah, his brother, completed oversight of the temple wall reconstruction (see Nehemiah 12:36).

Hanani Anointing: a seer anointing to stand strong in the face of persecution

Hananiah: a false prophet who opposed Jeremiah and died (see Jeremiah 28)

Handwriting: when you see words in the spirit realm that show you what the Lord is doing or saying or wants to do or say; We see a biblical example of this in Daniel 5:1-8:

"In the same hour the fingers of a man's hand appeared and wrote opposite the lampstand on the plaster of the wall of the king's palace; and the king saw the part of the hand that wrote. Then the king's countenance changed, and his thoughts troubled him, so that the joints of his hips were loosened and his knees knocked against each other.

"The king cried aloud to bring in the astrologers, the Chaldeans, and the soothsayers. The king spoke, saying to the wise men of Babylon, 'Whoever reads this writing, and tells me its interpretation, shall be clothed with purple and have a chain of gold around his neck; and he shall be the third ruler in the kingdom.' Now all the king's wise men came, but they could not read the writing, or make known to the king its interpretation."

Hard Heaven: *see Bronze Heaven*

Hard Vision: *see Grievous Vision*

Harvesting Angels: angels with an assignment to help bring in the harvest (see Acts 8:23; Acts 10:3)

Haughty Eyes: *see Arrogant Eyes*

Head of the Church: another name for Jesus found in Ephesians 1:22: "And He put all things under His feet, and gave Him to be head over all things to the church…"

Healing Angels: angels God sends on assignment at times to assist in healing ministry (see John 5:4)

Heart: the inner man; often a word used interchangeably with the spirit of a man in the Bible (see Romans 7:22; 2 Corinthians 4:16; Ephesians 3:16)

Heart of Evil: a wicked heart; a heart set on doing evil. Jesus said evil thoughts come from the heart of man (see Mark 7:1); In Genesis 6:5, "Then the Lord saw that the wickedness of man was great in the earth, and that every intent of the thoughts of his heart was only evil continually."

Heart of Gladness: a joyful heart; a heart full of the joy of the Lord; Exodus 4:14, shares, "So the anger of the Lord was kindled against Moses, and He said: 'Is not Aaron the Levite your brother? I know that he can speak well. And look, he is also coming out to meet you. When he sees you, he will be glad in his heart.'" Also see Isaiah 30:29; Deuteronomy 28:47: Song of Solomon 3:11; Acts 2:46. Seers can sometimes see the condition of someone's heart.

Heart of Hardness: a heart that will not receive the will of God; a heart that rejects the commands or ways of God; a heart that refuses to believe God; Exodus 4:21, "And the Lord said to Moses, 'When you go back to Egypt, see that you do all those wonders before Pharaoh which I have put in your hand. But I will harden his heart, so that he will not let the people go.'"

Heart of Integrity: a sound heart; a moral heart; a heart that holds God's Word as the standard; After Abimelech took Abraham's wife Sarah into his clan, God gave the foreign king a dream warning him; Genesis 20:5 shares Abimelech's conversation with God: "Did he not say to me, 'She is my sister'? And she, even she herself said, 'He is my brother.' In the integrity of my heart and innocence of my hands I have done this."

Heaven: the dwelling place of God and other heavenly beings; a place where those who died in Christ live until the new heaven and new earth are manifested

Heavenly Bodies: *see Celestial Bodies*

Heavenly Calling: a calling from heaven to believers as sons and citizens of the Kingdom, with the rights and responsibilities of the sons of God; Hebrews 3:1 reads, "Therefore, holy brethren, partakers of the heavenly calling, consider the Apostle and High Priest of our confession, Christ Jesus…"

Heavenly Dimension: a dimension in the spirit where you see heaven and heavenly things; (For more, get *The Seer Dimensions* book.)

Heavenly Gift: a gift from heaven; Jesus Christ Hebrews 6:4 reads, "For it is impossible for those who were once enlightened, and have tasted the heavenly gift, and have become partakers of the Holy Spirit, and have tasted the good word of God and the powers of the age to come, if they fall away, to renew them again to repentance, since they crucify again for themselves the Son of God, and put Him to an open shame."

Heavenly Host: a company of God's angels; Luke 2:13-14 reads, "And suddenly there was with the angel a multitude of the heavenly host praising God and saying: Glory to God in the highest, and on earth peace, goodwill toward men!"

Heavenly Jerusalem: *see New Jerusalem* (see Hebrews 12:22).

Heavenly Kingdom: God's Kingdom as it is in heaven; 2 Timothy 4:18 reads, "And the Lord will deliver me from every evil work and preserve me for His heavenly kingdom. To Him be glory forever and ever. Amen!"

Heavenly Minded: a mind more focused on what God wants to do than what the enemy is doing; a mind set on seeing God's will come to earth as it is in heaven; Paul wrote: "If then you were raised with Christ, seek those things which are above, where Christ is, sitting at the right hand of God. Set your mind on things above, not on things on the earth" (Colossians 3:1-2).

Heavenly Places: places in heaven; the place where Christ dwells at the right hand of the father; the place where believers are seated in Christ; Ephesians 1:3 reads, "Blessed be the God and Father of our Lord Jesus Christ, who has blessed us with every spiritual blessing in the heavenly places in Christ..."

Heavenly Things: activities that take place in heaven; things of a heavenly origin or nature; In John 3:12, Jesus said, "If I have told you earthly things and you do not believe, how will you believe if I tell you heavenly things?"

Heavenly Visions: a vision of heaven; a vision inspired by heaven; Acts 26:19 reads, "Therefore, King Agrippa, I was not disobedient to the heavenly vision..."

Heavens: space around and above the earth; a reference to the first, second and third heavens. Genesis 1:1, "In the beginning God created the heavens and the earth." (*See First Heaven; Second Heaven; Third Heaven*)

Hedge: a boundary or other means that protects or safeguards someone or something from danger; Satan spoke of the hedge God put around Job (see Job 1:10). God told Ezekiel, "And I sought for a man among them, that should make up the hedge, and stand in the gap before me for the land, that I should not destroy it: but I found none" (Ezekiel 22:30). The Greek word for a hedge in that verse is "a fence or wall."

Hedge of Thorns: a seer may see a hedge of thorns around a backslidden person whom God is trying to bring back to his heart; In the context of Israel's spiritual adultery, Hosea 2:6-

7 prophesies: "Therefore, behold, I will hedge up your way with thorns, and wall her in, so that she cannot find her paths. She will chase her lovers, but not overtake them; Yes, she will seek them, but not find them. Then she will say, 'I will go and return to my first husband, for then *it was* better for me than now.'"

Hell: *see Hades*

Helper: another name for the Holy Spirit; John 14:26 reads, "But the Helper, the Holy Spirit, whom the Father will send in My name, He will teach you all things, and bring to your remembrance all things that I said to you."

Heman: a seer whose name means faithful; The grandson of Samuel, Heman was marked for his wisdom (see 1 Kings 4:31; 1 Chronicles 2:6). He was the psalmist who wrote Psalm 88. Influential and multi-talented as a seer, songwriter, father and Levite, Heman is mentioned as one of the king David's seers in 2 Chronicles 25:5.

Heman Anointing: a seer anointing that stewards wisely and expresses itself creatively

Herald: one who announces a prophetic message; to make an announcement concerning prophetic revelation; an angel sent on assignment with a message of good news or judgment; *see also Prophetic Messenger*

Heresy: a doctrine or message contrary to the divine will of God as expressed in Scripture; destructive doctrines that lead people away from Christ; 2 Peter 2:1 reads, "But there were also false prophets among the people, even as there will be false teachers among you, who will secretly bring in destructive heresies, even denying the Lord who bought them, and bring on themselves swift destruction."

Heretic: one who propagates heresy

Hidden: something out of the seer's field of spiritual vision; something purposely concealed from view by God or the enemy; Ultimately, the enemy cannot conceal what God wants to reveal. Daniel 22 assures, "He reveals deep and hidden things; he knows what is in the darkness, and the light dwells with him."

Hidden From You: when the Lord hides something about the condition of someone with whom you are in relationship; In 2 Kings 4, we read of the woman to whom Elisha prophesied a son. The son was born but died in an accident in the field with his father. 2 Kings 4:25-27 reads:

"So it was, when the man of God saw her afar off, that he said to his servant Gehazi, 'Look, the Shunammite woman! Please run now to meet her, and say to her, 'Is it well with you? Is it well with your husband? Is it well with the child?'.

"And she answered, 'It is well.' Now when she came to the man of God at the hill, she caught him by the feet, but Gehazi came near to push her away. But the man of God said, 'Let her alone; for her soul is in deep distress, and the Lord has hidden it from me, and has not told me.'"

Hidden in His Quiver: a revelation kept as a secret weapon for God's use in the right time (see Isaiah 49:2)

Hidden in Your Heart: having God's Word, precepts and principles close to the heart (see Psalm 119:11)

Hidden Part of Man: the part of man that is not visible to the naked eye; the soul and the spirit (see Psalm 56:1)

Hidden Riches of Secret Places: seer revelation reserved and preserved in the secret place; Isaiah 45:3 reads, "I will give you the treasures of darkness and hidden riches of secret places, that you may know that I, the Lord, who call you by your name, am the God of Israel."

Hidden Snares: traps in the spirit demons set for prophets and seers to distract them, sabotage them, delay them, and ensnare them; Jeremiah 18:22 reads. "Let a cry be heard from their houses, when You bring a troop suddenly upon them; For they have dug a pit to take me, and hidden snares for my feet."

Hidden the Heart From Understanding: the condition of a heart from which God hides the meaning of a parable or spiritual truth; Job 17:4 reads, "For You have hidden their heart from understanding; Therefore You will not exalt them."

Hidden Treasures: valuable revelations God hides from the natural mind that must be searched out in the spirit

Hierarchy: a classification of angels, demons, or offices in the church; Paul outlines the hierarchy of demons in Ephesians 6.

Hierarchy of Angels: the divisions or classifications of angels, such as cherubim, seraphim, and archangels

Hierarchy of Demons: the divisions or classifications of demons, such as principalities, powers, rulers of darkness and spiritual wickedness in high places (see Ephesians 6:12)

High Places: places of worship, usually of foreign gods, that were elevated above ground level; places people worship God, such as on a mountain

High Priest: another name for Jesus found in Hebrews 4:14: "Seeing then that we have a great High Priest who has passed through the heavens, Jesus the Son of God, let us hold fast our confession."

Holy: set apart; 1 Peter 1:16 quotes God saying, "Be holy, for I am holy."

Holy Ground: quite literally, this means ground of holiness; ground made holy due to the manifest presence of God Himself; Exodus 3:5 reads, "Then He said, 'Do not draw near this place. Take your sandals off your feet, for the place where you stand is holy ground.'"

Holy Imagination: an imagination that is sanctified and set apart for God's use; an imagination overtaken by the Holy Spirit

Holy of Holies: the innermost chamber—and the most sacred part—of the temple, hidden behind the veil; a place where

God appears; In Leviticus 16:12, God told Moses, "Tell Aaron your brother not to come at just any time into the Holy Place inside the veil, before the mercy seat which is on the ark, lest he die; for I will appear in the cloud above the mercy seat." When Christ died on the cross, the veil was ripped in two from top to bottom (see Matthew 27:50-51). Believers now have direct access to God through Jesus Christ and can personally encounter His presence. Hebrews 19:20 reads, "Therefore, brethren, having boldness to enter the Holiest by the blood of Jesus, by a new and living way which He consecrated for us, through the veil, that is, His flesh…"

Holy Place: in the temple, the inner court, which is between the outer court and the Holy of Holy; a place made holy by the presence of God; Exodus 26:33 reads, "And you shall hang the veil from the clasps. Then you shall bring the ark of the Testimony in there, behind the veil. The veil shall be a divider for you between the holy place and the Most Holy."

Holy Servant: another name for Jesus found in Acts 4:29-30: "Now, Lord, look on their threats, and grant to Your servants that with all boldness they may speak Your word, by stretching out Your hand to heal, and that signs and wonders may be done through the name of Your holy Servant Jesus."

Holy Spirit: the third person in the Trinity; the power of God; the giver of the gifts of the Spirit

Horama: a Greek word for vision; sight divinely granted in an ecstasy or in a sleep; that which is seen; spectacle, according to *Thayer's Greek Lexicon. Strong's Concordance* defines it as something gazed at, spectacle (especially supernatural)—sight, vision; *Horama* is most typically used in the Book of Acts. In Acts 9, Paul had a vision (*horama*) of a prophet named Ananias that came to restore his sight after his encounter on the road to Damascus.

Horasis: gazing in the spirit; gazing on a vision, seeing behind the veil; This is the Greek word used in the Book of Revelation concerning John's epic vision. Revelation 4:3

reads, "And He who sat there was like a jasper and a sardius stone in appearance; and *there was* a rainbow around the throne, in appearance like an emerald."

Hosea: one of the 12 minor prophets in the Bible, and author of the Book of Hosea; the theme of his book was Israel's unfaithfulness to God, which was partially manifested in a prophetic act of the prophet marrying a prostitute

Hour: a specific time or season; a definite time, point of time or moment in time

House Prophet: a prophet whose jurisdiction in the spirit is confined to the local church; a prophet who has recognized authority in a local church

Huckster: one who sells prophetic words

Huldah: a prophetess who lived in the days of King Josiah; a prophetess who prophesied a word of judgment to Judah

I

I Am: another name for God as seen in Exodus 3:14: "And God said to Moses, 'I AM WHO I AM.' And He said, 'Thus you shall say to the children of Israel, 'I AM has sent me to you.'"; another name for Jesus seen in John 8:58: "Jesus said to them, 'Most assuredly, I say to you, before Abraham was, I AM.'"

I Will Not Keep Silent: the vow of a seer watchman in regards to prayer; Isaiah 62:1 reads, "For Zion's sake I will not hold My peace, and for Jerusalem's sake I will not rest, until her righteousness goes forth as brightness, and her salvation as a lamp that burns."

Ichabod: without glory; seers may see Ichabod written over churches or movements; In 1 Samuel 4:19:22 we read the only account:

"Now his daughter-in-law, Phinehas' wife, was with child, due to be delivered; and when she heard the news that the ark of God was captured, and that her father-in-law and her husband were dead, she bowed herself and gave birth, for her labor pains came upon her.

"And about the time of her death the women who stood by her said to her, 'Do not fear, for you have borne a son.' But she did not answer, nor did she regard it. Then she named the child Ichabod, saying, 'The glory has departed from Israel!' because the ark of God had been captured and because of her father-in-law and her husband. And she said, 'The glory has departed from Israel, for the ark of God has been captured.'"

Iddo Anointing: similar to an Issachar anointing, the Iddo anointing is a seer anointing that sees timely events

Iddo the Seer: a seer whose name means timely; 2 Chronicles 12:15 called Iddo a seer. Apparently, there was a book of visions he penned (see 2 Chronicles 13:22). He had visions concerning Jeroboam, son of Nebat (2 Chronicles 9:29).

Identificational Repentance: repentance on behalf of a people group or nation that strips Satan's right to operate; also called warfare repentance or the power to heal the past; We see this concept in several Scriptures, the foremost being Daniel's repentance for the sins of his ancestors (see Daniel 9:8, 20).

Idol: anything one worships apart from God (see Exodus 20:3-5)

Illegal Operation: a spiritual operation that is illegal according to the laws of the Spirit and the bounds of Scripture

Illuminate: brightened with the light of God; a spiritual enlightenment that opens up one's mind to divine truth; glorified

Illusion: a deceptive vision that appears true; visual revelation that has its source in the demonic realm

Image: the likeness or resemblance of an original; a picture one sees in the spirit; a spiritual representation of something in the real world; alternatively, a word often used to speak of idols in the Bible (see Jeremiah 51:52; Isaiah 45:20)

Imagination: picturing images in one's mind that are not yet reality; re-imaging visions or dreams God has given you in your mind, with dependence and guidance from the Holy Spirit

Impart: to "impart" or "give," according to *The KJV New Testament Greek Lexicon. Merriam-Webster's Dictionary* defines "impart" as "to give, convey or grant from as if from a store."

God has a great storehouse of gifts and He wants to impart what will strengthen you in your calling. *Young's Literal Bible* translates this "to give a share of." "Do not neglect the gift that is in you, which was given to you by prophecy, with the laying on of hands by the elders" (1 Timothy 4:14).

Impartation: a divine transfer that releases an ability one didn't have before; Through impartation, the Holy Spirit gives or grants one a spiritual gift, revelation, or power that one needs to fulfill his purpose.

Paul told the church in Rome: "For I am yearning to see you, that I may impart and share with you some spiritual gift to strengthen and establish you. That is, that we may be mutually strengthened and encouraged and comforted by each other's faith, both yours and mine" (Romans 1:11-12).

Importunity: an urgent persistence in prayer; In Luke 11:5-8, Jesus said, "And he said unto them, which of you shall have a friend, and shall go unto him at midnight, and say unto him, Friend, lend me three loaves; For a friend of mine in his journey is come to me, and I have nothing to set before him? And he from within shall answer and say, Trouble me not: the door is now shut, and my children are with me in bed; I cannot rise and give thee. I say unto you, Though he will not rise and give him, because he is his friend, yet because of his importunity he will rise and give him as many as he needeth."

Impression: the Holy Spirit's purposeful action to get our attention by influencing our thoughts, emotions or physical senses

In Theater: the place a seer may find himself in the spirit where a vision or encounters is unfolding

In the Body or Out of the Body: speaking of an encounter in heaven, Paul wrote, "And I know such a man—whether in the body or out of the body I do not know, God knows…" (2 Corinthians 12:3). Paul was indicating he could not be sure of whether his soul was up in heaven or if it were just a trance.

Matthew *Henry's* Commentary reads: "There can be no doubt the apostle speaks of himself. Whether heavenly things were brought down to him, while his body was in a trance, as in the case of ancient prophets; or whether his soul was dislodged from the body for a time, and taken up into heaven, or whether he was taken up, body and soul together, he knew not."

Infinity: unlimited time

Iniquity: perversity and depravity; the guilt or consequence of perversity or depravity; the issue prevalent in a generational curse; Exodus 34:7 reads, "Keeping mercy for thousands, forgiving iniquity and transgression and sin, by no means clearing the guilty, visiting the iniquity of the fathers upon the children and the children's children to the third and the fourth generation."

Inner Castle: also called The Mansions, a book by Teresa of Avila that acts as a guide for spiritual development through sacrifice and prayer

Inner Chamber: *see Secret Chamber*

Inner Man: the unseen man; the spirit man; the real you; (see Ephesians 3:16)

Inner Vision: a vision in which one sees with his mind's eye; a vision in which the Holy Spirit shows one something internally rather than an open vision or encounter

Innermost Being: the heart of a man; Jesus said, "He who believes in Me, as the Scripture said, 'From his innermost being will flow rivers of living water." (John 7:38, NASB).

Inquire of the Lord: to seek the Lord's counsel on a situation or something one has seen in the spirit; Jeremiah 21:2 reads, "Please inquire of the Lord for us, for Nebuchadnezzar king of Babylon makes war against us. Perhaps the Lord will deal with us according to all His wonderful works, that the king may go away from us."

Inspiration: the influence of the Holy Spirit that moves someone to act or speak in accordance with God's will; a prophetic revelation; 2 Peter 2:1 (Darby) reads, "For prophecy came not by the will of man at any time: but the holy men of God spoke, inspired by the Holy Ghost."

Instant: an infinitesimal space of time; a space of time so small that one cannot measure it; sometimes seers see something for a mere instant

Intense Vision: *see Great Vision*

Intercession: petitioning God on behalf of a person, place or circumstance; a type of prayer in which one cries out for another; a meeting with God over a third-party issue; 1 Timothy 2:1, "Therefore I exhort first of all that supplications, prayers, intercessions, and giving of thanks be made for all men…"

Internal Vision: *see Inner Vision*

Interpret: to unravel symbols, types, shadows and parables to offer the natural meaning or message contained in a dream, vision or encounter

Interpretation: the meaning of what you saw in a vision or experienced during a dream or encounter

Interpretation Belongs to God: the reality that God has the accurate interpretation of a dream or vision and all accurate interpretations come from His Spirit (see Genesis 40:8)

Interpretation of Tongues: the meaning of what someone, either you or someone else, has prayed in the spirit (see 1 Corinthians 12:10)

Interpreter of Dreams: one who has the gift of interpretation; Daniel and Joseph in the Bible were both spoken of as ones who had this gift

Interpreter of Tongues: one who has the gift of interpretation of tongues (see 1 Corinthians 12:10)

Invisible realm: *see Unseen Realm*

Invitation: a heavenly request for the seer's presence; At times, God will give the seer an auditory invitation that sounds something like this, "Come up here." We see John the Revelator receive such an invitation twice.

Inward Parts: the heart of a person; Psalm 51:6 reads, "Behold, You desire truth in the inward parts, and in the hidden part You will make me to know wisdom."

Isaiah: author of the Book of Isaiah whose name means "Yahweh is Salvation" a prophet who penned many judgment prophesies, as well as Messianic prophecies; a contemporary of the prophet Micaiah; Isaiah is also known as the prophet of hope

Isaiah 22:22 Key: *see Key of David*

Issachar Anointing: an anointing that was on the sons of Issachar (see 1 Chronicles 12:32)

J

Jacinth: an orangish precious stone John the Revelator saw on the foundations of the wall around the New Jerusalem (see Revelation 21:19-21)

Jacob's Ladder: the means by which angels ascend and descend to heaven by permission of the Captain of the Hosts; part of a vision Jacob had in Genesis 28:12

Jannes and Jambres: the names of the Egyptian sorcerers who opposed Moses in power demonstrations; The sin of these sorcerers was so great, Paul spoke of it in 2 Timothy 3:7-9, "Now as Jannes and Jambres resisted Moses, so do these also resist the truth: men of corrupt minds, disapproved concerning the faith; but they will progress no further, for their folly will be manifest to all, as theirs also was."

Jannes and Jambres give insight into the mindset of sorcerers and serve as a caution to seers.

Jasper: a stone used to visually describe the appearance of God on His throne (see Revelation 4:3), the holy city, Jerusalem, in the new earth (see Revelation 21:10-12); and the wall around the new Jerusalem (see Revelation 21:17-19)

Jeduthun: a seer whose name means praising; He was assigned to oversee the temple music service (see 1 Chronicles 16:31) and was known as one of the king's seers (see 2 Chronicles 35:15). Jeduthun is thought to have written the music that goes along with Psalms 39, 62, and 77. This musical prophet also bore six sons who were musical prophets (1 Chronicles 15:1-6). He was also the father of a gatekeeper (see 1 Chronicles 16:38).

Jeduthun Anointing: a seer anointing that sees the presence of the Lord and teaches others how to enter into his gates

Jehovah: an Old Testament name for God; a name by which God revealed Himself to the ancient Hebrews

Jehovah Adon Kol Ha-arets: a name for God that means "The Lord, the Lord of All the Earth," as seen in Joshua 3:11, "Behold, the ark of the covenant of the Lord of all the earth is crossing over before you into the Jordan."

Jehovah Chereb: a name for God that means "The Lord… the Sword," as seen in Deuteronomy 33:29, "Happy are you, O Israel! Who is like you, a people saved by the Lord, the shield of your help and the sword of your majesty! Your enemies shall submit to you, and you shall tread down their high places."

Jehovah El Elohim: a name for God that means "The Lord God of gods, the Lord, Mighty, Powerful, Strong One Over all," as seen in Joshua 22:22, "The Lord God of gods, the Lord God of gods, He knows, and let Israel itself know—if it is in rebellion, or if in treachery against the Lord, do not save us this day."

Jehovah El Emeth: a name for God that means "Lord God of Truth," as seen in Psalm 31:5, "Into Your hand I commit my spirit; You have redeemed me, O Lord God of truth."

Jehovah El Gemuwal: a name of God that means "The Lord God of Recompense," as seen in Jeremiah 51:56, "Because the plunderer comes against her, against Babylon, and her mighty men are taken. Every one of their bows is broken; For the Lord is the God of recompense, He will surely repay."

Jehovah Elohim Ab: a name for God that means "The Lord God of Your Forefathers," as seen in Joshua 18:3, "Then Joshua said to the children of Israel: 'How long will you neglect to go and possess the land which the Lord God of your fathers has given you?'"

Jehovah Elohim Yeshua: a name for God that means "The Son of God," as seen in Matthew 16:16, "Simon Peter answered and said, 'You are the Christ, the Son of the living God.'"

Jehovah Gibbor Milchama: a name for God that means "The Lord Mighty in Battle" as seen in Psalm 24:8, "Who is this King of glory? The Lord strong and mighty, the Lord mighty in battle."

Jehovah Goelekh: a name for God that means "The Lord Thy Redeemer," as seen in Isaiah 60:16, "You shall drink the milk of the Gentiles, and milk the breast of kings; You shall know that I, the Lord, am your Savior and your Redeemer, the Mighty One of Jacob."

Jehovah Ha-Melech: a name for God that means "The Lord the King," as seen in Psalm 98:6, "With trumpets and the sound of a horn; shout joyfully before the Lord, the King."

Jehovah Hashopet: a name for God that means "The Lord the Judge," as seen in Judges 11:27, "Therefore I have not sinned against you, but you wronged me by fighting against me. May the Lord, the Judge, render judgment this day between the children of Israel and the people of Ammon.'"

Jehovah Hoshiah: a name for God that means "O Lord Save," as seen in Psalm 20:9, "Save, Lord! May the King answer us when we call."

Jehovah Immeka: a name for God that means "The Lord is With You," as seen in Judges 6:12, "And the Angel of the Lord appeared to him, and said to him, 'The Lord is with you, you mighty man of valor!'"

Jehovah Jireh: a name of God that means, "The Lord Will Provide" (see Genesis 22:14) or "The God Who Sees" (see Genesis 16:13).

Jehovah Magen: a name for God that means "The Lord My Shield," according to Deuteronomy 33:29, "Blessed are you, Israel! Who is like you, a people saved by the Lord (Jehovah)? He is your shield (Magen) and helper and your glorious sword. Your enemies will cower before you, and you will tread on their heights."

Jehovah Maginnenu: a name of God that means "The Lord Our Defense," as seen in Psalm 89:18, "For our shield belongs to the Lord, and our king to the Holy One of Israel."

Jehovah Malakh: a name for God that means "The Angel of the Lord," as seen in Genesis 16:7, "Now the Angel of the Lord found her by a spring of water in the wilderness, by the spring on the way to Shur."

Jehovah Mauzzi: a name of God that means "The Lord My Fortress," as seen in Jeremiah 16:19, "O Lord, my strength and my fortress, my refuge in the day of affliction, the Gentiles shall come to You from the ends of the earth and say, 'Surely our fathers have inherited lies, worthlessness and unprofitable things.'"

Jehovah Mekoddishkem: a name of God that means, "the Lord who sanctifies you," as seen in Exodus 31:13, "Speak also to the children of Israel, saying: 'Surely My Sabbaths you shall keep, for it is a sign between Me and you throughout your generations, that you may know that I am the Lord who sanctifies you.'"

Jehovah Mephalti: a name for God that means "The Lord My Deliverer" as seen in Psalm 18:2, "The Lord is my rock and my fortress and my deliverer; My God, my strength, in whom I will trust; My shield and the horn of my salvation, my stronghold."

Jehovah Metsudhathi: a name for God that means "The Lord My High Tower," as seen in Psalm 18:2, "The Lord is my rock and my fortress and my deliverer; My God, my strength, in whom I will trust; My shield and the horn of my salvation, my stronghold."

Jehovah Moshiekh: a name for God that means "The Lord Your Savior," as seen in Isaiah 49:26, "I will feed those who oppress you with their own flesh, and they shall be drunk with their own blood as with sweet wine. All flesh shall know that

I, the Lord, am your Savior, and your Redeemer, the Mighty One of Jacob."

Jehovah Nissi: a name of God that means, "The Lord is my banner." Exodus 17:13-16 reads, "So Joshua defeated Amalek and his people with the edge of the sword. Then the Lord said to Moses, 'Write this for a memorial in the book and recount it in the hearing of Joshua, that I will utterly blot out the remembrance of Amalek from under heaven.' And Moses built an altar and called its name, The-Lord-Is-My-Banner; for he said, 'Because the Lord has sworn: the Lord will have war with Amalek from generation to generation.'"

Jehovah Ori: a name for God that means "The Lord My Light," as seen in Psalm 27:1, "The Lord is my light and my salvation; Whom shall I fear? The Lord is the strength of my life; Of whom shall I be afraid?"

Jehovah Raah: a name of God that means, "The Lord is my Shepherd." This name of God is found in Psalm 23.

Jehovah Rapha: a name for God that means, "The Lord that Heals." The first time this is in Exodus 15:26, "If you diligently heed the voice of the Lord your God and do what is right in His sight, give ear to His commandments and keep all His statutes, I will put none of the diseases on you which I have brought on the Egyptians. For I am the Lord who heals you."

Jehovah Sabaoth: a name for God that means "Lord of Hosts" (see 1 Samuel 1:3).

Jehovah Shalom: a name of God that means "The Lord is Peace." God reveals Himself to Gideon as Jehovah Shalom in Judges 6:22-24, "Now Gideon perceived that He was the Angel of the Lord. So Gideon said, 'Alas, O Lord God! For I have seen the Angel of the Lord face to face.' Then the Lord said to him, "Peace be with you; do not fear, you shall not die.' So Gideon built an altar there to the Lord, and called it

The-Lord-Is-Peace. To this day it is still in Ophrah of the Abiezrites."

Jehovah Shammah: a name for God that means, "The Existing One." The only time this is used in the Bible is Exodus 48:35: "All the way around shall be eighteen thousand cubits; and the name of the city from that day shall be: THE LORD IS THERE."

Jehovah Tsemach: a name for God that means "The Branch of the Lord," as seen in Isaiah 4:2, "In that day the Branch of the Lord shall be beautiful and glorious; And the fruit of the earth shall be excellent and appealing for those of Israel who have escaped."

Jehovah Tsidkenu: a name for God that means "the Lord our God spoke to us." This name is first used in Jeremiah 23:6: "In His days Judah will be saved, and Israel will dwell safely; Now this is His name by which He will be called: THE LORD OUR RIGHTEOUSNESS."

Jehu: a man God anointed as king to deal with the house of Ahab and confront Jezebel; Jehu commanded the eunuchs to throw Jezebel down. God sent a prophet to anoint and prophesy over Jehu; 2 Kings 9:5-10, "And he said, 'For you, Commander.' Then he arose and went into the house. And he poured the oil on his head, and said to him, "Thus says the Lord God of Israel: 'I have anointed you king over the people of the Lord, over Israel. You shall strike down the house of Ahab your master, that I may avenge the blood of My servants the prophets, and the blood of all the servants of the Lord, at the hand of Jezebel.

'For the whole house of Ahab shall perish; and I will cut off from Ahab all the males in Israel, both bond and free. So I will make the house of Ahab like the house of Jeroboam the son of Nebat, and like the house of Baasha the son of Ahijah. The dogs shall eat Jezebel on the plot of ground at Jezreel, and there shall be none to bury her.' And he opened the door and fled."

Jeremiah: author of the Book of Jeremiah and the Book of Lamentations

Jerusalem: the capital of Israel

Jesus: the Savior of the world; the Son of God; the ultimate Seer; In John 5:19, Jesus said, "Then Jesus answered and said to them, 'Most assuredly, I say to you, the Son can do nothing of Himself, but what He sees the Father do; for whatever He does, the Son also does in like manner.'"

Jezebel: a spirit of seduction that operates in the life of 1 Kings Queen Jezebel, and in the life of the Revelation 2 woman who called herself a prophetess

Jezreel: an ancient Israelite city whose name means "God scatters;" Jezreel was within the boundaries of the tribe of Issachar; a land of revelation; the place King Ahab and Jezebel lived.

Joel: one of the twelve minor prophets and author of the Book of Joel; One of the best-known Scriptures in Joel is Joel 2:27-28, "And it shall come to pass afterward that I will pour out My Spirit on all flesh; Your sons and your daughters shall prophesy, Your old men shall dream dreams, Your young men shall see visions. And also on My menservants and on My maidservants I will pour out My Spirit in those days."

John of the Cross: a 16th Century Spanish mystic, introduced the concept of the dark night of the soul in a book called Dark Night of the Soul. In it, he writes, "No matter how much individuals do through their own efforts, they cannot actively purify themselves enough to be disposed in the least degree for the divine union of the perfection of love. God must take over and purge them in that fire that is dark for them, as we will explain." *see also Dark Night of the Soul*

John the Baptist: a forerunner prophet who paved the way for the first coming of Christ; a transitional prophet between the Old and New Covenants. Jesus said John the Baptist was the greatest man born of a woman (see Matthew 11:11) and said, "And if you are willing to receive it, he is Elijah who is to come" (Matthew 11:4).

John the Revelator: one of the twelve apostles of Jesus; author of the Book of John, 1 John, 2 John, 3 John and the Book of Revelation, which outlines epic visions and encounters related to the end-times

Joint-Heirs: the reality that gives you permission to see in the spirit; seeing in the spirit is part of your spiritual inheritance in Christ; seeing in the spirit is one of the many spiritual blessings with which believers are blessed (see Ephesians 1:3)

Jonah: a rebellious prophet God sent to pronounce coming judgment on Nineveh; an example of a self-willed prophet who has a bias that leads to bitterness toward a people group; a prophet who would hinder revival for the sake of judgment

Joseph: a prophet and dreamer in the Bible who had the gift of interpreting dreams

Josephus: a Jewish priest, scholar, and historian who recorded significant events during the Jewish revolt of 66-70, as well as commentary and fact-finding on history from biblical days and characters, including Jezebel

Josiah: a king who brought revival to Israel after a period of reformation; an eight-year-old king whose name meant "Healed of the Lord" who saw the land healed in Judah after restoring the house of the Lord

Jubilee: a sabbatical year after 49 years (see Leviticus 25:9); a time of release from debt and the release of captives

Judge: another name for Jesus as seen in Acts 14:4, "And He commanded us to preach to the people, and to testify that it is He who was ordained by God to be Judge of the living and the dead."

Judge What You See: to discern the source of what you see as coming from God, your imagination, or an evil spirit

Judgment: a divine decision

Juncture: a critical point in time; a time of transition

Jurisdiction: the boundaries in which God allows one to exert their spiritual power or influence

K

Kadosh: a name for God that means "The Holy One," as seen in Isaiah 40:25, "'To whom then will you liken Me, Or to whom shall I be equal?' says the Holy One."

Kairos: a Greek word for time that means "a fitting season, opportunity, time, occasion;" It comes from the Greek word *kara*, referring to things "coming to a head" to take full advantage of. *Kairos* is the suitable time, the right moment, or favorable moment.

Keep on Looking: a seer's spiritual diligence to maintain seer focus until every detail of the vision is recorded or until everything you are supposed to see is revealed; In Daniel 7, the prophet kept on looking in the vision until he saw past the demons and into the glory of God.

Keep Silent: when you know something the Lord is about to do but do not have His permission to release it; when you discern something but elder prophets and seers tell you not to share it yet (see 2 Kings 2:3)

Keeper: another name for the Lord. Psalm 121:5 reads, "The Lord is your keeper; The Lord is your shade at your right hand."

Keeper of the Flame: a lead intercessor who oversees a group of intercessors on a schedule so that prayer continues to go forth day and night; Leviticus 6:9 reads, "Command Aaron and his sons, saying, 'This is the law of the burnt offering: The burnt offering shall be on the hearth upon the altar all night until morning, and the fire of the altar shall be kept burning on it.'"

Keeper of the Keys: a gatekeeper in the spirit; a steward of mysteries; one who holds secrets, revelation, wisdom, and strategies in the spiritual realms

Keeping Watch: watching in the spirit for the coming of the Lord (see Matthew 24:42)

Key: a prayer or strategy that unlocks something in the spirit or in the natural dimensions; wisdom that unlocks; authority that opens and shuts doors in the spirit

Key of David: a symbol of authority to allow or forbid access to gates; Isaiah 22:22 reads: "The key of the house of David I will lay on his shoulder; So he shall open, and no one shall shut; And he shall shut, and no one shall open." (Also see Revelation 3:7).

Key of Death: physical death; the separation of the soul from the body; In Revelation 1:18, Jesus said, "I am He who lives, and was dead, and behold, I am alive forevermore. Amen. And I have the keys of Hades and of Death."

Key of Hades: the keys to hell; In Revelation 1:18, Jesus said, "I am He who lives, and was dead, and behold, I am alive forevermore. Amen. And I have the keys of Hades and of Death."

Key of Knowledge: also known as the key to knowledge, a spiritual truth that opens the door to deeper revelation of the Kingdom of God and the Christ; In Luke 11:52, Jesus said, "Woe to you lawyers! For you have taken away the key of knowledge. You did not enter in yourselves, and those who were entering in you hindered."

Key to the Bottomless Pit: a key to the realm of the dead; Revelation 9:1 reads, "Then the fifth angel sounded: And I saw a star fallen from heaven to the earth. To him was given the key to the bottomless pit."

Keys to the Kingdom: power and authority to execute God's will in the earth; In Matthew 16:19, Jesus said: "And I will give you the keys of the kingdom of heaven, and whatever you bind on earth will be bound in heaven, and whatever you loose on earth will be loosed in heaven."

King of Kings: another name for Jesus as seen in Revelation 17:14: "These will make war with the Lamb, and the Lamb will overcome them, for He is Lord of lords and King of kings; and those who are with Him are called, chosen, and faithful."

Kingship: a reference to Christ as king; speaking of the authority of the believer; Peter called believers a royal priesthood, that is a priesthood of kings (see 1 Peter 2:9). Revelation 1:6 tells us Jesus made us kings and priests unto God and Revelation 20:6 reveals we will reign with Christ the King for 1,000 years after the Second Coming of Christ while Satan is imprisoned.

Kneeling: a posture of the body or of the heart to honor the Lord; a posture of worship or reverence; a posture of prayer in which one bows down on their knees; Psalm 95:6 says, "Oh come, let us worship and bow down; Let us kneel before the Lord our Maker."

Knock: a method of seeking entrance into the seer dimensions through prayer; a method of persistent prayer; In Matthew 7:7 (AMPC) Jesus says, "Keep on asking and it will be given you; keep on seeking and you will find; keep on knocking [reverently] and [the door] will be opened to you." Of course, you have to knock with respect and the right motive or you could find yourself going through a back door (*also see Back Door*).

Knowing: another way of seeing; to perceive in the spirit; to attain knowledge by the Spirit of God; a spiritual sense when one knows something about what is happening in the spirit or in the heart of a person by revelation, but cannot tell you definitively how they know;

Matthew 9:4 reads, "But Jesus, knowing their thoughts, said, 'Why do you think evil in your hearts?' And John 13:3 reads, "Jesus, knowing that the Father had given all things into His hands, and that He had come from God and was going to God…"

The Greek word for knowing in Matthew 9:4 and John 13:3 is *eido*, which means "see."

Know Them by the Spirit: to see someone how God sees them; to discern what spirit someone is operating in. Paul wrote, "And we urge you, brethren, to recognize those who labor among you…" (1 Thessalonians 5:12). The Greek word for "recognize" in that verse is also translated "know" in other versions of the Bible. That Greek word *eido* means "see."

Know Them by Their Fruits: a biblical means by which you can judge false prophets, false visions, false dreams, and false utterances (see Matthew 7:15-20)

Knowledge: as it relates to seer dimensions, knowing, understanding, or awareness of what is happening in the spirit and what to do with the revelation you see; Ecclesiastes 1:8 tells us he who increases in knowledge increases with sorrow. That's because seers take responsibility for the knowledge (or light) they have, often through an intercessory prayer burden.

Knowledge of God's Ways: understanding the manner in which God makes decisions or takes action; Job 21:14 reads, "Yet they say to God, 'Depart from us, for we do not desire the knowledge of Your ways.'"

Knowledge of Good and Evil: an aspect of discernment (see Deuteronomy 1:39)

Knowledge of the Glory: referring to a time of Christ's return when God's glory will be known throughout the earth; Habakkuk 2:14 reads, "For the earth will be filled with the knowledge of the glory of the Lord, as the waters cover the sea."

Knowledge of the Holy: a modern classic book by A.W. Tozer; One of his famous quotes, "Acquaint thyself with God." A must-read for the seer.

Knowledge Puffs Up: an understanding that people who walk in prophetic revelation can easily step into spiritual pride; 1 Corinthians 8:1, "Knowledge puffs up, but love edifies." Speaking of himself, Paul explained, "And lest I should be exalted above measure by the abundance of the revelations, a thorn in the flesh was given to me, a messenger of Satan to buffet me, lest I be exalted above measure" (2 Corinthians 12:7).

L

Labor in the Spirit: working with the Holy Spirit to do God's will; In 1 Corinthians 15:10, Paul said, "But by the grace of God I am what I am, and His grace toward me was not in vain; but I labored more abundantly than they all, yet not I, but the grace of God which was with me."

Ladder: *see Jacob's Ladder*

Lake of Fire: also known as the second death (see Revelation 20:6) or hell, the lake of fire is the final judgment; The lake of fire is a place of eternal punishment reserved for anyone whose name is not written in the Lamb's Book of Life (see Revelation 20:10,14,15).

Lamb of God: another name for Christ; John the Baptist said in John 1:29, "The next day John saw Jesus coming toward him, and said, 'Behold! The Lamb of God who takes away the sin of the world!'"

Lamb Slain from the Foundation of the World: another name for Christ; Revelation 13:8 reads, "All who dwell on the earth will worship him, whose names have not been written in the Book of Life of the Lamb slain from the foundation of the world."

Lamentations: a book in the Bible penned by Jeremiah the prophet that laments the destruction of Jerusalem; an expression of grief or sorrow and mourning

Landmarks: boundary markers in the spirit; a characteristic or object that helps one identify where he is in the spirit, such as a gate or an angel; The Bible speaks of ancient landmarks (see Proverbs 22:28). There are ancient landmarks in the spirit.

Laodicea: a city in biblical times that lies about miles east of Ephesus; it was a prosperous city in Asia Minor

Laodicean Church: a church in the ancient city of Laodicea to which Jesus wrote a scathing letter because of its compromised spiritual condition; a symbol for the lukewarm church;

Revelation 3:13-22, "And to the angel of the church of the Laodiceans write, 'These things says the Amen, the Faithful and True Witness, the Beginning of the creation of God: 'I know your works, that you are neither cold nor hot. I could wish you were cold or hot. So then, because you are lukewarm, and neither cold nor hot, I will vomit you out of My mouth.

"Because you say, 'I am rich, have become wealthy, and have need of nothing'—and do not know that you are wretched, miserable, poor, blind, and naked—I counsel you to buy from Me gold refined in the fire, that you may be rich; and white garments, that you may be clothed, *that* the shame of your nakedness may not be revealed; and anoint your eyes with eye salve, that you may see.

"As many as I love, I rebuke and chasten. Therefore be zealous and repent. Behold, I stand at the door and knock. If anyone hears My voice and opens the door, I will come in to him and dine with him, and he with Me To him who overcomes I will grant to sit with Me on My throne, as I also overcame and sat down with My Father on His throne."

Last Days: the era after which Christ ascended to the right hand of the father but before the end-times

Latter Rain Movement: a movement that started in 1907 but gained momentum in the 1940s; The movement focused on the baptism of the Holy Spirit, five-fold ministry, the manifestations of the sons of God, and the imminent return of Jesus. The Latter Rain movement taught that God was pouring out His "latter rain" in modern times just as He did on the Day of Pentecost to ready the world for the Second Coming of Christ.

While many Pentecostals and Charismatics affirm that the church will see the greatest outpouring of the Holy Spirit before the Second Coming of Christ, most deny other aspects of Latter Rain theology, such as shepherding discipleship methods that lean toward control, Kingdom Now eschatology (Amillennialism, Post-millennialism, and Preterist interpretations of the Olivet Discourse and the book of Revelation), and Manifested Sons of God, which promises the fullness of our inheritance as sons of God before Jesus returns.

Latter Times: a term speaking of the last days (see Last Days); 1 Timothy 4:1 reads, "Now the Spirit expressly says that in latter times some will depart from the faith, giving heed to deceiving spirits and doctrines of demons."

Legion: technically, a large group of foot soldiers numbering in the thousands; In the context of Mark 5:9, a legion is a group of thousands of demons that inhabited a man Jesus set free. In the context of the Garden of Gethsemane at Jesus's arrest, it spoke of an angel army. Jesus said, "Or do you think that I cannot now pray to My Father, and He will provide Me with more than twelve legions of angels?" (Matthew 26:53). Seers may see legions of demons in people, in an atmosphere, or legions of angels.

Leper: *see Spiritual Leper*

Let Two or Three Judge: allowing what you see in the spirit to be judged by elders, according to 1 Corinthians 14:29, which reads, "Let two or three prophets speak, and let the others judge."

Liar: another name for Satan (see John 8:44)

Liberty in the Spirit: freedom to follow the Holy Spirit's leading in a ministry setting. 2 Corinthians 3:17 reads, "Now the Lord is the Spirit; and where the Spirit of the Lord is, there is liberty."

Lid: cap or limitation in the spirit; something preventing you from ascending in the spirit to see what God wants to show you

Lift up Your Eyes: God's call to elevate your spiritual sight; to see into higher dimensions in the spirit; to see further into the seer dimensions; to ascend; Genesis 13:14, "And the Lord said to Abram, after Lot had separated from him: 'Lift your eyes now and look from the place where you are—northward, southward, eastward, and westward.'"

Light from Heaven: light that emanates from heaven during encounters. Saul, who later became Paul, experienced this light first hand and it caused him to fall to the ground;

Acts 9:3-4 reads, "As he journeyed he came near Damascus, and suddenly a light shone around him from heaven. Then he fell to the ground, and heard a voice saying to him, 'Saul, Saul, why are you persecuting Me?'"

While angels appear as light, sometimes God appears in light. Metaphorically, God is light and there is no darkness in him (see 1 John 1:5).

We see Jesus appearing in light again at the Mount of Transfiguration. In Matthew 17:1-2, we read, "Now after six days Jesus took Peter, James, and John his brother, led them up on a high mountain by themselves; and He was transfigured before them. His face shone like the sun, and His clothes became as white as the light."

Light of the World: another name for Jesus as seen in John 8:12 and John 9:5; John 8:12 reads, "Then Jesus spoke to them again, saying, 'I am the light of the world. He who follows Me shall not walk in darkness, but have the light of life.'"

Lightning: along with thunder and voices, part of the scenery around God's throne (see Revelation 4:5); a marker signifying the Second Coming of Jesus (see Matthew 24:27); A picture of Satan's fall from heaven (see Luke 10:18).

Likeness: seer language used to describe something for which there are no human words; verbiage that seeks to give a mental image of something in the spirit that carries similarities to something in the natural;

In Daniel 10:16, Daniel wrote, "And suddenly, *one* having the likeness of the sons of men touched my lips; then I opened my mouth and spoke, saying to him who stood before me, 'My lord, because of the vision my sorrows have overwhelmed me, and I have retained no strength.'"

Lion of the Tribe of Judah: another name for Jesus as seen in Revelation 5:5: "But one of the elders said to me, 'Do not weep. Behold, the Lion of the tribe of Judah, the Root of David, has prevailed to open the scroll and to loose its seven seals.'"

Listening in the Spirit: intentionally inclining your ear to hear not just the voice of God but the chatter of demons, the sound of angels and other spiritual beings moving in the seer dimensions in order to gain more detailed revelation

Little Scroll: also called a little book; a document containing revelation; Revelation 10:1-2, "I saw still another mighty angel coming down from heaven, clothed with a cloud. And a rainbow was on his head, his face was like the sun, and his feet like pillars of fire. He had a little book open in his hand. And he set his right foot on the sea and his left foot on the land…"

Living Creatures: four spiritual creatures that minister around the throne of God in heaven' These living creatures are mentioned first in Ezekiel 1:12-20, next in Isaiah 6:1-3, then later in Revelation 4:6-9; 5:6-14; 6:1-8; 14:3; 15:7; and 19:4. Revelation 4:6-9 reads:

"Before the throne there was a sea of glass, like crystal. And in the midst of the throne, and around the throne, were four living creatures full of eyes in front and in back. The first living creature was like a lion, the second living creature like a calf, the third living creature had a face like a man, and the fourth living creature was like a flying eagle. The four living creatures, each having six wings, were full of eyes around and within. And they do not rest day or night, saying: 'Holy, holy, holy, Lord God Almighty, Who was and is and is to come!' Whenever the living creatures give glory and honor and thanks to Him who sits on the throne, who lives forever and ever…'"

Locked: a mystery that is shut up from view; a mystery that is inaccessible

Lofty Eyes: *see Arrogant Eyes*

Look: to engage your spiritual eyes to see something in the spirit; to exercise the gift of spiritual vision

Look Again: *see Keep on Looking*

Look at the Heart: looking at the condition, whether pure or impure, of someone's heart (see 1 Samuel 16:7)

Look Into: seer terminology for "pray into;" When the seer says they are going to look into something, it means they are going to pray and ask the Lord to show them what they need to see in the spirit realm so they can intercede or war or otherwise act effectively, by faith, to bring God's will into a situation.

Looking at Worthless Things: a decision that causes you to lose visual purity (see Psalm 119:37)

Loose: to deliver someone from bondage; to declare unlawful; an operation of seer deliverance; In Matthew 18:18, Jesus said, "Assuredly, I say to you, whatever you bind on earth will be bound in heaven, and whatever you loose on earth will be loosed in heaven."

Lord's Day: a day of worship; in modern times this is Sunday but in the Old Testament the Sabbath was on Sunday

Loud in the Spirit: a voice, clashing, wail or cry in the spirit that demands attention; a loud sound in the spirit only those with spiritual ears can hear; John recalls in Revelation 1:10,

"I was in the Spirit on the Lord's Day, and I heard behind me a loud voice, as of a trumpet…"

Lurking: to lie in wait out of the seer's field of vision for evil purposes; Psalm 17:12 reads, "As a lion is eager to tear his prey, And like a young lion lurking in secret places."

Lying Spirit: a spirit with a specific agenda to communicate lies (see 2 Chronicles 18:21)

Lying Vision: *see False Vision*

M

Macrocosm: the universe; something at a large scale. Seers who see into the macrocosm are seeing beyond the earth realm into other dimensions of the universe God created

Magic: *see Secret Arts*

Magic Arts: *see Secret Arts*

Magic Spells: *see Secret Arts*

Magician: a word the Bible uses interchangeably with diviner and astrologer; Moses had a showdown with Pharaoh's magicians in the Book of Exodus. And Daniel 2:10 reads, "The Chaldeans answered the king, and said, 'There is not a man on earth who can tell the king's matter; therefore no king, lord, or ruler has ever asked such things of any magician, astrologer, or Chaldean.'"

Magnificent Vision: *see Great Vision*

Major Prophet: prophets who wrote some of the longer books contained in the Bible; Isaiah; Jeremiah; Ezekiel and Daniel

Maker: another name for God; Psalm 95:6 reads, "Oh come, let us worship and bow down; Let us kneel before the Lord our Maker."

Making Process: the process a prophet walks through to be sculpted into the voice God created him to be; a process of being formed into the image of Christ the Prophet; a pruning and shaping the prophet endures that causes suffering, loss of worldly pleasures, and a change in desires; For more, read the book *The Making of a Prophet*.

Malachi: one of the twelve minor prophets who penned the Book of Malachi; Malachi is the last book in the Old Testament, and Malachi was the last prophetic voice until

John the Baptist arrived on the scene 400 years later. Malachi labored in the days of Nehemiah and Ezra.

Man of Sin: another name for Satan (see 2 Thessalonians 2:3).

Mandate: heaven's command over your life; a divine mission with heaven's authority

Manifest: to make recognizable or seen

Manifestation: the fulfillment of prophetic revelation; the felt or seen presence of a spirit, either the Holy Spirit, an angel or an evil spirit; 1 Corinthians 12:7 reads, "But the manifestation of the Spirit is given to each one for the profit of all…"

Manna: bread from heaven God rained down in the wilderness as food for the Israelites (see Exodus 16:33); symbolic of revelation from the Throne Room; an eternal reward promised to overcome the doctrines of Balaam and the Nicolaitans;

In Revelation 2:17 Jesus said to the church at Pergamos: "He who has an ear, let him hear what the Spirit says to the churches. To him who overcomes I will give some of the hidden manna to eat. And I will give him a white stone, and on the stone a new name written which no one knows except him who receives it" (Revelation 2:17).

Manner of Time: *see Kairos Time*; 1 Peter 1:10-11 reads, "Of this salvation the prophets have inquired and searched carefully, who prophesied of the grace that would come to you, searching what, or what manner of time, the Spirit of Christ who was in them was indicating when He testified beforehand the sufferings of Christ and the glories that would follow."

Mantle: a sign of one's call, authority and responsibility in the Kingdom of God; a symbol of the Holy Spirit's anointing on the life of a minister

Mark: author of the Gospel of Mark who penned an action-packed account of Jesus' ministry in the earth; also known as John Mark

Marketplace: a public place where Christians mix with unbelievers; any public place outside the four walls of the church, such as the workplace, universities, grocery stores, etc.; a harvest field for the lost

Marred in the Hand of the Potter: to crush the clay and start over again; a phrase used to describe prophets and seers who rebel against the hand of the Lord and miss their highest calling;

Jeremiah 18:1-4 reads: "The word which came to Jeremiah from the Lord, saying: 'Arise and go down to the potter's house, and there I will cause you to hear My words.' Then I went down to the potter's house, and there he was, making something at the wheel. And the vessel that he made of clay was marred in the hand of the potter; so he made it again into another vessel, as it seemed good to the potter to make."

Martyr: one who suffers or dies for the sake of the gospel; Stephen was the first recorded martyr in Christianity (see Acts 7; Acts 22:20); Revelation 17:6 speaks of the blood of the martyrs. For more, Read Fox's *Book of Martyrs*.

Matrix: a womb; something that produces or births something else

Meaning: discernment revealed in the interpretation of a dream or vision; understanding what the dream or vision means at various levels and how to respond; Daniel 8:15 reads, "Then it happened, when I, Daniel, had seen the vision and was seeking the meaning, that suddenly there stood before me one having the appearance of a man."

Mediator: another name for Jesus found in 1 Timothy 2:5: "For there is one God and one Mediator between God and men, the Man Christ Jesus..."

Meditate: a gateway into the seer dimension; to muse on the Word of God; to imagine scenes in the Word of God; to speak the Word of God over and over; to think deeply about God

Meditation: the act of meditating on God and His Word

Melchizedek: a king of Salem (Jerusalem) whose name means "king of righteousness" and a priest of God. Psalm 110 speaks of Melchizedek, a type of Christ, to whom Abraham paid a tenth of the spoils of war; Hebrews 6:20 says Jesus came in the order of Melchizedek.

Memory: the seer's capacity for storing information about their dreams and visions for quick recollection; the seer's capacity to remember the meanings of numbers, symbols, and other facets of interpreting seer revelation

Message: the theme of one's auditory or visual revelation; information shared publicly based on revelation from God; Daniel 10:1 reads, "In the third year of Cyrus king of Persia a message was revealed to Daniel, whose name was called Belteshazzar. The message was true, but the appointed time was long; and he understood the message, and had understanding of the vision."

Messenger Angels: angels that bring messages, such as Gabriel (see Luke 31)

Messiah: the Savior of the world; Jesus Christ

Metaphor: a symbol representing reality; a phrase not meant to be taken literally, such as "a mighty fortress is our God." God is not a mighty fortress; He is a Spirit, but metaphorically we can run into Him and be safe in the same way we would run into a mighty fortress.

Metaphysics: realities outside objective experience; The world studies these issues with curiosity, but the seer understands metaphysical proof of God by subjective experience that is proved objectively by creation.

Paul wrote, "For since the creation of the world His invisible attributes are clearly seen, being understood by the things that are made, even His eternal power and Godhead, so that they are without excuse" (Romans 1:20).

Methuselah: the son of Enoch and the grandfather of Noah; his name means man of the javelin; the oldest person in human history

Metron: a Greek word for a measured sphere of authority or territory; Paul said, "We, however, will not boast beyond measure, but within the limits of the sphere which God appointed us—a sphere which especially includes you" (2 Corinthians 10:13).

Micah: one of the twelve minor prophets in the Bible; the author of the Book of Micah, which offers a significant prophecy about Christ's birth

Micaiah: the prophet of whom Ahab said, "I hate him, because he does not prophesy good concerning me, but evil" (1 Kings 22:8); the prophet who Ahab ordered arrested after he prophesied the king's death instead of agreeing with the "yes man" prophets that surrounded Ahab

Michael: an archangel, or chief angel, mentioned in Jude 9; the angel that stands guard over Israel (see Daniel 12:1); an angel that directly opposed Satan (see Jude); an angelic military commander (see Revelation 12:7-9); a warrior angel (see Daniel 10:21)

Microcosm: seeing things at a granular level; seeing something very small

Midwife: a type of intercessor who helps people birth that with which God has impregnated them

Mighty One of Jacob: another name for Jesus seen in Isaiah 60:16: "You shall drink the milk of the Gentiles, and milk the breast of kings; You shall know that I, the Lord, am your Savior and your Redeemer, the Mighty One of Jacob."

Milk: a metaphor for simple spiritual truths; Hebrews 5:13 reads, "For everyone who partakes only of milk is unskilled in the word of righteousness, for he is a babe." And 1 Peter

2:2 says, "as newborn babes, desire the pure milk of the word, that you may grow thereby."

Millennial Kingdom: the one-thousand-year reign of Jesus Christ on the earth; Revelation 20:2-7 paints a picture of the Millennial Kingdom:

"He laid hold of the dragon, that serpent of old, who is the Devil and Satan, and bound him for a thousand years; and he cast him into the bottomless pit, and shut him up, and set a seal on him, so that he should deceive the nations no more till the thousand years were finished. But after these things he must be released for a little while.

"And I saw thrones, and they sat on them, and judgment was committed to them. Then I saw the souls of those who had been beheaded for their witness to Jesus and for the word of God, who had not worshiped the beast or his image, and had not received his mark on their foreheads or on their hands.

"And they lived and reigned with Christ for a thousand years. But the rest of the dead did not live again until the thousand years were finished. This is the first resurrection. Blessed and holy is he who has part in the first resurrection. Over such the second death has no power, but they shall be priests of God and of Christ, and shall reign with Him a thousand years."

Mind of Christ: thinking the way Jesus thinks; to understand how Christ thinks about a particular matter; to be in agreement with the way Christ views an issue;

Philippians 2:5-8 reads, "Let this mind be in you which was also in Christ Jesus, who, being in the form of God, did not consider it robbery to be equal with God, but made Himself of no reputation, taking the form of a bondservant, and coming in the likeness of men. And being found in appearance as a man, He humbled Himself and became obedient to the point of death, even the death of the cross."

Mind's Eye: a mental picture conceived in the imagination

Minor Prophet: a shorter prophetic book in the Bible, named after the prophet who penned it; there are 12 minor prophets in the Old Testament: Hosea, Joel, Amos, Obadiah, Jonah, Micah, Nahum, Habakkuk, Zephaniah, Haggai, Zechariah, and Malachi

Minstrel: technically, one who plays a stringed instrument; used today generally for singers and musicians. 2 Kings 13:15-16, "But now bring me a minstrel. And it came to pass, when the minstrel played, that the hand of the Lord came upon him. And he said, Thus saith the Lord…"

Miracle: supernatural manifested power that interrupts natural events; an extraordinary divine intervention into the affairs of man

Miracle Realm: a realm in the spirit where the miraculous is waiting for someone with faith to pull down divine interventions

Miriam: a prophetess and the sister of Moses and Aaron; Miriam helped preserve the life of Moses when his mother set him to float on the Nile River (see Exodus 2:5-10). Miriam released a song of the Lord, sometimes called the Song of the Sea or the Song of Moses, in Exodus 15 after the Israelites escaped Pharaoh.

Miss It: to misinterpret what you've seen in the spirit; to misunderstand what you've seen in the spirit; to misapply what you've seen in the spirit

Mixture: something profane mixed in with something holy; a combination of evil with good; the quality of a compromised seer; Paul wrote in 2 Corinthians 6:14, "For what fellowship has righteousness with lawlessness? And what communion has light with darkness?"

Moment: a brief period of time in history

Monitoring Agents: *see Monitoring Spirits*

Monitoring Spirits: spirits that monitor you. Monitoring spirits watch, keep track of, or check usually for a special purpose; They are spiritual peeping toms and evil eavesdroppers. They are satanic watchdogs. They are illegal informants. They are part of a demonic network that watches and reports information back to higher ranking demonic powers so they can devise plans to steal, kill and destroy you. Monitoring spirits work in the realm of witchcraft.

Morning Star: another name for Lucifer (see Isaiah 14:12)

Moses: many consider Moses the most important prophet; he goes down in Bible history as the meekest man to walk the face of the earth (see Numbers 12:3); He led the Israelites out of Egyptian captivity and wrote the Torah as inspired by God.

Most Holy Place: *see Holy of Holies*

Multi-Layered Meaning: when a dream or vision has two or more meanings or levels of meaning that may manifest at different times

Multiplied Visions: a season of increase in visions; numerous visions; a strong increase in visions; Hosea 12:10 reveals, "And have multiplied visions; I have given symbols through the witness of the prophets."

Murder: another name for Satan (see John 8:44)

Muse: to think deeply about a seer revelation; a state of deep thought

Muttering Spirits: spirits that moan, growl, devise and plot against God's people through divination; Isaiah 8:19 reads, "And when they say to you, 'Seek those who are mediums and wizards, who whisper and mutter,' should not a people seek their God? Should they seek the dead on behalf of the living?"

Mystery: a hidden or secret truth; a truth not obvious to human understanding; a truth that is spiritually discerned through revelation; secret counsels of God;

Ephesians 3:2-6 reads, "If indeed you have heard of the dispensation of the grace of God which was given to me for you, how that by revelation He made known to me the mystery (as I have briefly written already, by which, when you read, you may understand my knowledge in the mystery of Christ), which in other ages was not made known to the sons of men, as it has now been revealed by the Spirit to His holy apostles and prophets: that the Gentiles should be fellow heirs, of the same body, and partakers of His promise in Christ through the gospel…"

Mysteries of the Kingdom: mystic truths in the form of words, dreams and visions available for download to Christ's true disciples; In Matthew 13:11 Jesus said to His disciples, "Because it has been given to you to know the mysteries of the kingdom of heaven, but to them it has not been given."

Mysterious Sayings: *see Dark Sayings*

Mystery of Time: the concept that God moves in and out of time and has our times in His hands; 2 Peter 3:8 reads, "But, beloved, do not forget this one thing, that with the Lord one day is as a thousand years, and a thousand years as one day." And Psalm 90:4 reads, "For a thousand years in Your sight are like yesterday when it is past, and like a watch in the night."

Also, the mystery of time is showcased in Ecclesiastes 3, which offers a prophetic calendar. Ecclesiastes 3:1 reads, "To everything there is a season, a time for every purpose under heaven." Seers discern times and timing.

Mystic: truths that inspire an awe of God; one who understands deeper revelations about the presence and union with God

Mysticism: theories of how one enters into union with God through practices such as contemplation and silence which may lead to ecstatic visions, revelations and encounters;

1 Corinthians 2:12-16 reads, "Now we have received, not the spirit of the world, but the Spirit who is from God, that we might know the things that have been freely given to us by God.

"These things we also speak, not in words which man's wisdom teaches but which the Holy Spirit teaches, comparing spiritual things with spiritual. But the natural man does not receive the things of the Spirit of God, for they are foolishness to him; nor can he know them, because they are spiritually discerned.

"But he who is spiritual judges all things, yet he himself is rightly judged by no one. For 'who has known the mind of the Lord that he may instruct Him?' But we have the mind of Christ."

N

Nabi prophet: a type of prophet who speaks the prophetic word of the Lord by the moving of the Spirit; The word "nabi," is one of the words used for prophet in the Old Testament. Nabi means "spokesman, speaker and prophet," according to *The KJV Old Testament Hebrew Lexicon*. Noteworthy is the fact that it can also mean false prophet or heathen prophet. Nabi is used in 316 Old Testament verses.

This word "nabi" means "to bubble forth, as from a fountain," according to *Easton's Bible Dictionary*. *Smith's Bible Dictionary* reads, "The ordinary Hebrew word for prophet is nabi, derived from a verb signifying 'to bubble forth' like a fountain; hence the word means one who announces or pours forth the declarations of God." This bubbling forth is an unction from the Holy Spirit.

The nabi prophet functions mostly by hearing the still small voice of the Lord. Forty-five times in Scripture—including in the books of Jeremiah, Ezekiel, and Zechariah—we see the phrase, "the word of the Lord came unto me saying."

Nahum: a minor prophet whose name means "comforter"–author of the Book of Nahum; Nahum's message was one of judgment against Nineveh.

Names: a seer may see names written in the spirit, which could signify a call to pray for a person or could be a visual clue that will unlock further revelation; a seer could see the name of a person written in the Lamb's Book of Life, or see a name written over someone's head

Nanosecond: one billionth of a second (see *Instant; Glimpse*)

Narrow Gate: a way of life on earth that leads to eternal life in heaven; a gate that is constricted by pressure and so conforms us into the image of Christ;

In Matthew 7:13-14, Jesus said, "Enter by the narrow gate; for wide is the gate and broad is the way that leads to destruction, and there are many who go in by it. Because narrow is the gate and difficult is the way which leads to life, and there are few who find it."

Nathan: an Old Testament prophet who was an advisor to David; the prophet who privately rebuked David for his sin with Bathsheba

Nazarite: a person consecrated to God's service and living under a strict vow (see Numbers 6). Samson, Samuel, and John the Baptist were Nazarites

Nazarite Vow: a vow to abstain from alcohol, to let one's hair grow long, and to avoid contact with the dead (see Numbers 6)

Nebuchadnezzar: a king of Babylon who had two significant dreams; a king who consulted the Israeli prophet Daniel to interpret his dreams

Necromancer: the practice of talking to the dead to get information from the spirit realm; In Leviticus 19:31 (ESV) God warns, "Do not turn to mediums or necromancers; do not seek them out, and so make yourselves unclean by them: I am the Lord your God."

Necromancy: communicating with the dead

Nephilim: the offspring of fallen angels and human women. Nephilim are directly mentioned twice in Scripture;

Genesis 6:4 (ESV), reads, "The Nephilim were on the earth in those days, and also afterward, when the sons of God came in to the daughters of man and they bore children to them. These were the mighty men who were of old, the men of renown." And Numbers 13:33 reads, "And there we saw the Nephilim (the sons of Anak, who come from the Nephilim), and we seemed to ourselves like grasshoppers, and so we seemed to them."

Nest: a group or hub designed for seers and prophets to be birthed, grow, and launch out from; a home base for seers and prophets

New Jerusalem: a city that comes down from heaven to the new earth that is home to the bride of Christ after the Second Coming of Jesus; Ezekiel had a vision of the New Jerusalem in Ezekiel 8; Two scriptures speak directly of "New Jerusalem" in detail:

Revelation 3:12 reads, "He who overcomes, I will make him a pillar in the temple of My God, and he shall go out no more. I will write on him the name of My God and the name of the city of My God, the New Jerusalem, which comes down out of heaven from My God. And I will write on him My new name."

Revelation 21:2 reads, "Then I, John, saw the holy city, New Jerusalem, coming down out of heaven from God, prepared as a bride adorned for her husband."

Night Seasons: seasons of gloom; Psalm 16:7 reads, "I will bless the Lord who has given me counsel; My heart also instructs me in the night seasons."

Night Visions: visions that occur during the time when one begins to rouse from sleep and the time one is fully awake; that period between sleep and wakefulness. Job 4:13, reads "In disquieting thoughts from the visions of the night, when deep sleep falls on men…"

Night-Eyed: equipped with spiritual eyes that are able to see well in the dark

Nightmare: a dream of dark or scary nature inspired by the soul or by demon powers; a method by which the enemy tempts a seer to shut down his dream life (see Psalm 91:5)

Noah: the last of the pre-flood patriarchs; the man who built an arc through divine revelation from God to save a remnant of humanity before the flood

Nocturnal Attacks: spiritual attacks that often come through nightmares, night visions, or sleep disturbances

Noise: confusion in the spirit; distracting noises in the spirit that interfere with hearing the voice of God or angels; audible disturbances in the spirit; a sound that is too far away to clearly distinguish; a sudden sound that attracts attention; demonic static

North Wind: a pleasant wind that brings blessings; Proverbs 25:23 says, "The north wind brings forth rain…" Song of Solomon 4:16 says, "Awake, O north wind, And come, O south! Blow upon my garden, that its spices may flow out."

Nostrils of God: a phrase that typically relates in Scripture to anger, rebuke, and judgment; The Hebrew word for nose is anger; sin is like smoke to God in that it is offensive and unpleasant; (see Psalm 18:8; Psalm 18:15; Exodus 15:8).

Nothing Hidden Except to be Revealed: Jesus' promise that at some point in time, everything we haven't seen will be seen and every secret thing we have not learned will be revealed; Seer revelation is progressive based on what God wants to show the seer, but we can be patient knowing that one day we will see and know more completely.

Mark 4:22 reads, "For there is nothing hidden which will not be revealed, nor has anything been kept secret but that it should come to light." And Luke 8:17 confirms, "For nothing is secret that will not be revealed, nor *anything* hidden that will not be known and come to light."

Now: in the present moment; visual revelation that is immediately relevant for prayer or action

Numerology: the study of numbers to interpret dreams and visions; Biblical numerology is based strictly on the Bible through the study of patterns in Scripture. Occult numerology can deceive seers looking for truth outside of the Bible.

O

Oath: a vow or promise usually calling on God as a witness; oaths are serious in God's eyes; Numbers 30:2 reads, "If a man makes a vow to the Lord, or swears an oath to bind himself by some agreement, he shall not break his word; he shall do according to all that proceeds out of his mouth."

This is why Jesus warned in Matthew 5:33-37, "Again you have heard that it was said to those of old, 'You shall not swear falsely, but shall perform your oaths to the Lord.'.

"But I say to you, do not swear at all: neither by heaven, for it is God's throne; nor by the earth, for it is His footstool; nor by Jerusalem, for it is the city of the great King. Nor shall you swear by your head, because you cannot make one hair white or black. But let your 'Yes' be 'Yes,' and your 'No,' 'No.' For whatever is more than these is from the evil one."

Obadiah: a man who served in Ahab's kingdom that hid 100 true prophets from Jezebel, sustaining them with food and water; 1 Kings 18:4 reads, "For so it was, while Jezebel massacred the prophets of the Lord, that Obadiah had taken one hundred prophets and hidden them, fifty to a cave, and had fed them with bread and water."

Obadiah Phenomenon: when prophets are divided in the name of preservation from Jezebel; where there is no cross-pollination among prophetic camps

Obscure: difficult to see, understand or immediately interpret without further revelation; a parabolic revelation the Holy Spirit must explain after showing; In John 16:25 (NET), Jesus said to His disciples, "I have told you these things in obscure figures of speech; a time is coming when I will no longer speak to you in obscure figures, but will tell you plainly about the Father."

Observe: to watch; to take notice; Speaking of God, the psalmist wrote: "He rules by His power forever; His eyes observe the nations; Do not let the rebellious exalt themselves. Selah" (Psalm 66:7).

Occult: to shut off from view or exposure, not revealed, secret, not easily apprehended or understood, abstruse, mysterious, or concealed, according to *Merriam-Webster's Dictionary*; Another definition is "matters regarded as involving the action or influence of supernatural or supernormal powers or some secret knowledge of them." The occult uses witchcraft, but the occult is more than witchcraft.

Occult Practices: *see Secret Arts*

Odor: a smell in the spirit, either good or bad, that helps you discern what is happening in the seer dimensions. *Also, see Smelling in the Spirit*

Office: a duty in the church; a position given through Christ Himself, such as a five-fold office of apostle, prophet, evangelist, pastor or teacher (see Ephesians 4:11); a position given by the election of a presbytery, such as a deacon

Old Serpent: another name for Satan (see Revelation 12:9; 20:2)

Omega: the last; a word Jesus used to describe Himself in the context of being the eternal God who was and is and is to come. In Revelation 1:8, Jesus said, "I am the Alpha and the Omega, the Beginning and the End," says the Lord, "who is and who was and who is to come, the Almighty."

Omni perspective: a God's eye view; seeing from multiple perspectives in a single encounter

Omnipotence: all-powerful; having unlimited power and authority; an attribute of God

Onar: a Greek word for dream: The word *onar* is used five times in Scripture, all in the Book of Matthew. *Onar* was the word for *dream* that was used for each of the five dreams in which God gave Joseph direction to keep the baby Jesus safe.

Open Heaven: a prerequisite to Throne Room visions and visitations; Ezekiel 1:1 reads, "Now it came to pass in the thirtieth year, in the fourth month, on the fifth day of the month, as I was among the captives by the River Chebar, that the heavens were opened and I saw visions of God."

Both John the Baptist and Stephen the evangelist experienced open heavens. Matthew 3:16 reads, "When He had been baptized, Jesus came up immediately from the water; and behold, the heavens were opened to Him, and He saw the Spirit of God descending like a dove and alighting upon Him." And when Stephen was being stoned, he said, "Look! I see the heavens opened and the Son of Man standing at the right hand of God!"

When heaven is near earth and a strong sense of God's manifest presence is felt; a manifestation of Isaiah 64:1, "Oh, that You would rend the heavens! That You would come down! That the mountains might shake at Your presence…"

Open Vision: a vision that appears to the seer like a movie or imagery acting out before one's very eyes; The seer's eyes are open and he is immune to what is going on around him. It's like the world around you stops. Paul had an open vision on the road to Damascus (see Acts 9:3-9) and also in the night when he received the Macedonian call (see Acts 16:9).

Operations: how a seer moves in his ministry; how a seer functions in his gifting

Operative: a seer who works in secret for the Kingdom of God; a demon power who spies

Opportune Time: *see Kairos Time*

Optasia: a vision, either while awake or asleep. The Bible uses this word four times; Paul wrote, "It is doubtless not profitable for me to boast. I will come to visions and revelations of the Lord" (2 Corinthians 12:1). Luke 1:22 says of John the Baptist's father, "But when he came out, he could not speak to them; and they perceived that he had seen a vision in the temple, for he beckoned to them and remained speechless."

Luke 24:23 reads, "When they did not find His body, they came saying that they had also seen a vision of angels who said He was alive." And Acts 26:19 Paul shares, "Therefore, King Agrippa, I was not disobedient to the heavenly vision..."

Optics: the immediate perceptions of what you see in the spirit; Optics are not always accurate so you need to press into the interpretation with the Holy Spirit.

Oracles: the words of God; 1 Peter 4:10-12, "As each one has received a gift, minister it to one another, as good stewards of the manifold grace of God. If anyone speaks, let him speak as the oracles of God. If anyone ministers, let him do it as with the ability which God supplies, that in all things God may be glorified through Jesus Christ, to whom belong the glory and the dominion forever and ever. Amen."

Ordain: to establish someone in a church office; to appoint someone to religious duty; God told Jeremiah, "Before I formed you in the womb I knew you; Before you were born I sanctified you; I ordained you a prophet to the nations" (Jeremiah 1:5).

Order in the Spirit: according to protocols; absent of chaos and disorder; In 1 Corinthians 14:40 Paul wrote, "Let all things be done decently and in order."

'Or Goyim: a name for God that means "Light of the Nations," a seen in Isaiah 42:6, "I, the Lord, have called You in righteousness, and will hold Your hand; I will keep You and give You as a covenant to the people, as a light to the Gentiles."

Orion: technically a constellation, but spiritual warriors understand Orion in the second heavens is a principality that attacks deliverance ministries and releases the power of death (see Job 9:9; Job 38:31; Amos 5:8)

Out-of-Body Dimension: a realm in the spirit where someone is transported in the spirit to heaven or a physical place while their body stays stationary

Out-of-Body Experience: being caught up in the spirit; 2 Corinthians 12:2 reads, "I know a man in Christ who fourteen years ago—whether in the body I do not know, or whether out of the body I do not know, God knows—such a one was caught up to the third heaven."

P

Panoptic: a comprehensive view of the spirit realm; a big picture view

Panoramic Vision: a vision that offers an extremely wide view of the spirit realm

Parable: something you hear or see that illustrates a spiritual truth

Parabolic: expressed by or being a parable (*Merriam-Webster's dictionary*); Jesus often spoke in parables. In Matthew 13:10-11 we read: "The disciples came and said to Him, 'Why do You speak to them in parables?' He answered them, 'It is given to you to know the mysteries of the kingdom of heaven, but to them it is not given." The Greek word for parables in this verse is *parabole.*

According to *The KJV New Testament Dictionary*, it means, "a placing of one thing by the side of another, juxtaposition, as of ships in battle.

Metaph. a comparing, comparison of one thing with another, likeness, similitude' an example by which a doctrine or precept is illustrated; a narrative, fictitious but agreeable to the laws and usages of human life, by which either the duties of men or the things of God, particularly the nature and history of God's kingdom are figuratively portrayed in a parable: an earthly story with a heavenly meaning; a pithy and instructive saying, involving some likeness or comparison and having preceptive or admonitory force an aphorism, a maxim; a proverb; an act by which one exposes himself or his possessions to danger, a venture, a risk."

Parabolic Prophet: a prophet or seer who becomes his message, such as Ezekiel

Passing on a Mantle: imparting to someone the gifts and anointings you carry. Elijah passed his mantle to Elisha (see 2 Kings 2:3)

Passover: a sacred Jewish holiday commemorating the Israelites exodus out of the bondage of Egypt

Past: a realm of the spirit God can allow you to look into for revelation; a completed period of time, whether yesterday or an ancient age; the former time; times of old. Seers may see into a person's past in ministering encouragement for the future or healing or deliverance for the present

Pastor: one of the five-fold offices mentioned in Ephesians 4:11; a shepherd of God's people who cares for their needs

Pathways in the Spirit: lines of clear communication between the seer and God; a familiar path to encountering God a seer can travel upon time and again because he knows the way

Patterns in the Spirit: a blueprint for building; a series of repetitive characteristics or objects, such as symbols, colors, numbers, people, etc.

Paul the Apostle: an apostle of Jesus Christ who wrote two-thirds of the New Testament by way of revelation; Paul was a man of supernatural encounters, falling into trances, ascending to heaven, casting out demons, healing the sick, and raising the dead.

Pay the Price: the seer's willingness to endure hardships to fulfill his calling; Paul said in Philippians 3:8, "Yet indeed I also count all things loss for the excellence of the knowledge of Christ Jesus my Lord, for whom I have suffered the loss of all things, and count them as rubbish, that I may gain Christ."

Pedigree: your seer ancestry; the lineage of seers or seer anointing impartations you have received from people who went before you

Peeping Spirits: divining spirits that release a quiet sound in the spirit; Isaiah 8:19, (KJV), reads "And when they shall say unto you, Seek unto them that have familiar spirits, and unto wizards that peep, and that mutter: should not a people seek unto their God? for the living to the dead?"

Peleh Yo'etz: a name for God that means "Wonderful Counselor," as seen in Isaiah 9:6, "For unto us a Child is born, unto us a Son is given; And the government will be upon His shoulder. And His name will be called Wonderful, Counselor, Mighty God, Everlasting Father, Prince of Peace."

Pen: to author or record; to scribe

Pen of a Ready Writer: a phrase used for an articulate, experienced scribe; Psalm 45:1, "My heart is overflowing with a good theme; I recite my composition concerning the King; My tongue is the pen of a ready writer."

Pentecost: a Jewish feast day known as Feast of the Harvest or Feast of Weeks to celebrate the first fruits of the harvest; The feast is mentioned in Exodus 23, Exodus 24, Leviticus 16, Numbers 28, and Deuteronomy 16. In the New Testament, Pentecost represents the birth of the church in Acts 2, when the Holy Spirit came into the Upper Room where 120 disciples were waiting on Christ's promise.

Pentecostal: believers who ascribe to the beliefs put forth in the Pentecostal movement, including spiritual gifts and speaking in tongues

Pentecostal Movement: a movement birthed in a holiness revival during the second half of the 19th Century; One emphasis of the Pentecostal movement is the baptism of the Holy Spirit with the evidence of speaking in tongues and a belief in the full gospel, including the gifts of the Spirit, healing, miracles, and deliverance.

Perceive: to become aware through discernment; to gain knowledge through your spiritual senses; Mark 2:7-9 reads, "'Why does this Man speak blasphemies like this? Who can forgive sins but God alone?' But immediately, when Jesus perceived in His spirit that they reasoned thus within themselves, He said to them, 'Why do you reason about these things in your hearts? Which is easier, to say to the paralytic, 'Your sins are forgiven you,' or to say, 'Arise, take up your bed and walk'?"

Perception: awareness and sensitivity that leads to observation and discernment about activities in the spirit realm

Period: a division of time marked by specific events, such as the Renaissance, Ancient Greece or the Stone Age; Seers may see into periods past or periods future.

Peripheral Vision: also called side vision, peripheral vision is the ability to see what is to either side of you while you're looking straight ahead; While our natural vision is strongest looking forward, God can open the periphery in the spirit to the eyes of our heart. Put another way, He can allow our spiritual eyes to see at angles our natural eyes can't reach.

Permission: approval from someone to look into their life; authorization for someone to pray and seek to see what the enemy or the Lord is doing in your life

Perpetual: a continual occurrence; certain visions in heaven unfold perpetually, such as the four living creatures around the throne crying "holy, holy, holy" (see Revelation 4:8).

Persecution: a byproduct of the seer ministry; mistreatment, harassment, or hostility toward a seer; Jezebel persecuted the prophets, and so did the Pharisees

Perspective: the vantage point from which a seer sees into the spirit, such as from below, from above, or from some other angle

Perversion: corruption of the seer gift; misuse of the seer gift; twisting the meaning of a dream or vision to suit the seer's purposes; the state of a seer who has turned away from what is morally correct

Peter the Apostle: one of the first Christ-followers and later given revelation that Jesus is the Christ; Peter was known to be especially outspoken, bold, strong-willed, and rash in his youth. He was a pillar of the earth church who worked miracles in the Book of Acts.

Peter entered the seer dimensions through a vision during a trance. Acts 10:9-16 reads, "The next day, as they went on their journey and drew near the city, Peter went up on the housetop to pray, about the sixth hour. Then he became very hungry and wanted to eat; but while they made ready, he fell into a trance and saw heaven opened and an object like a great sheet bound at the four corners, descending to him and let down to the earth.

"In it were all kinds of four-footed animals of the earth, wild beasts, creeping things, and birds of the air. And a voice came to him, 'Rise, Peter; kill and eat.' But Peter said, 'Not so, Lord! For I have never eaten anything common or unclean.' And a voice spoke to him again the second time, 'What God has cleansed you must not call common.' This was done three times. And the object was taken up into heaven again."

Petition: an earnest prayer; Daniel 6:13 reads, "So they answered and said before the king, 'That Daniel, who is one of the captives from Judah, does not show due regard for you, O king, or for the decree that you have signed, but makes his petition three times a day.'"

Pharisee: a religious leader in Jewish culture; a modern symbol of someone who has a religious spirit

Philadelphia: one of the seven churches in Asia to which Jesus wrote a letter; a metaphor for a faithful church (see Revelation 3:7-13)

Philip: an evangelist who was transported in the spirit in Acts 8; *see also Transported in the Spirit*

Philosophy: the seer's worldview; the pursuit of seer wisdom

Physical Realm: Located within the earth realm, the physical realm is specific to the physical body or perceived through the natural senses

Picosecond: one trillionth of a second; the measure of a faint impression in the spirit

Pictorial Vision: *see Pictures*

Pictures: visual impressions or images that may spring forth when praying over someone or even in your own private prayer time; a quick flash of an image that appears randomly in your field of vision

Piercing Serpent: another name for Satan (see Isaiah 27:1)

Pilgrim: *see Sojourner*

Pilgrimage: our lifetime on earth

Plots: storylines that appear in visual revelation; the main theme of a dream or vision

Plumbline: a chord with a weight at one end used to determine an exact vertical line, typically used in building; allegorically, it means God is measuring His people against righteousness;

Amos 7:6-8 reads, "The Lord repented for this: This also shall not be, saith the Lord God. Thus he shewed me: and, behold, the Lord stood upon a wall made by a plumbline, with a plumbline in his hand. And the Lord said unto me, Amos, what seest thou? And I said, A plumbline. Then said the Lord, Behold, I will set a plumbline in the midst of my people Israel: I will not again pass by them any more…"

Pneumatology: the study of the Holy Spirit

Ponder: to weigh a dream or vision in the mind; to think about or meditate visual revelation in hopes of gaining a greater understanding of the message and its application

Portal: an opening, gateway or doorway into the spirit realm.

Potter: another name for God

Potter's Wheel: a metaphor for God's process of shaping the seer and molding his character; a place of pruning that results in greater revelation;

Jeremiah 18:2-4 reads, "'Arise and go down to the potter's house, and there I will cause you to hear My words.' Then I went down to the potter's house, and there he was, making something at the wheel. And the vessel that he made of clay was marred in the hand of the potter; so he made it again into another vessel, as it seemed good to the potter to make."

Pour Life Out as a Drink Offering: pouring out one's life as a sacrifice to Christ in service of His people; pouring out one's God-given strength, power and wisdom to the next generation;

In Philippians 2:17, Paul said, "Yes, and if I am being poured out as a drink offering on the sacrifice and service of your faith, I am glad and rejoice with you all."

Power: the ability, strength and power to perform miracles; 1 Corinthians 4:20 reads "For the kingdom of God is not in word but in power."

Power of the Highest: another name for the Holy Spirit; Luke 1:35 reads, "And the angel answered and said to her, 'The Holy Spirit will come upon you, and the power of the Highest will overshadow you; therefore, also, that Holy One who is to be born will be called the Son of God.'"

Prayer: petitioning God; making a request made known to God; talking to and listening to God

Prayer Angels: angels on assignment to bring prayer answers (See Daniel 9:21-31; Daniel 10:12-13)

Prayer Closet: a private place of prayer; Jesus said in Matthew 6:6, "But thou, when thou prayest, enter into thy closet, and when thou hast shut thy door, pray to thy Father which is in secret; and thy Father which seeth in secret shall reward thee openly."

Prayer Strike: targeted intercession to tear down enemy strongholds; We get this concept from 2 Kings 13:18, which reads, "Then he said, 'Take the arrows;' so he took them. And he said to the king of Israel, 'Strike the ground'; so he struck three times, and stopped."

Praying in the Spirit: the act of praying in tongues or praying Spirit-inspired words in your native language; *see also Praying in Tongues*

Praying in Tongues: praying in the heavenly language you receive when you are baptized in the Holy Spirit; Romans 8:26 reads, "Likewise the Spirit also helps in our weaknesses. For we do not know what we should pray for as we ought, but the Spirit Himself makes intercession for us with groanings which cannot be uttered;" *see also Baptism of the Holy Spirit.*

Preappointed Times: a God-ordained time for nations to rise and fall; Acts 17:27 reads, "And He has made from one blood every nation of men to dwell on all the face of the earth, and has determined their preappointed times and the boundaries of their dwellings…"

Predestined: something God decided beforehand; predetermined; God's will decreed before the foundations of the earth; foreordained; Romans 8:29 reveals, "For whom he did foreknow, he also did predestinate to be conformed to the image of his Son, that he might be the firstborn among many brethren." (See also Ephesians 1:5; Ephesians 1:11; 1 Peter 1:2.)

Presbytery: a body of apostles, prophets and teachers who make up the governing body in the church; 1 Timothy 4:14 (KJV) reads, "Neglect not the gift that is in thee, which was given thee by prophecy, with the laying on of the hands of the presbytery."

Prescribed Time: *see Appointed Time*

Presence of God: a term used to describe the manifest or tangible presence of God; While God is technically everywhere, you can enter into His manifest presence through portals in the Spirit. He rends the heavens and floods the atmosphere with Himself, often in response to prayer or worship.

Present Time: *see Kairos Time*

Present Truth: truth God reveals for the current generation; mysteries that unfold in a particular age of Christianity; spiritual warfare present-day truth emerged in the 1980s; apostolic present-day truths emerged in the 1990s; 2 Peter 1:12 reads, "For this reason I will not be negligent to remind you always of these things, though you know and are established in the present truth."

Presume: to draw conclusions about situations in the natural realm based on what you've seen in dreams or visions, without any hard evidence to draw an accurate parallel

Presumption: the act of presuming

Presumptuous: overstepping one's authority in the seer dimensions; one who draws conclusions based on soulish dot connections rather than waiting on the Holy Spirit's help to interpret visual revelation; to offer one's opinion in the name of prophecy;

Deuteronomy 18:20 declares, "The prophet who presumes to speak a word in My name, which I have not commanded him to speak, or who speaks in the name of other gods, that prophet shall die" We are in a new covenant and prophets are not struck dead for presumption, but God still hates presumption.

Prevision: a seer forecast; to foresee

Prince of Peace: another name for Jesus seen in Isaiah 9:6, "For unto us a Child is born, unto us a Son is given; And the government will be upon His shoulder. And His name will be called Wonderful, Counselor, Mighty God, Everlasting Father, Prince of Peace."

Prince of Persia: a principality that was hindering an angel from bringing Daniel a prayer answer (see Daniel 10); This is evidence of the war in the heavens that is released when we pray.

Prince of the Devils: another name for Satan (see Matthew 12:24)

Prince of the Power of the Air: another name for Satan. Paul wrote in Ephesians 2:2: "And you He made alive, who were dead in trespasses and sins, in which you once walked according to the course of this world, according to the prince of the power of the air, the spirit who now works in the sons of disobedience…"

Prince of This World: another name for Satan (see John 14:30)

Principality: the highest in the ranks of demon powers listed in Ephesians 6:12; also called territorial demons, principalities influence the mindsets of people in cities, states or nations

Process: *see Making of a Seer*

Process of Time: the end of a time period set forth by God; Genesis 4:3 reads, "And in the process of time it came to pass that Cain brought an offering of the fruit of the ground to the Lord."

Proclaim: to make a formal declaration of revelation; In Jeremiah 50:2, God told Jeremiah, "'Declare among the nations, Proclaim, and set up a standard; Proclaim—do not conceal it—Say, 'Babylon is taken, Bel is shamed. Merodach is broken in pieces; Her idols are humiliated, her images are broken in pieces.'"

Profane: something unholy; part of the seer's mandate. Ezekiel 44:23 (KJV) reads, "And they shall teach my people the difference between the holy and profane, and cause them to discern between the unclean and the clean."

Profound: visual revelation that carries weight in the spirit; visual revelation that offers deep spiritual insight. Psalm 92:5 (NET) reads, "How magnificent are Your works, Lord, how profound Your thoughts!"

Promotion: an elevation of rank in the spirit that comes through humility and obedience in God's timing; Psalm 75:7 reads, "But God is the Judge: He puts down one, and exalts another."

Proof: evidence of seer accuracy; evidence of a spiritual encounter

Prophecy: the revelation and verbal expression of the heart, mind and will of God; the testimony of Jesus is the spirit of prophecy (see Revelation 19:10)

Prophesy: to speak forth the oracles of God; to speak under the influence of the spirit of prophecy

Prophet: a mouthpiece for God

Prophetes: the Greek word for prophets in the New Testament. *Prophetes* appears 143 times in the Bible; *Strong's* defines *prophetes* as, "one who speaks forth by the inspiration of God; a prophet" and explains, "a prophet declares the mind (message) of God, which sometimes predicts the future (foretelling)—and more commonly, speaks forth His message for a particular situation. A prophet then is someone inspired by God to foretell or tell-forth (forthtell) the Word of God."

Prophetic: an insight or message emanating from the Holy Spirit; of or relating to revelation from the Holy Spirit

Prophetic Act: an action God asks one to take in order to illustrate a principle or act out His will in a situation.; According to the book *Waging Prophetic Warfare*, the Bible is full of prophetic acts, which should give us a clue as to how God uses people in the earth realm as a point of contact through intercessory prayer and action in spiritual warfare.

All prophetic acts don't relate to spiritual warfare. Prophetic acts can be used to bring a warning (see Ezekiel 4–5); to announce a call into ministry (see 1 Kings 19:19); to facilitate healing (see 2 Kings 5:9–14), and much more.

Prophetic Activation: to bring the prophetic anointing alive in someone through an exercise that puts a demand on the gifting

Prophetic Anointing: an anointing or empowerment to tap into prophetic insight; an anointing to prophesy

Prophetic Dance: a language of movement that communicates what God is saying or doing in an atmosphere; also, spontaneous dance

Prophetic Edge: the sharpness, or accuracy, of someone's prophetic ministry

Prophetic Movement: a movement in the Church that saw the beginning of the restoration of the office of the prophet and the rise of prophetic people in the church in the 1980s

Prophetic Streams: different flows of the prophetic anointing; different camps within the prophetic movement that demonstrate a particular flow of the prophetic anointing

Prophetic Swirl: a frenzy of prophetic anointing and revelation; a series of prophetic events manifesting one after another that demands attention

Prophetic Vessels: a person through whom the prophetic spirit flows; 2 Timothy 2:20-21 reads, "But in a great house there are not only vessels of gold and silver, but also of wood and clay, some for honor and some for dishonor. Therefore if anyone cleanses himself from the latter, he will be a vessel for honor, sanctified and useful for the Master, prepared for every good work."

Prophetic Warning: a Spirit-inspired admonition of impending danger

Prostitute the Gift: one who sells the gifts of God for greedy gain; one who exchanges prophecy for money; Leviticus 20:6

warns, "And the person who turns to mediums and familiar spirits, to prostitute himself with them, I will set My face against that person and cut him off from his people."

Protocol: wise guidelines, procedures or rules that govern the release of seer revelation to ensure spiritual accuracy, proper interpretation, release and application of visual revelation (See the book *Prophetic Protocols & Ethics* for more on protocols).

Proverb: a short, practical saying that offers wisdom for life

Providence: the reality is that our Sovereign God is in control and intervenes in the lives of His people; Romans 8:28 is an example of God's providence: "And we know that all things work together for good to those who love God, to those who are the called according to His purpose."

Pruning: to cut off parts that are hindering growth; to trim so as to make more fruitful; part of the seer's making process. Jesus said in John 15:1-4:

"I am the true vine, and My Father is the vinedresser. Every branch in Me that does not bear fruit He takes away; and every branch that bears fruit He prunes, that it may bear more fruit. You are already clean because of the word which I have spoken to you. Abide in Me, and I in you. As the branch cannot bear fruit of itself, unless it abides in the vine, neither can you, unless you abide in Me."

Psalm: a Spirit-inspired song or hymn used in worship

Psalmist: one who pens or sings a psalm

Puffed Up: a class of pride often connected to prophetic revelation; Paul wrote, "We know that we all have knowledge. Knowledge puffs up, but love edifies" (1 Corinthians 8:1).

Pure: absent of mixture; holy; In Matthew 5:8, Jesus said, "Blessed *are* the pure in heart for they shall see God."

Pure Knowledge: untainted knowledge from God; Job 33:3 reads, "My words come from my upright heart; My lips utter pure knowledge."

Purify: to be cleansed from defilement, and unrighteousness

Q

Quanna: a name for God that means jealous (see Genesis 22:14)

Queen of Heaven: another name for Ashtoreth, the goddess of the wicked Queen Jezebel from 1 Kings; The Queen of Heaven also goes by various other names, including Inanna, Anat, Isis, Nut, Astarte and Asherah. Ashtoreth was thought to be the wife of Bal, a Babylonian God. Catholics call Mary, mother of Jesus, the Queen of Heaven.

The prophet Jeremiah refers to the Queen of Heaven twice: "The children gather wood, the fathers kindle the fire, and the women knead dough, to make cakes for the queen of heaven; and *they* pour out drink offerings to other gods, that they may provoke Me to anger" (Jeremiah 7:18). And Jeremiah 44:17-15 reads:

"But we will certainly do whatever has gone out of our own mouth, to burn incense to the queen of heaven and pour out drink offerings to her, as we have done, we and our fathers, our kings and our princes, in the cities of Judah and in the streets of Jerusalem. For then we had plenty of food, were well-off, and saw no trouble. But since we stopped burning incense to the queen of heaven and pouring out drink offerings to her, we have lacked everything and have been consumed by the sword and by famine."

"The women also said, "And when we burned incense to the queen of heaven and poured out drink offerings to her, did we make cakes for her, to worship her, and pour out drink offerings to her without our husbands' permission?"

"Then Jeremiah spoke to all the people—the men, the women, and all the people who had given him that answer—saying: 'The incense that you burned in the cities of Judah and in the streets of Jerusalem, you and your fathers, your kings and your princes, and the people of the land, did not the Lord remember them, and did it not come into His mind?"

"So the Lord could no longer bear it, because of the evil of your doings and because of the abominations which you committed. Therefore your land is a desolation, an astonishment, a curse, and without an inhabitant, as it is this day. Because you have burned incense and because you have sinned against the Lord, and have not obeyed the voice of the Lord or walked in His law, in His statutes or in His testimonies, therefore this calamity has happened to you, as at this day."

"Moreover Jeremiah said to all the people and to all the women, "Hear the word of the Lord, all Judah who are in the land of Egypt! Thus says the Lord of hosts, the God of Israel, saying: 'You and your wives have spoken with your mouths and fulfilled with your hands, saying, "We will surely keep our vows that we have made, to burn incense to the queen of heaven and pour out drink offerings to her." You will surely keep your vows and perform your vows!'"

Quench the Spirit: spiritual malpractice in which one interferes or puts a stop to what the Holy Spirit is saying or doing in an atmosphere; 1 Thessalonians 5:19 simply says, "Do not quench the Spirit." The AMPC version says, "Do not quench (suppress or subdue) the [Holy] Spirit." The New Living Translation says, "Don't stifle the Holy Spirit."

Quick Flash: something you see in the spirit realm for mere seconds; something that flashes by, disappearing as fast as it appeared

Quickened: to make alive; filled with Holy Spirit power that revitalizes

Quiet: still; tranquil; calm

Quiet Habitation: a peaceful home; a prayer closet; a place where one meets God; Isaiah 33:20, "Look upon Zion, the city of our appointed feasts; Your eyes will see Jerusalem, a quiet home, a tabernacle that will not be taken down; Not one of its stakes will ever be removed, nor will any of its cords be broken."

Quiet Resting Places: *see Quiet Habitation*

Quiet Spirit: a spirit ready in a tranquil state in full readiness to receive revelation from God; Psalm 131:2 reads, "Surely I have calmed and quieted my soul, like a weaned child with his mother; Like a weaned child is my soul within me." And 1 Peter 3:3-4 reads, "Do not let your adornment be merely outward—arranging the hair, wearing gold, or putting on fine apparel—rather let it be the hidden person of the heart, with the incorruptible beauty of a gentle and quiet spirit, which is very precious in the sight of God."

R

Rain: a sign of God's blessing (see Leviticus 6:4)

Rainbow: a sign of God's covenant; In Genesis 9:13, God said, "This is the sign of the covenant which I am making between Me and you and every living creature that is with you, for all future generations. I have set My rainbow in the cloud, and it shall be a sign of a covenant between Me and the earth.

"When I bring a cloud over the earth, the rainbow will be seen in the cloud; then I will remember My covenant, which is between Me and you and every living creature of all flesh, and the waters will never again become a flood to destroy all flesh. The rainbow will appear in the cloud, and I will see it and remember the everlasting covenant between God and every living creature of all flesh that is on the earth."

Also, an arc with various colors in bands that is over the throne of God (see Revelation 4:3). The description of an angel in the Book of Revelation. John wrote, "Then I saw another mighty angel coming down from heaven, clothed with a cloud and a rainbow on his head. His face was like the sun, and his feet like pillars of fire" (Revelation 10:1).

Ezekiel saw a rainbow in his vision of the glory of God. Ezekiel 1:27-28 reads: "Then I saw as glowing metal, as the appearance of fire all around within it, from the appearance of His loins and upward; and from the appearance of His loins and downward I saw as it were the appearance of fire, and there was a brightness around Him. As the appearance of the rainbow that is in the cloud on a day of rain, so was the appearance of the brightness all around. This was the appearance of the likeness of the glory of the Lord. And when I saw it, I fell on my face and heard a voice of one speaking."

Ramah: a place from which Samuel administered justice as a judge of Israel (see 1 Samuel 8:4)

Range of View: *see Visual Field*

Rank in the Spirit: someone's position or degree of authority in the spirit realm

Ranks: an orderly formation of soldiers or angels

Raphael: an archangel mentioned in the Book of Enoch

Ravenous Wolves: how Jesus symbolized false prophets (see Matthew 7:15)

Realm: a domain, whether in the earth or in the spirit; seer realms or dimensions such as dreams, visions, trances, spirit travel, and out of body experiences; (See the book, *The Seer Dimensions*, for more.)

Reaper: a type of end-times angel that gathers the tares and the wheat—the true and the false; Matthew 13:39-41 (NASB) reads: "And the field is the world; and as for the good seed, these are the sons of the kingdom; and the tares are the sons of the evil one; and the enemy who sowed them is the devil, and the harvest is the end of the age; and the reapers are angels. So just as the tares are gathered up and burned with fire, so shall it be at the end of the age."

Revelation 14:14-16 records John's vision of reaper angels: "Then I looked, and behold, a white cloud, and sitting on the cloud was one like a son of man, having a golden crown on His head and a sharp sickle in His hand. And another angel came out of the temple, crying out with a loud voice to Him who sat on the cloud, 'Put in your sickle and reap, for the hour to reap has come, because the harvest of the earth is ripe.' Then He who sat on the cloud swung His sickle over the earth, and the earth was reaped."

Reassuring Angels: angels that bring reassurance in times of stress (see Luke 2:10)

Rebuke: to warn or reprimand; God can give seers visions or dreams of rebuke

Receipt: written or recorded proof of a prophetic revelation that was released before it came to pass; a means of establishing a prophetic track record

Record: to put down in writing, or make an audio or video of a seer revelation so as to remember its details, preserve the encounter and share it with appropriate parties; written, audible or visible evidence of your seer revelation

Recurring Dream: a dream that one has over and over again, either every now and again, or consistently; a dream that indicates God is urgently trying to get you a message; (For more, see the book *Decoding Your Dreams*.)

Redeemer: another name for Jesus as seen in Job 19:25, "For I know that my Redeemer lives, and He shall stand at last on the earth…"

Refining: to deliver from moral flaws; to perfect through melting away what is not like the character of Christ; Jeremiah 9:7 reads, "Therefore thus says the Lord of hosts: 'Behold, I will refine them and try them; For how shall I deal with the daughter of My people?'"

Refiner's Fire: supernatural fire of God that burns or melts away everything that hinders the seer from advancing in his calling; Malachi 3:2 reads, "But who can endure the day of His coming? And who can stand when He appears? For He is like a refiner's fire and like launderers' soap."

Reformation: sweeping change for the better; dealing with flaws in systems

Reformer: one who seeks reformation; Prophets have a reformer's edge

Reinvasion: to envision a seer encounter again; to read through your record and live the encounter again in your mind with the Holy Spirit's help

Release: to discharge seer revelation

Religious Spirit: a demonic spirit that is legalistic, judgmental and puts traditions over the Word of God; a demonic spirit that has a form of godliness but denies the power of God (see 2 Timothy 3:5); the spirit that influenced the Pharisees in the New Testament accounts of Jesus' ministry

Remembrance: recalling a dream, vision or supernatural encounter with the help of the Holy Spirit; John 14:26 reads, "But the Helper, the Holy Spirit, whom the Father will send in My name, He will teach you all things, and bring to your remembrance all things that I said to you."

Remnant: the church within the church; a small number of people among a large crowd; a group of survivors with boldness to do and say what the Lord wants done and said despite the personal cost

Rend the Heavens: when God breaks into earth's atmosphere; a prayer for God's presence to manifest among a people; only God Himself can rend the heavens; Isaiah 64:1, "Oh, that You would rend the heavens! That You would come down! That the mountains might shake at Your presence."

Rend Your Heart Not Your Garments: to repent deeply from within rather than merely demonstrating an outward repentance that does not match the condition of the heart; Joel 2:13 reads, "And rend your heart not your garments. Return to the Lord your God, for He is gracious and merciful, slow to anger, and of great kindness; and He relents from doing harm."

Renounce: a formal declaration of resignation; breaking agreement with a demon power; a decree of divorce with demons in which one declares a separation and refusal to follow or submit any longer

Repairer of the Breach: one God uses to restore what the enemy has torn down; an intercessor who rebuilds a gap in a wall under enemy siege; Isaiah 58:12 reads, "Those from among you shall build the old waste places; You shall raise up the foundations of many generations; And you shall be called the Repairer of the Breach, The Restorer of Streets to Dwell In."

Repent: to change one's mind for the better, heartily to amend with abhorrence of one's past sins, according to *The KJV New Testament Greek Lexicon*

Repentance: a gift from God; the act of repenting

Report: a detailed statement about visual revelation the seer receives; the act of giving an account of seer revelation

Resemblance: the shape or form of something in the spirit that can be best described by using a natural example

Resistance: the presence of opposition to receiving or processing visual revelation; enemy interference in your ministry

Rest: an important factor in receiving divine revelation; a state of quiet, calm expectation; in Matthew 11:28 Jesus said, "Come to Me, all you who labor and are heavy laden, and I will give you rest."

Resurrection and Life: another name for Jesus as seen in John 11:24: "I am the resurrection and the life. He who believes in Me, though he may die, he shall live."

Retrace: to review the events in a dream or vision's timeline as part of interpreting the visual revelation

Retro vision: the seer's ability to see in the distant past

Revealed: intelligence or knowledge made known through divine revelation; Genesis 41:39 reads, "Then Pharaoh said to Joseph, 'Since God has revealed the meaning of the dreams to you, clearly no one else is as intelligent or wise as you are.'"

Revealed Things: to open up revelation that has been previously hidden; Ephesians 3:5 reads, "by which, when you read, you may understand my knowledge in the mystery of Christ, which in other ages was not made known to the sons of men, as it has now been revealed by the Spirit to His holy apostles and prophets."

Revealer of Secrets: a description of God as seen in Daniel 2:47, "The king answered Daniel, and said, 'Truly your God is the God of gods, the Lord of kings, and a revealer of secrets, since you could reveal this secret.'"

Revelation: the manifestation of a divine truth; visual communication from God; 1 Corinthians 14:26 (NLT) reads, "Well, my brothers and sisters, let's summarize. When you meet together, one will sing, another will teach, another will tell some special revelation God has given, one will speak in tongues, and another will interpret what is said. But everything that is done must strengthen all of you."

Riddles of the Wise: *see Dark Sayings*

River of Life: a river in heaven; Revelation 22:1-2 reads, "And he showed me a pure river of water of life, clear as crystal, proceeding from the throne of God and of the Lamb. In the middle of its street, and on either side of the river, was the tree of life, which bore twelve fruits, each tree yielding its fruit every month. The leaves of the tree were for the healing of the nations."

Rivers of Living Water: a metaphor for the Holy Spirit; John 7:37-39, "On the last day, that great day of the feast, Jesus stood and cried out, saying, 'If anyone thirsts, let him come to Me and drink. He who believes in Me, as the Scripture has said, out of his heart will flow rivers of living water.' But this He spoke concerning the Spirit, whom those believing in Him would receive; for the Holy Spirit was not yet given, because Jesus was not yet glorified."

Roaring Lion: another name for Satan (see 1 Peter 5:8)

Rock: another name for Jesus seen in 1 Corinthians 10:4: "And all drank the same spiritual drink. For they drank of that spiritual Rock that followed them, and that Rock was Christ."

Roeh Prophet: We see the word *roeh* used for a prophet beginning in Samuel's day (see 2 Samuel 24:11); *Roeh* is used seven times to describe Samuel's gift. Although we know that Samuel heard "the word of the Lord come unto him saying," in his ministry, the use of the word *roeh* reveals another level of prophetic function in the office of the prophet. It appears 12 times in the Old Testament.

Roeh simply means "seer." Abstractly, it also means to perceive. *Vine's Dictionary* defines it also as "vision" while Brown Driver & Briggs Hebrew Lexicon defines it as seer, prophet, or prophetic vision.

Rooms in Heaven: also called mansions, dwelling places, and resting places, spaces in heaven designated for specific uses; The rooms in heaven are part of the mystical realm of the seer dimension. Beyond places for believers to dwell, there are many rooms in heaven, such as prayer rooms and records rooms, and of course, the throne room.

In John 14:2-3, Jesus said, "In My Father's house are many mansions; if it were not so, I would have told you. I go to prepare a place for you. And if I go and prepare a place for you, I will come again and receive you to Myself; that where I am, there you may be also."

Root: something unseen that feeds what is seen; Seers can often see the roots of issues in the realm of deliverance. John the Baptist said, "And even now the ax is laid to the root of the trees. Therefore every tree which does not bear good fruit is cut down and thrown into the fire" (Matthew 3:9).

Root of David: another name for Jesus as seen in Revelation 5:5: "But one of the elders said to me, 'Do not weep. Behold, the Lion of the tribe of Judah, the Root of David, has prevailed to open the scroll and to loose its seven seals."

Ruach Elohim: a name for God that means Spirit of God, as seen in 1 Samuel 10:10, "When they came there to the hill, there was a group of prophets to meet him; then the Spirit of God came upon him, and he prophesied among them."

Ruach Hakkodesh: a name for the Holy Spirit, as seen in Psalm 51:11, "Do not cast me away from Your presence, and do not take Your Holy Spirit from me."

Ruler of this World: another name for Satan (see John 12:31)

S

Salve: *see Eyesalve*

Samson: a Nazarite and judge of Israel whose anointing was connected to his long hair; a warrior whose strength was tied to his hair; a victim of the Delilah spirit who sold him out for money

Samuel: a seer prophet who was dedicated to the Lord from his mother's womb and anointed Israel's first two kings; His name means "name of God" or "heard of God."

Samuel's prophetic ministry was marked by uncanny accuracy. The Bible says the Lord would not let any of his words fall to the ground (see 1 Samuel 3:19). Samuel was a miracle child from the tribe of Levi and the last judge in Israel.

Samuel Anointing: a seer anointing bent toward raising up other seers in holiness

Sanctification: a purification for service to the Lord; 1 Thessalonians 4:3 says, "For this is the will of God, your sanctification: that you should abstain from sexual immorality..." Seers must pursue a lifestyle of sanctification.

According to *The KJV New Testament Greek Lexicon*, the Greek word for sanctification is *hagiasmos*, which means, "consecration, purification; the effect of consecration; sanctification of heart and life."

Merriam-Webster defines sanctification as "the state of growing in divine grace as a result of Christian commitment after baptism or conversion" and "the act of being sanctified."

The same dictionary defines sanctified as "to set apart to a sacred purpose or to religious use : consecrate; to free from sin : purify; to impart or impute sacredness, inviolability, or respect to; to give moral or social sanction to; to make productive of holiness or piety."

Sapphire: a gemstone of deep purplish-blue color; the appearance of the throne of God (see Ezekiel 1:26); a stone in the foundation of the walls around the New Jerusalem; gemstones on the breastplate of judgment the Old Testament priests wore (see Exodus 28:18);

Also, a gemstone under the feet of God: Exodus 24:9-11 reads, "Then Moses went up, also Aaron, Nadab, and Abihu, and seventy of the elders of Israel, and they saw the God of Israel. And there *was* under His feet as it were a paved work of sapphire stone, and it was like the very heavens in its clarity. But on the nobles of the children of Israel He did not lay His hand. So they saw God, and they ate and drank."

Sar Shalom: a name for God that means Prince of Peace as seen in Isaiah 9:6, "For unto us a Child is born, unto us a Son is given; And the government will be upon His shoulder. And His name will be called Wonderful, Counselor, Mighty God, Everlasting Father, Prince of Peace."

Sardius: a reddish-brown precious stone John the Revelator saw on the foundations of the wall around the New Jerusalem (see Revelation 21:19-21)

Sardonyx: onyx stone with a banded appearance due to its mixture with sardius stone; a precious stone John the Revelator saw on the foundations of the wall around the New Jerusalem (see Revelation 21:19-21)

Satan: formerly called Lucifer, a created being that once dwelled in the presence of God; the prince of the power of the air, the ruler of darkness; a fallen angel who organizes demonic armies to fight against the will of God, to deceive believers, and to steal, kill and destroy (see John 10:10).

Satanic Eyes: *see Monitoring Spirits*

Scales on the Eyes: a visual obstruction; a blinding of the eyes; Acts 9:18 reads, "Immediately there fell from his eyes something like scales, and he received his sight at once; and he arose and was baptized."

Scent: one of many fragrances you may smell in the spirit; Psalm 45:8 reads, "All Your garments are scented with myrrh and aloes and cassia, out of the ivory palaces, by which they have made You glad," suggesting that David smelled the presence of the Lord in the spirit dimensions.

School of the Prophets: schools where prophets are trained in the Word of God and the operations of the Spirit; We see schools of the prophets in 1 Samuel 19 with Samuel raising up prophets; 2 Kings 2 points Elijah's school of the prophets and 2 Kings 4 points to Elisha's school of the prophets.

Scribe: a writer in the Kingdom of God; one who writes down the words of God

Scriptural: a truth that lines up completely with the Holy Scriptures

Scroll: papers that contained important information, including dictated prophetic words; Seers can look into scrolls as the Holy Spirit escorts them (see Jeremiah 36:4)

Sea of Glass: a scene in the Throne Room of God; Two Scriptures mention the sea of glass: Revelation 4:6 and Revelation 15:2;

Revelation 4:6 reads, "Before the throne there was a sea of glass, like crystal. And in the midst of the throne, and around the throne, were four living creatures full of eyes in front and in back."

Revelation 15:2 reads, "And I saw something like a sea of glass mingled with fire, and those who have the victory over the beast, over his image and over his mark and over the number of his name, standing on the sea of glass, having harps of God."

Seal: to keep visual revelation secret

Seal Up the Vision: to lock up; to secure; to authenticate with a mark; Daniel 9:24 reads," Seventy weeks are determined for your people and for your holy city, to finish the transgression, to make an end of sins, to make reconciliation for iniquity, to bring in everlasting righteousness, to seal up vision and prophecy, and to anoint the Most Holy."

Search Out: to seek an interpretation of visual revelation through prayer and Bible study; Proverbs 25:2 tells us, "It is the glory of God to conceal a thing, but the honor of kings is to search out a matter." Seers must search out the matters of God in the spirit.

Season: a set time, an appointed time; Ecclesiastes 3:1 reads, "To everything there is a season, a time for every purpose under heaven."

Season and a Time: a biblical way to say 1,000 years; Daniel 7:12, "As for the rest of the beasts, they had their dominion taken away, yet their lives were prolonged for a season and a time."

Second Heaven: Satan's domain; a sphere above the earth's atmosphere but below heaven, where God's throne sits;

Common sense informs us if there is a third heaven, there must be a second heaven and a first heaven. The concept of the second heaven is found in Revelation 8:13: "Then I looked, and I heard an eagle flying in midheaven, saying with a loud voice, 'Woe, woe, woe to those who dwell on the earth, because of the remaining blasts of the trumpet of the three angels who are about to sound!'"

We see supernatural activity in the midheaven, or second heaven, with other references found in Revelation 14:6 and Revelation 19:17. Spiritual conflicts take place in the second heaven. When the Prince of Persia withstood the angel seeking to deliver Daniel's prayer answers, this skirmish took place in the midheaven. Much of the spiritual warfare with which we are familiar is taking place in the second heaven.

Second Watch: a watch that runs from 9 pm to 12 am; This watch starts with thanksgiving to the Lord as Protector and petitions for divine intervention in the battle for the coming day. Spiritual warfare marks this watch. The enemy wants to stand against the revelation God is trying to show you about planned attacks. (See the book, *The Making of the Seer*, for more.)

Secret: something hidden or concealed; Amos 3:7 reads, "Surely the Lord God does nothing, unless He reveals His secret to His servants the prophets." But the Bible also says, "The secret of the Lord is with those who fear Him, and He will show them His covenant" (Psalm 25:14).

Secret Arts: to influence one's mind or circumstances through incantations and spells; to bewitch with witchcraft

Secret Chamber: prayer closet; a secret room

Secret Counsel of God: an intimate place of conversation between the seer and the Holy Spirit; Proverbs 3:32 reads, "For the perverse person is an abomination to the Lord, but His secret counsel is with the upright."

Secret Counsel of the Wicked: a hidden assembly of evil spirits; Psalm 64:2 (KJV) reads, "Hide me from the secret counsel of the wicked; from the insurrection of the workers of iniquity."

Secret Dimension: a dimension in the spirit where God reveals His secrets to those who fear Him

Secret Faults: faults known only between you and God that, if left uncleansed, can compromise your spiritual vision; David prayed in Psalm 19:12, "Who can understand his errors? Cleanse me from secret faults."

Secret Message: knowledge hidden from sight until God chooses to reveal it

Secret Messengers: prophets who discreetly share a hidden message; a function of some angels on assignment

Secret of the Kingdom of God: mystic truths about the Kingdom of God and its operations; hidden revelations about God's Kingdom; Mark 4:11 reads, "He replied, 'You are permitted to understand the secret of the Kingdom of God. But I use parables for everything I say to outsiders…'"

Secret Place: a hidden place in the presence of God; a place of protection from the enemy; a place of revelation of God Himself; Psalm 91:1 reads, "He who dwells in the secret place of the Most High shall abide under the shadow of the Almighty."

Secret Place of Thunder: a pillar of clouds that hides God's people from evil; Psalm 81:7 reads, "You called in trouble, and I delivered you; I answered you in the secret place of thunder; I tested you at the waters of Meribah. Selah."

Secret Plan: a hidden plot of the enemy revealed to the seer; Psalm 64:6, (Berean Study Bible) reads, "They devise injustice and say, 'We have perfected a secret plan.' For the inner man and the heart are mysterious."

Secret Powers: *see Secret Arts*

Secret Sins: sins that only God sees, unless God reveals them to the seer for the purpose of intercession; Psalm 90:8, "You have set our iniquities before You, our secret sins in the light of Your countenance."

Secret Things: truths God has chosen to hide from those who are not part of the covenant; Deuteronomy 29:29 reads, "The secret things belong to the Lord our God, but those things which are revealed belong to us and to our children forever, that we may do all the words of this law."

Secrets of Men: realities of the mind men hide in their souls; Romans 2:16 reads, "in the day when God will judge the secrets of men by Jesus Christ, according to my gospel."

Secrets of the Heart: thoughts and intentions hidden in the heart; unspoken desires and plans sometimes revealed to seers to forward God's purposes through prayer; Psalm 44:21 reads, "Would not God search this out? For He knows the secrets of the heart." And 1 Corinthians 14:25, "And thus the secrets of his heart are revealed; and so, falling down on his face, he will worship God and report that God is truly among you."

Secrets of Wisdom: skillful wisdom revealed prophetically; Job 11:6 reads, "That He would show you the secrets of wisdom! For they would double your prudence."

See: an ability to perceive things in the spirit realm through dreams, visions, impressions or trances

See in Part: incomplete revelation; Often seers will get one part of the spiritual puzzle and other seers will have another part; This is why it's so important to have a community that can deliberate seer revelation. 1 Corinthians 13:12 (NLT) says, "Now we see things imperfectly…"

See Through a Glass Darkly: to see in part; *see also Darkly*

Seer: a prophet who sees in the spirit; all seers are prophets, not all prophets are seers

Seer Activation: to bring the seer anointing alive in someone through an exercise that puts a demand on the gifting

Seer Anointing: a God-given anointing to see in the spirit; a special endowment to see behind the veil

Seer Aptitude: a seer's capacity for learning spiritual truths; the inclinations or tendencies of the seer

Seer Authority: the authority a seer carries in the spirit realm

Seer Company: *see Company of Seers*

Seer Continuum: a series of dreams or visions that make up an entire revelatory storyline

Seer Counsel: visual revelatory counsel seers disperse

Seer Culture: a culture that welcomes, appreciates, honors and celebrates and heeds seers and revelations seers release

Seer Deliverance: the ability to see the spirits oppressing a person as a prerequisite for casting them out

Seer Depth: the measure of a seer's visual revelation, often relating to shallow perception or profoundness

Seer Famine: when visual revelation is rare; when seers in the land are rare; 1 Samuel 3:1 reads, "Now the boy Samuel ministered to the Lord before Eli. And the word of the Lord was rare in those days; there was no widespread revelation."

Seer Focus: a seer skill developed through experience that allows one to focus primarily on what the Holy Spirit wants them to see amid an active spiritual background that could otherwise be overwhelming

Seer Functions: actions seers perform as part of their ministry, such as dreams, visions, trances, prophesying, interpreting dreams, etc.

Seer Guard: a seer that watches over another person in the spirit, typically for the purpose of warning, warring and interceding for them

Seer Instincts: automatic reactions and behaviors that are innate to the seer gifting, such as intercession and discernment

Seer Intelligence: seeing with the intention of learning or understanding what you are seeing; Seer intelligence comes through seer focus and helps you comprehend at times not only what you are seeing, but what it means and how to apply the visual revelation.

Seer Intercession: intercession seers engage in based on what they see in the spirit; the seer's bent to stand in the gap over visual revelation God showed them

Seer Journey: the seer's passage from one dimension to another; the seer's travel through the stages of their ministry.

Seer Jots: quick pictures or words written down following an encounter

Seer Language: language seers use to describe the gift, calling, warfare, dreams, visions and other revelations

Seer Lineage: the spiritual line from which a seer descends; the spiritual parents of the seer, and the spiritual parents of the spiritual parents of the seer, and so on; the seer's family tree

Seer Mantle: the mantle of the seer; see also *Mantle*

Seer Movement: a stream of the prophetic movement focused on the restoration of seers and seeing people

Seer Operations: *see Seer Functions*

Seer Paradigm: a seer's theological framework, such as how he views Jesus, prophetic ministry or the end-times

Seer Protocols: a set of wisdom-inspired guidelines for operating in the seer anointing that assure one's ministry is safe and effective

Seer Purpose: the distinct reason God created a seer, understanding that not all seers have the same purpose just because they have the same category of anointing

Seer Ranking: the rank of a seer; there are newly-minted seers and elder seers in the Kingdom. *see also Rank in the Spirit*

Seer Realm: the unseen world

Seer Release: the sharing of visual revelation publicly

Seer Scribes: a seer who releases revelation predominantly through writing; a seer who records his revelations and the revelations of other seers

Seer Streams: various facets of the seer movement, including dreamers, visionaries, and those known for heavenly encounters and out-of-body experiences

Seer Swirl: a whirl of revelation that turns the seer's head

Seer Talk: language relevant to seers; language sometimes only seers understand; expressions relevant to describing seer realities; the ways seers speak about visual revelation

Seer Territory: see *Metron*

Seer Training: spiritual education specific to the seer gift

Seer Vocabulary: a collection of words that make up the seer language; *see also Seer Language*

Seer Warfare: spiritual warfare particular to seers and seeing people, such as nightmares and persecution

Seer Wisdom: wisdom in receiving, interpreting, releasing and applying visual revelation

Seership: the position, office, or dignity of a seer; the personality of a seer

Selah: a pause to consider the revelation one has received; an interlude between seer revelations

Semiramis: the Queen of Heaven, the false god Jezebel serves

Sentinel: *see Watchman*

Seraphim: winged creatures seated above God's throne (see Isaiah 6:1-2)

Serpent: another name for Satan (see Genesis 3:4, Genesis 3:16; 2 Corinthians 11:3)

Set Time: *see Season*

Seven Bowls: the final judgments in the tribulation period of the end-times John saw in an epic vision; Revelation 16:1-21 outline the wrath of God poured out with the seven bowls.

Seven Seals: a series of judgments in the end-times John saw in an epic vision; Revelation 6:1-17 and Revelation 8:1-5 outline what is released when each of the seven seals is broken.

Seven Spirits of God: the seven manifestations of the Holy Spirit listed in Isaiah 11:2: "The Spirit of the Lord shall rest upon Him, the Spirit of wisdom and understanding, the Spirit of counsel and might, the Spirit of knowledge and of the fear of the Lord."

Seven Trumpets: after the seventh seal is broken on the end-times scrolls, angels blow seven trumpets, which release God's judgements on the earth; Revelation 8:6-9:19 and Revelation 11:15-19 outline what is released when each of the seven trumpets blast.

Seventh Watch: a watch that runs from noon to 3 pm. After Jesus gave up His Spirit at noon, darkness covered the earth until 3 pm. This is when Peter and John went up to the temple for the hour of prayer, the ninth hour (see Acts 3:1). This is a time to take authority over the powers of darkness in prayer. Watch for enemy activity in this day division from the secret place. (See the book, *The Making of the Seer*, for more.)

Severe Vision: *see Grievous Vision*

Shadow: a dark reflection of what is hidden in the seer dimensions; obscurity in the spirit

Shadow of Death: thick darkness

Shadow of God's Wings: a place of protection in God; Psalm 17:8 reads, "Keep me as the apple of Your eye; Hide me under the shadow of Your wings…"

Shadow of Heavenly Things: a faint picture of the things of heaven; Hebrews 8:5 reads, "who serve the copy and shadow of the heavenly things, as Moses was divinely instructed when he was about to make the tabernacle. For He said, 'See that you make all things according to the pattern shown you on the mountain.'"

Shadow of His Hand: the protection of God's hand; Isaiah 49:2 reads, "In the shadow of His hand He has hidden Me, And made Me a polished shaft; In His quiver He has hidden Me."

Shadow of the Almighty: the protection of God; Psalm 91:1 reads, "He who dwells in the secret place of the Most High Shall abide under the shadow of the Almighty."

Shadow of Things to Come: an outline of something that we will see fully at a later time; Colossians 2:17 reads, "which are a shadow of things to come, but the substance is of Christ."

Shamar: a Hebrew word for watchman that means "to observe, keep, heed, preserve, beware, mark, wait, regard and save;" Nehemiah 3:29 reads, "After them Zadok the son of

Immer made repairs in front of his own house. After him Shemaiah the son of Shechaniah, the keeper of the East Gate, made repairs." The word "keeper" in this verse comes from the Hebrew word *shamar*.

Shape: the appearance of something you see in the spirit that you can't readily name; a way the seer describes something he sees in the spirit that resembles something in the natural; Ezekiel 10:1 reads, "sapphire, resembling the shape of a throne, appearing above them."

Sharpen: to hone; to make more accurate, as in sharpen one's visual accuracy

Sheol: *see Hell*

Shock: an emotional state that results from seeing something dramatic in the seer dimensions

Shut Down the Gift: when the seer gift is overwhelming and one asks God to shut it down or shut it off; Warning: do not do this. If you have done it, repent and ask God to restore the full capacity and use of the gift. The gifts and callings of God are irrevocable (see Romans 11:29).

Shut up Vision: *see Seal Up the Vision*

Side Vision: *see Peripheral Vision*

Sift: the trying of one's faith; Luke 22:31 reads, "And the Lord said, 'Simon, Simon! Indeed, Satan has asked for you, that he may sift you as wheat."

Sift a Vision: to separate the themes in a vision; to separate a Spirit-inspired dream or vision from the soulish elements it may contain

Sigh in the Spirit: the sound of one that is grieving or mourning in the Spirit; a deep heard breath; *see also Groan;* Mark 7:32-35 reads, "Then they brought to Him one who was deaf and had an impediment in his speech, and they begged Him to put His hand on him. And He took him aside from the multitude, and put His fingers in his ears, and He spat and touched his tongue. Then, looking up to heaven, He sighed, and said to him, 'Ephphatha,' that is, 'Be opened.' Immediately his ears were opened, and the impediment of his tongue was loosed, and he spoke plainly."

Sight of the Lord: the eyes of the Lord upon a person, place or thing; Genesis 38:7 reads, "But Er, Judah's firstborn, was wicked in the sight of the Lord, and the Lord killed him."

Sight worthy: worth seeing

Sign: visual revelation that points to future events

Signs of the Times: signs that point to the generation that lives in the end-times; Jesus spoke at length about the end times in Matthew 24; You can learn more about the end-times in Discerning the Signs of the Times at schoolofthespirit.tv.

Silence: the absence of sound

Silence in Heaven: absence of sound in heaven; Revelation 8:1 says, "When He opened the seventh seal, there was silence in heaven for about half an hour."

Silent and Listen: remaining quiet and listening to what the Lord is saying (see Deuteronomy 27:9)

Silent Dimension: a dimension in the spirit where there is absolute silence; the destination of one who practices silence as a gateway to the seer dimensions; (For more, see the book *The Seer Dimensions*.)

Silent Groan: an inward groan in response to something grievous; Ezekiel 24:17 (NASB) reads, "Groan silently; make no mourning for the dead. Bind on your turban and put your shoes on your feet, and do not cover your mustache and do not eat the bread of men."

Silent to Discern: remaining quiet in soul and calm in spirit in order to discern what is happening in the spirit (see Genesis 24:21)

Simon the Sorcerer: a sorcerer who got born again but not delivered; Simon tried to buy the power of the Holy Spirit (see Acts 8:9-24).

Simple Gift of Prophecy: the simple gift of prophecy is a gift of the Spirit available to all believers; a gift of the spirit that edifies, exhorts and comforts people with Holy Spirit-inspired words (see 1 Corinthians 14:1-12).

Singing in the Spirit: singing in your heavenly language; singing in tongues; Ephesians 5:19 says, "speaking to one another in psalms and hymns and spiritual songs, singing and making melody in your heart to the Lord."

Sixth Watch: a watch that runs from 9 am to noon; a watch where promises are fulfilled; This was the watch during which Jesus was crucified. Jesus hung on a cross at 9 am (see Mark 15:25). This is the watch where God delivers people out of darkness and into His light (see Colossians 1:3). It's a time to meditate on the power of the cross, who we are in Christ, and the yes-and-amen promises of God in Christ. (For more see *The Making of a Watchman*).

Smelling in the Spirit: the ability to smell the presence of God or demon spirits; an aspect of the gift of discerning of spirits (see 1 Corinthians 12:10)

Sojourner: a temporary resident; our status on earth as people of God; Hebrews 13:14 reads, "For this world is not our permanent home; we are looking forward to a home yet to come."

Solitude: being alone in order to fellowship with the Holy Spirit or pray

Solving Spiritual Riddles: a gift Daniel possessed; Daniel 5 reveals Daniel solving a spiritual riddle in handwriting on the wall

Son of Perdition: another name for Satan (see 2 Thessalonians 2:3)

Son of the Highest: another name for Jesus as seen in Luke 1:32: "He will be great, and will be called the Son of the Highest; and the Lord God will give Him the throne of His father David."

Song of the Lord: a prophetic song; Miriam released a song of the Lord in Exodus; Deborah released a song of the Lord in Judges; Zephaniah 3:14-17 is another strong example.

Soothsayer: one who predicts the future through familiar spirits; While a seer gains access to the spirit world through the door of Jesus and by the will of the Holy Spirit, a soothsayer goes in through a backdoor in the spirit (see Backdoor).

Soothsaying: foretelling future events through demonic intelligence

Sorcerer: one who practices sorcery; Acts 13:6 shares, "Now when they had gone through the island to Paphos, they found a certain sorcerer, a false prophet, a Jew whose name *was* Bar-Jesus…"

Sorcery: divination; tapping into information from the supernatural realm illegally; Jeremiah 27:9 reads, "Therefore do not listen to your prophets, your diviners, your dreamers, your soothsayers, or your sorcerers, who speak to you, saying, 'You shall not serve the king of Babylon.'" In this instance, prophets are false and lumped in with other false operators.

Soul Realm: the realm of the mind, will, emotions, imaginations, reasoning and intellect

Soul Senses: responses to what we see, hear, touch, taste, smell or know based on reactions in our mind, will, imaginations, reasonings, intellect and emotions; Unrenewed areas of one's soul and past positive or negative experiences in life can skew what one sees or thinks he sees in the spirit or what he discerns.

Sound the Alarm: to give a warning about impending danger; Joel 2:1 reads, "Blow the trumpet in Zion, and sound an alarm in My holy mountain! Let all the inhabitants of the land tremble; For the day of the Lord is coming, for it is at hand…"

South Wind: a wind representing calm; the south wind is mentioned in the Bible five times; a still land (Job 37:17); in association with discerning times (Luke 12:55); Paul's ship being driven by the wind (Acts 27:13; Acts 28:13); and God directing the south wind (Psalm 78:26).

Sovereign: supreme power; a characteristic of God

Speak a Vision: to share the vision with the Body of Christ; Jeremiah 23:16 reads, "Thus says the Lord of hosts 'Do not listen to the words of the prophets who prophesy to you. They make you worthless; They speak a vision of their own heart, not from the mouth of the Lord."

Speaking in Tongues: speaking in one's heavenly language

Spies: to watch in secret, usually with ill intent; Galatians 2:4 reads, "And this occurred because of false brethren secretly brought in (who came in by stealth to spy out our liberty which we have in Christ Jesus, that they might bring us into bondage)."

Spirit Beings: angels, demons, living wheels (see Ezekiel 1:20); a winged woman (see Zechariah 5:9); there may be other spirit beings not recorded in the Bible

Spirit of Adoption: another name for the Holy Spirit. Romans 8:15 reads, "For you did not receive the spirit of bondage again to fear, but you received the Spirit of adoption by whom we cry out, 'Abba, Father.'"

Spirit of Burning: another name for the Holy Spirit; Isaiah 4:4 reads, "When the Lord has washed away the filth of the daughters of Zion, and purged the blood of Jerusalem from her midst, by the spirit of judgment and by the spirit of burning…"

Spirit of Counsel: one of the seven spirits of God; another name for the Holy Spirit (see Isaiah 11:12)

Spirit of Deep Sleep: deep sleep; a trance; Isaiah 29:10 reads, "For the Lord has poured out on you the spirit of deep sleep, and has closed your eyes, namely, the prophets; and He has covered your heads, namely, the seers."

Spirit of Error: a spirit that deceives people; 1 John 4:6 points out this spirit, "We are of God. He who knows God hears us; he who is not of God does not hear us. By this we know the spirit of truth and the spirit of error;" *see also Error*

Spirit of Glory: another name for the Holy Spirit; 1 Peter 4:14 reads, "If you are reproached for the name of Christ, blessed are you, for the Spirit of glory and of God rests upon you. On their part He is blasphemed, but on your part He is glorified."

Spirit of God: another name for the Holy Spirit; Genesis 1:2 reads, "The earth was without form, and void; and darkness was on the face of the deep. And the Spirit of God was hovering over the face of the waters."

Spirit of Grace: another name for the Holy Spirit; Hebrews 10:29 reads, "Of how much worse punishment, do you suppose, will he be thought worthy who has trampled the Son of God underfoot, counted the blood of the covenant by which he was sanctified a common thing, and insulted the Spirit of grace?"

Spirit of Holiness: another name for the Holy Spirit; Romans 1:4 reads, "and declared to be the Son of God with power according to the Spirit of holiness, by the resurrection from the dead."

Spirit of Justice: another name for the Holy Spirit; Isaiah 28:6 reads, "For a spirit of justice to him who sits in judgment, and for strength to those who turn back the battle at the gate."

Spirit of Knowledge: another name for the Holy Spirit (see Isaiah 11:2).

Spirit of Life: another name for the Holy Spirit; Romans 8:2 reads, "For the law of the Spirit of life in Christ Jesus has made me free from the law of sin and death."

Spirit of Might: another name for the Holy Spirit (see Isaiah 11:2).

Spirit of Prophecy: another name for the Holy Spirit; Revelation 9:10 reads, "For the testimony of Jesus is the spirit of prophecy."

Spirit of Revelation: another name for the Holy Spirit; Ephesians 1:17 reads, "that the God of our Lord Jesus Christ, the Father of glory, may give to you the spirit of wisdom and revelation in the knowledge of Him…"

Spirit of Supplication: another name for the Holy Spirit; Zechariah 12:10 reads, "And I will pour on the house of David and on the inhabitants of Jerusalem the Spirit of grace…"

Spirit of the Father: another name for the Holy Spirit; Matthew 10:20 reads, "for it is not you who speak, but the Spirit of your Father who speaks in you."

Spirit of the Fear of the Lord: another name for the Holy Spirit (see Isaiah 11:2)

Spirit of the Living God: another name for the Holy Spirit; 2 Corinthians 3:3 reads, "Clearly you are an epistle of Christ, ministered by us, written not with ink but by the Spirit of the living God, not on tablets of stone but on tablets of flesh, that is, of the heart."

Spirit of the Lord: another name for the Holy Spirit; Isaiah 61:1 reads, "The Spirit of the Lord God is upon Me, because the Lord has anointed Me to preach good tidings to the poor; He has sent Me to heal the brokenhearted, to proclaim liberty to the captives, and the opening of the prison to those who are bound…"

Spirit of the Prophets is Subject to the Prophets: a prophet can control his or her own spirit and utterance (see 1 Corinthians 14:32)

Spirit of the Son: another name for the Holy Spirit; Galatians 4:6 reads: "And because you are sons, God has sent forth the

Spirit of His Son into your hearts, crying out, 'Abba, Father!'"

Spirit of Truth: another name for the Holy Spirit; John 14:17 reads, "the Spirit of truth, whom the world cannot receive, because it neither sees Him nor knows Him; but you know Him, for He dwells with you and will be in you."

Spirit of Understanding: another name for the Holy Spirit (see Isaiah 11:2)

Spirit of Wisdom: another name for the Holy Spirit (see Isaiah 11:2)

Spirit Travel: *see Translated by the Spirit*

Spiritual Aromas: fragrances in the spirit that are being discerned through the natural sense of smell

Spiritual Atmosphere: the spirits influencing an environment, whether the Holy Spirit, angels or demons

Spiritual Attack: an affront or ambush by spiritual enemies

Spiritual Awareness: an awareness of the spiritual realm around you

Spiritual Climate: the prevailing spiritual atmosphere of a place.

Spiritual Conflict: opposition in the spirit realm; a war in the heavens

Spiritual Curiosity: being inquisitive about the things of the spirit

Spiritual Environment: the conditions and influences in one's life, church, family, business, school, etc.

Spiritual Eyes: *see Eyes of Your Heart*

Spiritual Famine: when moves of God are rare due to a lack of hunger or a grieving or quenching of the Holy Spirit

Spiritual Frustration: a spiritual sensation that occurs when you cannot discern the will of the Lord or demonic interference; a feeling one experiences when they hit a spiritual plateau and cannot seem to ascend higher; a feeling a seer encounters when they are being held back or not accepted in a church

Spiritual Laws: also laws of the Spirit; spiritual laws outline the rules of the Kingdom of God, such as the law of sin and death (see Romans 8:2), the law of the Spirit of life in Christ Jesus (see Romans 8:2), and the law of sowing and reaping (see Galatians 6:7)

Spiritual Phenomena: a rare occurrence or event in the spirit dimensions

Spiritual Senses: senses in the spirit that correlate to natural senses, including see, hear, touch, feel and smell; Hebrews 5:14 reads, "But solid food belongs to those who are of full age, that is, those who by reason of use have their senses exercised to discern both good and evil."

Spiritual Sensitivity: being sensitive to the spiritual realm, including angels, demons, God, spiritual atmospheres and spiritual climates

Spiritual Spying: *see Monitoring Spirits*

Spiritual Vocabulary: words that relate to or describe things of the spirit realm

Spiritually-Minded: having a mind set on things above; having a mind set on the things of God

Spoiler: an agent of darkness that works to destroy, corrupt, ruin, decay, or pervert; Isaiah 54:16 reads, "Behold, I have created the blacksmith who blows the coals in the fire, who brings forth an instrument for his work; And I have created the spoiler to destroy."

Spoils: valuables gained after victory in battle, i.e. the spoils of war; I Chronicles 26:27 reads, "Some of the spoils won in battles they dedicated to maintain the house of the Lord."

Spy Out: *see Surveying*

Squinting in the Spirit: concentrating deeply, or staring at something in the spirit realm that is difficult to see

Stalk: the enemy's pursuit of his prey; the activity of harassing demons; 1 Peter 5:8 reads, "Be sober, be vigilant; because your adversary the devil walks about like a roaring lion, seeking whom he may devour."

Standby: another name for the Holy Spirit

Stare: to fix one's eyes upon something in the seer dimensions; to gaze

Static in the Spirit: noise in the spiritual atmosphere, manifesting as audible noise that prevents one from hearing clearly what is happening or visual noise that keeps one from seeing clearly what is happening

Station: *see Watchtower*

Stephen: a disciple of Christ who was stoned to death and saw into heaven during the assault; Acts 7:55-56 gives the account: "But he, being full of the Holy Spirit, gazed into heaven and saw the glory of God, and Jesus standing at the right hand of God, and said, 'Look! I see the heavens opened and the Son of Man standing at the right hand of God!'"

Steward Visual Revelation: judging, interpreting, praying through and applying what you see in the spirit

Stewarding the Gift: to manage one's spiritual gifts under the leadership of the Holy Spirit; 1 Peter 4:10 reads, "As each one has received a gift, minister it to one another, as good stewards of the manifold grace of God."

Stir up the Gift: to activate; to press into the use of the gift God has given you; In 2 Timothy 1:6 Paul tells his spiritual son Timothy: "Therefore I remind you to stir up the gift of God, which is in you by the laying on of my hands." The Greek word for stir in this verse is *anazopureo*, which means "to kindle up, inflame one's mind, strength, zeal."

Stirring: a movement in the spirit

Strange Eyes: *see Monitoring Spirits*

Strange Fire: profane fire, or unauthorized fire; a counterfeit prophetic operation; a counterfeit move of the Spirit; Leviticus 10:1-3 reads, "And Nadab and Abihu, the sons of Aaron, took either of them his censer, and put fire therein, and put incense thereon, and offered strange fire before the Lord, which he commanded them not. And there went out fire from the Lord, and devoured them, and they died before the Lord. Then Moses said unto Aaron, This is it that the Lord spake, saying, I will be sanctified in them that come nigh me, and before all the people I will be glorified. And Aaron held his peace."

Streets of Gold: an attribute of heaven; Revelation 21:21 reads, "The twelve gates were twelve pearls: each individual gate was of one pearl. And the street of the city was pure gold, like transparent glass."

Strengthening Angels: angels that come to strengthen God's people (see Luke 22:40-44)

Suffering: affliction, distress, demonic attacks; James 5:10 reads, "My brethren, take the prophets, who spoke in the name of the Lord, as an example of suffering and patience."

Supernatural: the realm of miracles; an unseen realm where God exists

Surveying: to examine the landscape in the spirit realm

Suspended Sentences: an occurrence that happens during a trance, when all natural senses are suspended

Symbol: something in the spirit that represents something in the natural

Symbolic: seer revelation that relies on symbols to understand

Symbiotic Vision: *Merriam-Webster* defines symbiotic as "characterized by or being a close, cooperative, or interdependent relationship;" Seers who move in companies become symbiotic. Their collective visions unlock greater revelation.

T

Tapestry: a rich landscape in the spirit; designs in the spirit; Psalm 104:12 (TPT) reads: "You wrap yourself with a shimmering, glistening light. You wear sunshine like a garment of glory. You stretch out the starry skies like a tapestry."

Tare: weeds; deceptions of the enemy; false revelations the enemy sows in a seer's soul; In Matthew 13:24-25, Jesus said, "Another parable He put forth to them, saying: 'The kingdom of heaven is like a man who sowed good seed in his field; but while men slept, his enemy came and sowed tares among the wheat and went his way.'"

Target: the object of enemy attack; a prayer goal

Tarry: to wait with expectation; to linger in the Lord's presence

Taste: experience something in the spirit; Psalm 34:8 connects tasting with seeing: "Oh, taste and see that the Lord is good…"

Tasting in the Spirit: a form of discernment in which one can taste good or evil

Teacher: an Ephesians 4:11 five-fold minister who teaches the Word of God; one who expounds upon and breaks the Word of God into practical keys and steps that believers can apply to see their mind renewed and their life changed

Tears: an expression of desperate prayer; sometimes a byproduct of deep travail; Psalm 6:6 reads, "I am weary with my groaning; All night I make my bed swim; I drench my couch with my tears."

Tempest: a violent storm; Isaiah 29:6, reads, "You will be punished by the Lord of hosts with thunder and earthquake and great noise, with storm and tempest and the flame of devouring fire."

Temporal: things seen; things you can see and feel in the earth realm that will one day pass away

Tempter: another name for Satan; Matthew 4:3 reads, "Now when the tempter came to Him, he said, 'If You are the Son of God, command that these stones become bread.'"

Terrestrial: something related to the earth realm

Terrifying Vision: a grievous vision; Isaiah 21:2 (NLT) reads, "I see a terrifying vision: I see the betrayer betraying, the destroyer destroying. Go ahead, you Elamites and Medes, attack and lay siege. I will make an end to all the groaning Babylon caused."

Terror by Night: *see Nightmares*

Test the Spirits: examine the source of the visual revelation; judge the root of the revelation, whether it comes from God, the enemy or one's soul; 1 John 4:1 reads, "Beloved, do not believe every spirit, but test the spirits, whether they are of God; because many false prophets have gone out into the world."

Testify: something you see in the natural that bears witness to what you see in the spirit realm; a person who bears witness to a seer revelation's validity, either through confirming independent revelation or physical evidence of a manifestation; In John 5:39 Jesus said, "You search the Scriptures, for in them you think you have eternal life; and these are they which testify of Me."

Testimony of Jesus: what Jesus is saying to the church; the office committed to the prophets of testifying concerning future events, according to *The KJV New Testament Greek Lexicon*

Revelation 19:10 reads, "For the testimony of Jesus is the spirit of prophecy." Revelation 1:9 reads, "I, John, both your brother and companion in the tribulation and kingdom and patience of Jesus Christ, was on the island that is called

Patmos for the word of God and for the testimony of Jesus Christ."

The Door: another name for Jesus as seen in John 10:19: "I am the door; If anyone enters by Me, he will be saved, and will go in and out and find pasture."

The Life: another name for Jesus as seen in John 14:6: "Jesus said to him, 'I am the way, the truth, and the life. No one comes to the Father except through Me.'"

The Mansions: see *The Inner Castle*

The Spirit: another name for the Holy Spirit

The Truth: another name for Jesus as seen in John 14:6: "Jesus said to him, 'I am the way, the truth, and the life. No one comes to the Father except through Me.'"

The Vision of the Horns and Craftsmen: one of Zechariah's visions; Zechariah 1:18-21 reads:

"Then I raised my eyes and looked, and there were four horns. And I said to the angel who talked with me, 'What are these?' So he answered me, 'These are the horns that have scattered Judah, Israel, and Jerusalem.' Then the Lord showed me four craftsmen. And I said, 'What are these coming to do?'.

"So he said, 'These are the horns that scattered Judah, so that no one could lift up his head; but the craftsmen are coming to terrify them, to cast out the horns of the nations that lifted up their horn against the land of Judah to scatter it.'"

The Way: another name for Jesus as seen in John 14:6: "Jesus said to him, 'I am the way, the truth, and the life. No one comes to the Father except through Me.'"

The Word: another name for Jesus as seen in John 1:1: "In the beginning was the Word, and the Word was with God, and the Word was God."

Theresa of Avila: a Spanish mystic who wrote *The Inner Castle*, containing many deep seer revelations

Thick Darkness: *see Deep Darkness*

Thief: another name for Satan (see John 10:9-10)

Things That Are Above: heavenly things; Colossians 3:1 tells us: "If you then were raised with Christ, desire those things which are above, where Christ sits at the right hand of God."

Christ is seated "above." The Greek word for above in this verse is *ano*. According to *The KJV New Testament Greek Lexicon*, it means "up, upwards, above, on high; of the quarters of the heaven, northward; of time, formerly."

Things That Have Been Kept Secret Since the Foundation of the World: mysteries of the gospel Jesus shared in parables when He walked the earth; In Matthew 13:35 Jesus said, quoting Psalm 78:2, "That it might be fulfilled which was spoken by the prophet, saying: 'I will open My mouth in parables; I will utter things kept secret from the foundation of the world." Also, spiritual allegories and parables God reveals as present-day truth. Everything Jesus did and taught was not recorded in Scripture, so present-day truth continues to unfold.

Things Which Are Not Seen: hidden revelation; truth not apparent to the natural eye or knowledge that does not make sense to the natural ear; truths one must have spiritual eyes and ears to receive or discern;

2 Corinthians 4:18 tells us "While we do not look at the things which are seen, but at the things which are not seen." The Greek word for seen in that verse is *blepo*. According to *The KJV New Testament Greek Lexicon*, it means "to see, discern, of the bodily eye; with the bodily eye: to be possessed of sight, have the power of seeing; perceive by the use of the eyes: to see, look descry; to turn the eyes to anything: to look

at, look upon, gaze at; to perceive by the senses, to feel; to discover by use, to know by experience;

"Metaph. to see with the mind's eye; to have (the power of) understanding; to discern mentally, observe, perceive, discover, understand to turn the thoughts or direct the mind to a thing, to consider, contemplate, to look at, to weigh carefully, examine."

Third Eye: a concept in false religions of an invisible eye that offers insight into spiritual things; an expression of divination

Third Heaven: the heaven where Father God sits on the throne and where Christ is seated as His right hand; Paul's words in 2 Corinthians 12:2-4 speaks of the third heaven:

"I know a man in Christ who fourteen years ago—whether in the body I do not know, or out of the body I do not know, God knows—such a man was caught up to the third heaven. And I know how such a man—whether in the body or apart from the body I do not know, God knows—was caught up into Paradise and heard inexpressible words, which a man is not permitted to speak."

Third Watch: also called "the witching hour," the third watch is from 12 am to 3 am; Principalities, powers, rulers of the darkness and spiritual wickedness in high places are overactive during this watch. Therefore, this watch is usually reserved for more seasoned watchmen who are experts in spiritual warfare and understand their authority. Some also call this the cockcrowing watch. During this watch is when Peter denied Christ three times (see John 13:38). (See the book, *The Making of a Watchman*, for more.)

Thirst: a painful awareness of the need of God; In Matthew 5:6 Jesus said, "Blessed are those who hunger and thirst for righteousness, for they shall be filled." And in John 4:14 He said, "Whoever drinks of the water that I shall give him will never thirst. But the water that I shall give him will become in him a fountain of water springing up into everlasting life."

This Time Next Year: part of the language God uses to indicate time

Thorns and Thistles: a sign of the curse (see Genesis 3:18; Hosea 10:8)

Thorns in the Eyes: when the enemy afflicts the seer's eyes through temptation; Numbers 33:55 reads, "But if you don't drive out the inhabitants of the land before you, those you allow to remain will become thorns in your eyes and in your sides; they will harass you in the land where you will live."

Threats: an expression of evil intentions; Jezebel threatened to murder Elijah (see 1 Kings 19:2)

Three-Hundred-Sixty Degree: a full range of seer view from all angles

Threshing Floor: symbolic of a seer's sifting; *see also Sift*

Thrones: a place where high-ranking demons are seated; a counterfeit for God's throne reserved for demonic powers;

Colossians 1:13-17 reads: "He has delivered us from the power of darkness and has transferred us into the kingdom of His dear Son, in whom we have redemption through His blood, the forgiveness of sins. He is the image of the invisible God and the firstborn of every creature. For by Him all things were created that are in heaven and that are in earth, visible and invisible, whether they are thrones, or dominions, or principalities or powers. All things were created by Him and for Him. He is before all things, and in Him all things hold together."

Most spiritual warriors are familiar with principalities and powers, but not as much with dominions and thrones. The word "throne" in that verse comes from the Greek word *thronos*, which means "a throne seat, a chair of state having a footstool." We know that Christ's enemies will one day be made a footstool under His feet (see Hebrews 10:13). Right now, some of them are sitting on demonic thrones.

Throne Room: the place in heaven where God dwells. Isaiah and others had visions of the throne room; Isaiah 6:1-5 reads:

"In the year that king Uzziah died I saw also the Lord sitting upon a throne, high and lifted up, and his train filled the temple. Above it stood the seraphims: each one had six wings; with twain he covered his face, and with twain he covered his feet, and with twain he did fly.

"And one cried unto another, and said, Holy, holy, holy, is the Lord of hosts: the whole earth is full of his glory. And the posts of the door moved at the voice of him that cried, and the house was filled with smoke.

"Then said I, Woe is me! for I am undone; because I am a man of unclean lips, and I dwell in the midst of a people of unclean lips: for mine eyes have seen the King, the Lord of hosts."

Throne Room Scenes: visions of the throne room; (See Daniel 7:9-14; Revelation 4-5; 8:2-6; 11:19; 15; 16:17-17:3; 19:1-10; 21:5)

Thunder: one expression of the voice of the Lord (see Psalm 29:3); noise around the throne (see Revelation 4:5)

Time: a measurable period or span during which something occurs

Time and Times and Half a Time: 1,260 days, or 42 months; Daniel 7:25, "Then the saints shall be given into his hand For a time and times and half a time."

Time Kings Go to War: springtime; a period where kings in Old Testament times typically went to war; 2 Samuel 11:1 reads, "It happened in the spring of the year, at the time when kings go out to battle, that David sent Joab and his servants with him, and all Israel; and they destroyed the people of Ammon and besieged Rabbah. But David remained at Jerusalem."

Time of Reformation: the time of Christ's coming; the ultimate reformation is when Christ comes again; Hebrews 9:9-11 reads, "It was symbolic for the present time in which both gifts and sacrifices are offered which cannot make him who performed the service perfect in regard to the conscience—concerned only with foods and drinks, various washings, and fleshly ordinances imposed until the time of reformation."

Time of Sowing: a time to plant; Leviticus 26:5 reads, "Our threshing shall last till the time of vintage, and the vintage shall last till the time of sowing; you shall eat your bread to the full, and dwell in your land safely."

Time of the Dead: Judgment Day; Revelation 11:18 reads, "The nations were angry, and Your wrath has come, and the time of the dead, that they should be judged, and that You should reward Your servants the prophets and the saints, and those who fear Your name, small and great, and should destroy those who destroy the earth."

Time of the End: the end times; Daniel 8:17 reads, "So he came near where I stood, and when he came I was afraid and fell on my face; but he said to me, 'Understand, son of man, that the vision refers to the time of the end.'"

Time of the Latter Rain: symbolically, the final outpouring of the Holy Spirit; Zechariah 10:1, "Ask the Lord for rain In the time of the latter rain. The Lord will make flashing clouds; He will give them showers of rain, Grass in the field for everyone."

Time of Vintage: harvest time; Leviticus 26:5 reads, "Our threshing shall last till the time of vintage, and the vintage shall last till the time of sowing; you shall eat your bread to the full, and dwell in your land safely."

Time of Your Visitation: a time when the Lord visits a person or a church; Luke 19:43-45 reads, "For days will come upon you when your enemies will build an embankment around you, surround you and close you in on every side, and level you, and your children within you, to the ground; and they will not leave in you one stone upon another, because you did not know the time of your visitation."

Time to Come: the future not yet revealed; Isaiah 42:23, "Who among you will give ear to this? Who will listen and hear for the time to come?"

Times in God's Hands: an understanding of the sovereignty of God to direct our steps into experiences and occasions that fit into His purpose; David wrote, "My times are in Your hand; Deliver me from the hand of my enemies, and from those who persecute me" (Psalm 31:15).

Times of Refreshing: a replenishing, restoration, renewal or revival; Acts 3:19 reads, "Repent therefore and be converted, that your sins may be blotted out, so that times of refreshing may come from the presence of the Lord…"

Times of Restoration of All Things: a coming time when mankind will experience the perfect state before the fall; Acts 3:21 reads, "Whom heaven must receive until the times of restoration of all things, which God has spoken by the mouth of all His holy prophets since the world began."

Times of the Gentiles: the time between the destruction of the temple in 586 B.C. and the Second Coming of Christ; Luke 21:24 reads, "And Jerusalem will be trampled by Gentiles until the times of the Gentiles are fulfilled."

Times Past: part of the time language of God speaking

Topaz: a yellow transparent precious stone John the Revelator saw on the foundations of the wall around the New Jerusalem (see Revelation 21:19-21)

Trace: barely noticeable evidence of something in the spirit realm that has already taken place; the residue of an encounter; to search out a pathway in the spirit through landmarks or signs left behind

Trance: the state of one who is "out of himself," according to *Easton's Bible Dictionary*; The word *trance* comes from the Greek word *ekstasis*, from which the word ecstasy is derived.

Peter fell into a trance in Acts 10:10 that opened his eyes to preach the gospel to the Gentiles. Paul fell into a trance in Acts 22:17 in which the Lord gave Him a warning and a commission to preach the gospel to the Gentiles.

Smith's Bible Dictionary goes a little deeper, saying a trance is: "The state in which a man has passed out of the usual order of his life, beyond the usual limits of consciousness and volition, being rapt in causes of this state are to be traced commonly to strong religious impressions. Whatever explanation may be given of it, it is true of many, if not of most, of those who have left the stamp of their own character on the religious history of mankind, that they have been liable to pass at times into this abnormal state."

Trance Dimension: a dimension in the spirit where natural senses are suspended while God pours out visual revelation; (For more, see the book, *The Seer Dimensions*.)

Transfiguration: a drastic change in one's appearance, such as Jesus at the Mt. of Transfiguration; Matthew 17:1-2 speaks of Christ's transfiguration: "After six days Jesus took with him Peter, James and John the brother of James, and led them up a high mountain by themselves. There he was transfigured before them. His face shone like the sun, and his clothes became as white as the light."

Translated by the Spirit: when God supernaturally transports someone from where they are to another place, typically a faraway place; This happened to Philip in Acts 8:39-40, "Now when they came up out of the water, the Spirit of the Lord caught Philip away, so that the eunuch saw him no more; and he went on his way rejoicing. But Philip was found at Azotus. And passing through, he preached in all the cities till he came to Caesarea."

Transparent Glass: an element of heaven; the appearance of the streets in the New Jerusalem

Travail: a genuine form of prayer that can break through in warfare or to birth God's will; The Greek word *travail* is found several times in the New Testament (and many more times in the Old Testament). When Jesus talked about the pregnant woman who had sorrow in travail (see John 16:21), He was referring to *tikto*, which means "to bring forth, bear, produce (fruit from the seed); of a woman giving birth; of the earth bringing forth its fruits."

When Paul was talking about interceding for the Thessalonians (see 1 Thessalonians 2:9), the Greek word for travail is *mochthos*, which means a hard and difficult labor, toil, travail, hardship, distress.

Hebrew words for travail include *yalad*, which also brings in the connotation of helping: "to cause or help to bring forth; to assist or tend to as a midwife" (See Genesis 38:27); *t@la'ah*, which implies seeking deliverance from toil, hardship, distress, weariness (see Exodus 18:8); *inyan*, which refers to an occupation, task, job (see Eccl. 1:13); *amal* which refers to toil, trouble, labor (see Isaiah 23:4); and *challah*, which means to be or become grieved, be or become sorry (see Isaiah 53:11).

Tree of Life: a tree in heaven that brings life and healing; Revelation 22:2 reads, "In the middle of its street, and on either side of the river, was the tree of life, which bore twelve fruits, each tree yielding its fruit every month. The leaves of the tree were for the healing of the nations."

Triennium: a period of three years

True Vine: another name for Jesus as seen in John 15:1: "I am the true vine, and My Father is the vinedresser."

Trumpet: to issue a warning; to proclaim the word of the Lord

Try the Spirits: *see Test the Spirits*

Tune In: to listen or watch in the spirit; to be deeply focused on what is happening in the seer dimensions

Tunnel Vision: a narrow visual field that prohibits peripheral vision in the spirit; a deep focus on what is set directly before the seer's eyes

Turn Aside to Look: when you aren't sure what you are seeing in the spirit, so you stop to take another look (see Exodus 3:4)

Twilight: that period between sleeping and waking up when you have a dream or vision

Twinkling of an Eye: a beat in time; 1 Corinthians 15:51-52, reads "Behold, I tell you a mystery: We shall not all sleep, but we shall all be changed—in a moment, in the twinkling of an eye, at the last trumpet. For the trumpet will sound, and the dead will be raised incorruptible, and we shall be changed."

Two Witnesses: two prophets in the end-times who are martyred in the Book of Revelation; Revelation 11:3-6 reads, "And I will give *power* to my two witnesses, and they will prophesy one thousand two hundred and sixty days, clothed in sackcloth. These are the two olive trees and the two lampstands standing before the God of the earth.

"And if anyone wants to harm them, fire proceeds from their mouth and devours their enemies. And if anyone wants to harm them, he must be killed in this manner. These have power to shut heaven, so that no rain falls in the days of their prophecy; and they have power over waters to turn them to blood, and to strike the earth with all plagues, as often as they desire."

U

Unawares: the condition of sight that allows the enemy to creep in; spiritual ignorance.

Unbelief: an enemy to your spiritual sight; a miracle-stopper; weakness of faith; skepticism

Unchangeable: a vision or dream for which the outcome cannot be changed; an attribute of the God who does not change (see Malachi 3:6)

Unclean Spirit: a foul spirit that defiles; a spirit of impurity; Jesus said in Matthew 10:1, "And when He had called His twelve disciples to Him, He gave them power over unclean spirits, to cast them out, and to heal all kinds of sickness and all kinds of disease."

Uncover: to reveal something in the spirit that was hidden; to expose; to shed light on a matter

Unction: an anointing; a bubbling up in your spirit to prophesy or move in spiritual gifts; 1 John 2:20 (KJV) reads, "But ye have an unction from the Holy One, and ye know all things."

Understand the Vision: to have the right interpretation and application of a vision; Daniel 8:16 reads, "And I heard a man's voice between the banks of the Ulai, who called, and said, 'Gabriel, make this man understand the vision.'"

Understanding: to comprehend a visual revelation or dream

Understanding of the Times: discernment into the times and seasons of God; 1 Chronicles 12:32 speaks of "the sons of Issachar who had understanding of the times, to know what Israel ought to do, their chiefs were two hundred; and all their brethren were at their command…"

Unknown: the part of the vision, dream or prophetic revelation that is yet to be revealed

Unknown Prophet: prophets in the Bible who are not named, like the 1 Kings 20 prophet who spoke to the King of Israel or the prophet who anointed Jehu as king at Elijah's direction

Unrecognized Appearance: something that appears in the seer realm that is unrecognizable; something the seer has never seen before in the spirit realm; something one sees in the spirit realm that cannot be explained (see Job 4:16)

Unroll the Scroll: open an ancient revelation; In Luke 4:17 we read: "The scroll of Isaiah the prophet was handed to him. He unrolled the scroll and found the place where this was written…"

Unseen Realm: the realm of creation not seen with the human eye

Unspeakable: prophetic revelation for which you cannot find adequate words to describe; prophetic revelation that God tells you not to speak

Unweighted: seer revelation that is not judged

Urgency in the Spirit: a state of heart where the Holy Spirit is compelling you to take action

Uriah: a prophet who was martyred; Jeremiah 26:20-23 reads, "Now there was also a man who prophesied in the name of the Lord, Urijah the son of Shemaiah of Kirjath Jearim, who prophesied against this city and against this land according to all the words of Jeremiah.

"And when Jehoiakim the king, with all his mighty men and all the princes, heard his words, the king sought to put him to death; but when Urijah heard *it*, he was afraid and fled, and went to Egypt.

"Then Jehoiakim the king sent men to Egypt: Elnathan the son of Achbor, and *other* men *who went* with him to Egypt. And they brought Urijah from Egypt and brought him to Jehoiakim the king, who killed him with the sword and cast his dead body into the graves of the common people."

Utterance: a vocal expression; articulating what you have seen in a dream, vision or encounter

V

Vacuum: *see Void*

Vain Imagination: demonic arguments launched against the mind; subtle enemy whispers that seek to erect strongholds in the mind; 2 Corinthians 10:5 (KJV), "Casting down imaginations, and every high thing that exalteth itself against the knowledge of God, and bringing into captivity every thought to the obedience of Christ…"

Vain Vision: see *False Vision*

Vanish: something you see in the spirit that suddenly disappears right before your eyes

Vault: a secret room in heaven where valuable mysteries are stored

Veil: something that blocks or hinders visual revelation; The Greek word for veil in the New Testament of the Bible is *kalupto*. It means "to hide, veil, to hinder the knowledge of a thing," according to *The KJV New Testament Greek Lexicon*. *Merriam-Webster's Dictionary* defines veil as something used to cover, provide, obscure, or conceal.

Maclaren's Expositions writes, "A veil is but a thin partition. We can hear the voices on the other side of a woolen curtain, we can catch the gleams of light through it, A touch will draw it aside. So we float in the midst of that solemn unseen present which is to us the future; and all the brightest and grandest objects of the Christian man's anticipation have a present existence and are real; just on the other side of that thin curtain that parts us from them."

Verses: scriptures seers see in the spirit to indicate what God is doing, saying, or warning about; God can show seers verses in the Spirit written in the air or on a wall

Vexed: to feel frustrated, agitated, worried, or otherwise troubled in spirit

View: the range of vision in the spirit; what you see in the seer dimensions

Virgin Eyes: eyes that have not been defiled by the lusts of the world

Visage: the characteristics or appearance of a face or animal you see in the spirit; Isaiah 52:14, "Just as many were astonished at you, so His visage was marred more than any man, and His form more than the sons of men."

Visible: something you can see with the naked eye or something the Lord allows you to see in the spirit realm

Visibility: how easy it is to see in the spirit; the clarity one has into the spiritual climate

Vision (Greek): The Greek word for vision is *horasis*, which means "the act of seeing, a vision, appearance," according to the NAS Exhaustive Concordance. *Thayer's Greek Lexicon* defines vision as "the act of seeing; the sense of sight; appearance, visible form, a vision, i.e., an appearance divinely granted in an ecstasy." And *Strong's* Exhaustive Concordance defines vision as "the act of gazing, i.e. (externally) an aspect or (internally) an inspired appearance – a sight, vision."

Vision (Hebrew): The Hebrew word for vision is *chazah*, which means "vision, a sight (mentally), i.e., a dream, revelation, or oracle – vision," according to *Strong's Concordance. Brown-Driver-Briggs* breaks it down as a "vision, as seen in an ecstatic state;" "vision, in the night;" and "divine communication in a vision, oracle, prophecy."

Vision Dimension: a dimension in the spirit realm where God communicates through visual revelation, such as pictures, open vision; (For more, see the book *The Seer Dimensions*.)

Vision is Yet for Many Days to Come: a vision of the end-times; Daniel 10:14 reads, "Now I have come to make you understand what will happen to your people in the latter days, for the vision refers to many days yet to come."

Vision of a Ram and a Goat: a vision of Daniel; Daniel 8:1 reads, "In the third year of the reign of King Belshazzar a vision appeared to me—to me, Daniel—after the one that appeared to me the first time."

Vision of Joshua the High Priest: a vision of Zachariah; Zachariah 3:1-5 reads, "Then he showed me Joshua the high priest standing before the Angel of the Lord, and Satan standing at his right hand to oppose him. And the Lord said to Satan, 'The Lord rebuke you, Satan! The Lord who has chosen Jerusalem rebuke you! Is this not a brand plucked from the fire?'.

"Now Joshua was clothed with filthy garments, and was standing before the Angel. Then He answered and spoke to those who stood before Him, saying, 'Take away the filthy garments from him.' And to him He said, 'See, I have removed your iniquity from you, and I will clothe you with rich robes.'.

"And I said, 'Let them put a clean turban on his head. 'So they put a clean turban on his head, and they put the clothes on him. And the Angel of the Lord stood by."

Vision of Nahum: the revelation recorded in the Book of Nahum.

Vision of Obadiah: a vision of the coming judgment of Edom in the Book of Obadiah

Vision of the Almighty: a vision of El Shaddai, the Almighty God; Numbers 24:4 reads, "The utterance of him who hears the words of God, Who sees the vision of the Almighty, Who falls down, with eyes wide open…"

Vision of the Ancient of Days: a vision of Daniel. Daniel 7:9-10, we read, "I watched till thrones were put in place, and the Ancient of Days was seated; His garment was white as snow, and the hair of His head was like pure wool. His throne was a fiery flame, its wheels a burning fire;

"A fiery stream issued and came forth from before Him. A thousand thousands ministered to Him; Ten thousand times ten thousand stood before Him. The court was seated, and the books were opened."

Vision of the Four Beasts: a vision of Daniel; Daniel 7:1-8 reads, "In the first year of Belshazzar king of Babylon, Daniel had a dream and visions of his head while on his bed. Then he wrote down the dream, telling the main facts.

"Daniel spoke, saying, 'I saw in my vision by night, and behold, the four winds of heaven were stirring up the Great Sea. And four great beasts came up from the sea, each different from the other. The first was like a lion, and had eagle's wings. I watched till its wings were plucked off; and it was lifted up from the earth and made to stand on two feet like a man, and a man's heart was given to it.

"And suddenly another beast, a second, like a bear. It was raised up on one side, and had three ribs in its mouth between its teeth. And they said thus to it: 'Arise, devour much flesh!' After this I looked, and there was another, like a leopard, which had on its back four wings of a bird. The beast also had four heads, and dominion was given to it.

"After this I saw in the night visions, and behold, a fourth beast, dreadful and terrible, exceedingly strong. It had huge iron teeth; it was devouring, breaking in pieces, and trampling the residue with its feet. It was different from all the beasts that were before it, and it had ten horns.

"I was considering the horns, and there was another horn, a little one, coming up among them, before whom three of the first horns were plucked out by the roots. And there, in this horn, were eyes like the eyes of a man, and a mouth speaking pompous words."

Vision of the Horsemen: a vision of Zachariah in which he sees the four horses of the Apocalypse; (see Zachariah 1:7-17)

Vision of the Locusts: a vision of Amos; Amos 7:1-3 reads, "Thus the Lord God showed me: Behold, He formed locust swarms at the beginning of the late crop; indeed it was the late crop after the king's mowings. And so it was, when they had finished eating the grass of the land, that I said: 'O Lord God, forgive, I pray! Oh, that Jacob may stand, for he is small!' So the Lord relented concerning this. 'It shall not be,' said the Lord.'"

Vision of the Man With the Measuring Line: a vision of Zachariah; Zachariah 2:1-5 reads, "Then I raised my eyes and looked, and behold, a man with a measuring line in his hand. So I said, 'Where are you going?' And he said to me, 'To measure Jerusalem, to see what is its width and what is its length.'.

"And there was the angel who talked with me, going out; and another angel was coming out to meet him, who said to him, 'Run, speak to this young man, saying: 'Jerusalem shall be inhabited as towns without walls, because of the multitude of men and livestock in it. For I,' says the Lord, 'will be a wall of fire all around her, and I will be the glory in her midst.'"

Vision of Their Own Heart: invented visions, or visions based on what is in their mind and heart rather than the spirit of God; Jeremiah 23:16 reads, "Thus says the Lord of hosts: 'Do not listen to the words of the prophets who prophesy to you. They make you worthless; They speak a vision of their own heart, not from the mouth of the Lord.'"

Vision of Your Head Upon Your Bed: a combination of dreams and internal visions; Daniel 2:28 reads, "But there is a God in heaven who reveals secrets, and He has made known to King Nebuchadnezzar what will be in the latter days. Your dream, and the visions of your head upon your bed, were these…"

Vision Refers to Many Days Yet to Come: a vision of events that take place in the end-times; Daniel 10:14 reads, "Now I have come to make you understand what will happen to your people in the latter days, for the vision refers to many days yet to come."

Vision That Concerns the Whole Multitude: a vision that applies to multitudes of people; Ezekiel 7:13 reads, "For the seller shall not return to what has been sold, though he may still be alive; For the vision concerns the whole multitude, and it shall not turn back; No one will strengthen himself Who lives in iniquity."

Vision That Deals With the Time of the End: a vision relating to the end-times; Daniel 8:17 reads, "So he came near where I stood, and when he came I was afraid and fell on my face; but he said to me, 'Understand, son of man, that the vision refers to the time of the end.'"

Vision Yet for an Appointed Time: a vision that will not come to pass immediately, but will be fulfilled at a specific time God decides; Habakkuk 2:3 a reads, "For the vision is yet for the appointed time; It hastens toward the goal and it will not fail. Though it tarries, wait for it; For it will certainly come, it will not delay."

Visionary States: different types, manifestations or expressions of visual revelation.

Visions of God: seeing different scenes of God in the Throne Room; Ezekiel 1:1 reads, "Now it came to pass in the thirtieth year, in the fourth month, on the fifth day of the month, as I was among the captives by the River Chebar, that the heavens were opened and I saw visions of God."

Visions of My Mind: dreams

Visions of the Dream: the contents of a dream; what was depicted in a dream; not to be confused with a vision within a dream' In Daniel 4:9, King Nebuchadnezzar said to Daniel, "Belteshazzar, chief of the magicians, because I know that the Spirit of the Holy God is in you, and no secret troubles you, explain to me the visions of my dream that I have seen, and its interpretation."

Visions That Cause Sorrow: a vision that causes pain or distress; Daniel 10:16 reads, "And suddenly, *one* having the likeness of the sons of men touched my lips; then I opened my mouth and spoke, saying to him who stood before me, 'My lord, because of the vision my sorrows have overwhelmed me, and I have retained no strength.'"

Visitation: when God's Spirit sweeps through a place where saints are gathered; a personal encounter with God's Spirit; a time when God displays His favor or judgment

Vista: an extensive view of the future

Visual Echo: the repetition of a vision in the spirit; seeing the same vision over and over, sometimes in one session or repeated at different intervals; The purpose of a visual echo is to get your attention, to let you see it again and again so you can gain seer intelligence on the matter or to warn you of its near manifestation so you can take appropriate action.

Visual Field: what you can see without intentionally looking around; what you can see with your spiritual eyes in the moment without further exploring the seer dimensions

Visual Metaphor: something you see in the spirit that is not really there but represents something that is, like a crack in the floor or a hole in the wall

Visual Revelation: revelation that flows through the channel of spiritual visions

Visual Word of Knowledge: a word of knowledge expressed visually; a word of knowledge you see with your eyes instead of hear with your ear; *see also Word of Knowledge*

Visual Word of Wisdom: a word of wisdom expressed visually. A word of wisdom is characterized by purity, peace, gentleness, reason, mercy, good fruits, impartiality and righteousness. A word of wisdom has to do with the past, present, or future; *see also Word of Wisdom*

Vocation: your calling in the Kingdom of God; your full-time occupation in the spirit; Paul wrote, "I, therefore, the prisoner of the Lord, beseech you to walk worthy of the calling with which you were called" (Ephesians 4:1).

Voice of a Stranger: the voice of a spirit that is not God; In John 10:1-6 Jesus said, "Most assuredly, I say to you, he who does not enter the sheepfold by the door, but climbs up some other way, the same is a thief and a robber. But he who enters by the door is the shepherd of the sheep.

"To him the doorkeeper opens, and the sheep hear his voice; and he calls his own sheep by name and leads them out. And when he brings out his own sheep, he goes before them; and the sheep follow him, for they know his voice. Yet they will by no means follow a stranger, but will flee from him, for they do not know the voice of strangers.'"

Voice of Healing Movement: a movement in the church from the mid-1940s to the late 1950s that saw miracles, signs and wonders starting in the United States and sweeping across the globe; Key figures were Oral Roberts, A.A. Allen, and Jack Coe.

Void: a vacant place in the spirit; a place without noticeable spiritual activity; Genesis 1:2 tells us the earth was once without form and void.

Volume: the intensity of the sound one hears in the spirit; the number of angels one sees in the seer dimensions

Vow: a promise to the Lord; to bind oneself with the words of one's mouth to an action or condition

W

Waging Prophetic Warfare: praying through and decreeing a prophetic word in the same way one would pray through or decree a Scripture; 1 Timothy 1:18 reads, "This charge I commit to you, son Timothy, according to the prophecies previously made concerning you, that by them you may wage the good warfare…"

Wait Silently: to wait on the Lord without music or any audible stimulation—without prayer or outwardly spoken words; Psalm 62:5 reads, "My soul, wait silently for God alone, for my expectation is from Him."

Waiting Upon the Lord: to quiet one's self and wait expectantly for the Lord to manifest His voice, His visions or His presence; to linger in prayer with hopeful anticipation that the Lord will reveal truth; Psalm 27:4 reads, "Wait on the Lord; Be of good courage, and He shall strengthen your heart; Wait, I say, on the Lord!"

Wakened: to rouse out of a trance or spiritual encounter with a new revelation; Zechariah 4:1-3 reveals the prophet's account: "Now the angel who talked with me came back and wakened me, as a man who is wakened out of his sleep. And he said to me, 'What do you see?' So I said, 'I am looking, and there is a lampstand of solid gold with a bowl on top of it, and on the stand seven lamps with seven pipes to the seven lamps. Two olive trees are by it, one at the right of the bowl and the other at its left.'"

Ward: *see Metron*

Warlike: seer terminology to help one describe what he sees in the spirit; 1 Maccabees 14:9 describes, "The ancient men sat all in the streets, communing together of good things, and the young men put on glorious and warlike apparel."

Warlock: the male equivalent of a witch; a sorcerer

Warning: to call out danger or evil in the spirit before it manifests in the natural; a function of the watchman; God told the prophet in Ezekiel 3:17, "Son of man, I have made you a watchman for the house of Israel; therefore hear a word from My mouth, and give them warning from Me."

Warring Angels: angels on assignment to war with and for God's people against dark forces (See 2 Kings 19:35)

Waster: *see Spoiler*

Watch: a designated time of prayer; to pay attention to what is going on in the spirit so you can respond swiftly and appropriately through prayer; In Mark 13:33 Jesus says, "Take heed, watch and pray; for you do not know when the time is."

Watches: divisions of the night set aside for prayer and watching in the spirit; there are eight watches in the night, each with specific purposes; You can read more about this in the book *The Making of a Watchman.*

Watch for What the Lord Will Say: the heart posture of a seer watchman standing in the watchtower in conversation with the Lord; Habakkuk 2:1 reads, "I will stand my watch and set myself on the rampart, and watch to see what He will say to me, and what I will answer when I am corrected."

Watcher Angels: angels whose assignment is to watch and record what people do (Malachi 3:6)

Watcher Demons: *see Monitoring Spirits*

Watchman: one who watches in the spirit for the coming King or demonic interference; one who keeps watch in the spirit realms; one who issues warnings based on what they see in the spirit

Watchtower: the station where a watchman stands on assignment; a lookout point for the watchman to watch into the spirit; Isaiah 21:8, "Then he cried, 'A lion, my Lord! I stand continually on the watchtower in the daytime; I have sat at my post every night.'"

Weighing: *see Judging and Testing the Spirits*

Weight: something that carries authority in the spirit; a profound revelation that is released with a sober spirit

West Wind: a wind associated with rescue, the west wind is only mentioned in the Bible once; Exodus 10:19, "And the Lord turned a very strong west wind, which took the locusts away and blew them into the Red Sea. There remained not one locust in all the territory of Egypt."

What Do You See? a question the Lord asked seers in the Bible to activate their spiritual vision or point them to a spiritual truth; When the Lord asks, "What do you see?" He's trying to activate your spiritual vision. Many times, the word of the Lord comes to a seer after he or she sees (see Jeremiah 1:11-15; Jeremiah 24:3; Amos 7:8; Amos 8:2; Zechariah 4:1-4; Zechariah 5:1-3).

What You See the Father Do: seeing what the Father is doing, as Jesus did when He walked the earth (see John 5:19)

Wheel within a Wheel: an element of Ezekiel's vision in Ezekiel 1:15-21; spirit beings Ezekiel saw in a dramatic vision;

Ezekiel 1:15;21 reads, "Now as I looked at the living creatures, behold, a wheel was on the earth beside each living creature with its four faces. The appearance of the wheels and their workings was like the color of beryl, and all four had the same likeness. The appearance of their workings was, as it were, a wheel in the middle of a wheel.

"When they moved, they went toward any one of four directions; they did not turn aside when they went. As for their rims, they were so high they were awesome; and their rims were full of eyes, all around the four of them. When the living creatures went, the wheels went beside them; and when the living creatures were lifted up from the earth, the wheels were lifted up.

"Wherever the spirit wanted to go, they went, because there the spirit went; and the wheels were lifted together with them, for the spirit of the living creatures was in the wheels. When those went, these went; when those stood, these stood; and when those were lifted up from the earth, the wheels were lifted up together with them, for the spirit of the living creatures was in the wheels."

Whirlwind: a tempest or storm; Elijah was taken up in a whirlwind (see 2 Kings 2:1)

Whirlwinds: visions that flash so suddenly that if you are not paying attention you could miss it; a flood of revelation that comes as an instantaneous supernatural download that you weren't expecting

Whisper: a faint impression of a vision; one way God speaks to people in dreams; Job 33:15-16 reads, "He speaks in dreams, in visions of the night, when deep sleep falls on people as they lie in their beds. He whispers in their ears and terrifies them with warnings."

Whispering Spirits: *see Peeping Spirits*

Wicca: a religion that worships both male and female gods of nature

Wiccan: one who practices Wicca

Wicked One: another name for Satan (see Matthew 13:19)

Wilderness: a parabolic term used to describe a dry season in someone's life; a period of transition from a place God is bringing a person from to the next land of promise

Wind of the Spirit: the Holy Spirit's grace or anointing on a person, place, or thing (see John 3:8)

Window: a portal into supernatural realms

Windows of Heaven: a portal in heaven through which either judgment or blessings rain down; Malachi 3:10 reads, "Bring all the tithes into the storehouse, that there may be food in My house, and try Me now in this," says the Lord of hosts, "If I will not open for you the windows of heaven and pour out for you such blessing that there will not be room enough to receive it."

Wisdom from Above: wisdom from above God's own insight on the right course of action (see James 3:17)

Witch: one who practices witchcraft

Witch at Endor: a witch Saul consulted when he could no longer find an answer by the prophets, dreams, visions or directly (see 1 Samuel 28)

Witchcraft: the work of magic, sorcery, and/or the cooperation with the operation of familiar spirits

Witness: to see something in the spirit that serves as evidence of demonic or angelic movement or of Holy Spirit visitation

Wizard: someone who flows in an illegal power; someone who orchestrates spiritual operations with spiritual power that does not originate from the Spirit of God

Women with Wind as Their Wings: a type of spiritual creature; Zechariah's vision in Zechariah 5:9-11, "there came out two women, and the wind was in their wings; for they had wings like the wings of a stork: and they lifted up the ephah between the earth and the heaven…"

Wonderful: another name for Jesus seen in Isaiah 9:6, "For unto us a Child is born, unto us a Son is given; And the government will be upon His shoulder. And His name will be called Wonderful, Counselor, Mighty God, Everlasting Father, Prince of Peace."

Word Famine: a condition that arises when there is a lack of study of the Word; Amos 8:11 reveals: "'Behold, the days are coming,' says the Lord God, "That I will send a famine on the land, not a famine of bread, nor a thirst for water, but of hearing the words of the Lord."

Word in Season: a prophetic utterance released with divine timing; Isaiah 50:4 reads, "The Lord God has given Me the tongue of the learned, that I should know how to speak a word in season to him who is weary. He awakens Me morning by morning, He awakens My ear to hear as the learned."

Word of Knowledge: revelation with information related to the past or present; God reveals a word or "fragment" of information related to people, places, or things; It can be manifested through a vision, angel, dream, or gift of prophecy (see 1 Corinthians 12).

Word of Wisdom: God's very own wisdom for a current situation, the past, or the future (see 1 Corinthians 12); The Greek word for wisdom in the 1 Corinthians 12 list of the gifts of the spirit is *sophia*. According to *The KJV New Testament Greek Lexicon*, it means "supreme intelligence, such as belongs to God."

Works of Darkness: actions that are carnal or demonic in nature and therefore do not produce the fruit of righteousness (see Ephesians 5:11)

Worshipping Angels: angels are on assignment to worship God (See Isaiah 6:30)

Worthless Vision: *see False Vision*

Write the Vision: record the vision in plain language for all to understand (see Habakkuk 2:2)

X

Xerox: a term used when someone plagiarizes your visual revelation

X-ray Vision: the ability of highly-gifted seers to see under the surface of a thing; to see what is going on inside a person, nation, room, business, church, or some other person, place or thing

Y

Yahweh: a name for God that means Lord, Master; The first time this name was used was in Genesis 2:4: "This is the history of the heavens and the earth when they were created, in the day that the Lord God made the earth and the heavens…"

Yeshua: a common name for the God of the Hebrews; the literal meaning is to rescue or to deliver

Yielding to the Spirit: to give way to the leading, guidance and desires of the Holy Spirit (see Galatians 5:16).

Yoctoseconds: one septillionth of a second; among the briefest of looks into the seer dimensions

Yoke: a form of enemy oppression that holds someone in bondage; as part of Seer Deliverance, seers can sometimes see the yoke of bondage; *see also Seer Deliverance*

Z

Zachariah: an Old Testament prophet and contemporary of Haggai; author of the Book of Zechariah; the prophet had dramatic prophetic visions

Zadok: a seer in the bible whose name means righteous and just; Zadok was a high priest during David's reign. When Absalom arranged the insurrection, Zadok wanted to follow David out of Jerusalem, but "The king also said to Zadok the priest, "Are you not a seer? Return to the city in peace, and your two sons with you, Ahimaaz your son, and Jonathan the son of Abiathar" (2 Samuel 15:27). David trusted Zadok to watch over the ark of the covenant.

Zadok anointing: a seer anointing to steward the presence and glory of God

Zebulon: a tribe of Israel. This tribe was known for warfare in the Book of Judges, but also the tribe that handles "the pen of the writer" (Judges 5:14); Some commentators say this was not in terms of literary skill, but in terms of gathering soldiers for battle.

Others, like Matthew Henry, say they were "even the scribes, who gave themselves to study and writing, whereby they were exempted from military service, did voluntarily enter into this service." Matthew Henry writes, "With the pen of the scribe or writer, i.e. who did not only go themselves, but by their letters invited and engaged others to go with them to the battle."

Gill's Exposition of the Entire Bible takes a dual approach: "but these through a zeal for the common cause dropped their pens, and took to the sword, in vindication of the rights and liberties of themselves and their brethren; for which they are justly commended."

In any case, this tribe had a scribe anointing. Seers with prolific dreams and visions need that scribe anointing to chronicle what they see in the spirit so others can run with the vision.

Zedekiah: a false prophet in 1 Kings who prophesied, "Thus says the Lord: 'With these you shall gore the Syrians until they are destroyed.' And all the prophets prophesied so, saying, "Go up to Ramoth Gilead and prosper, for the Lord will deliver it into the king's hand" (1 Kings 22:11-12).

Zenith: the culminating point of a dream or vision; the highest point in the heavens

Zephaniah: a prophet and the author of the Book of Zephaniah; He prophesied in the days of Josiah, king of Judah. Zephaniah issued warnings about the "Day of the Lord" but also saw into the future Messianic Kingdom.

Zeptosecond: one sextillion of a second; among the briefest of looks into the seer dimensions

Zillion: an uncountable, yet large number

Zion: the city of God; the city of David; God's spiritual kingdom (see Psalm 87:2-3; Hebrews 12:22)

Zodiac: a picture or object with markers of zodiac signs, which are based on the positioning of planet paths; a form of divination the seer should avoid

Zodiac Signs: any one of twelve symbols based on birth date ranges that promise to offer insight into one's temperament and preferences; a form of divination the seer should avoid

Zone: an area within the seer dimensions; the state of the seer who has tapped into the ecstatic realm

Zoom In: focusing your eyes on minute details of a vision

APPENDIX I

All the Visions in the Bible

Numbers 12:6, God says, "Hear now My words: if there is a prophet among you, I, the Lord, make Myself known to him in a vision; I speak to him in a dream."

Genesis 15:1-17 records Abraham's vision concerning his descendants

Genesis 28:12 records Jacob's vision of a ladder with angels ascending and descending

Genesis 46:2 records Jacob's visions of the night

Exodus 3:2 records Moses' encounter with the Angel of the Lord in the burning bush

Exodus 24:9-11 records when Moses and elders from Israel saw God

Exodus 24:17 records a vision of God's glory on top of a mountain

Exodus 33:18-33 records an encounter in which Moses saw God's glory

Joshua 5:13-15 records Joshua's encounter with the Captain of the Hosts

1 Samuel 3:11-15 records Samuel's encounter with the Lord where he received a word of judgment against the house of Eli

1 Kings 22:17 records Michaiah's vision of an Israelite defeat

1 Kings 22:19 records Michaiah's vision of the Lord sitting on the throne with His angels

2 Kings 6:17 records the Elisha's servant's vision of the chariots of fire

1 Chronicles 21:15-18 records David's vision of destroyer angels with a drawn sword stretched out over Jerusalem

Job 4:12-16 records Eliphaz's vision of the Spirit of God that caused him to tremble in fear and his bones shake

Isaiah 1 records the call of Isaiah, his vision of God and an angel with a burning coal of fire

Isaiah 6:1-13 records Isaiah's vision of God in His glorious temple

Isaiah 21:1-3 records Isaiah's distressing vision of treacherous dealer

Isaiah 2 records Isaiah's troubling vision of the Valley of Vision

Jeremiah 1:11 records Jeremiah's vision of the almond tree

Jeremiah 1:13 records Jeremiah's vision of the boiling pot

Ezekiel 1:4 records Ezekiel's vision of the glory of God

Ezekiel 1:5-25 records Ezekiel's vision of the four living creatures

Ezekiel 1:26-28 records Ezekiel's vision of God and His throne

Ezekiel 2:9 records Ezekiel's vision of a scroll

Ezekiel 10:1-7 records Ezekiel's vision of the glory of the Lord departing from the temple

Ezekiel 37:1-4 records Ezekiel's vision of the Valley of the Dry Bones

Ezekiel 40 records Ezekiel's vision of a new city and a new temple

Ezekiel 43:10 records Ezekiel's vision of the temple, God's dwelling place

Ezekiel 47:1-12 records Ezekiel's vision of the healing waters and trees

Daniel 7:9-27 records Daniel's vision of the Ancient of Days

Daniel 8 records Daniel's vision of the ram and the goat

Daniel 10 records Daniel's vision of an angel that brought him a prayer answer

Amos 7:1-3 records Amos' vision of the locusts swarming

Amos 7:4-6 records Amos' vision of God calling for conflict by fire

Amos 7:7-9 records Amos' vision of the man with the plumbline

Amos 8:1-2 records Amos' vision of a basket of summer fruit

Amos 9:1 records Amos' vision of the Lord standing on the altar releasing instructions

Zechariah 1:8-11 records Zechariah's vision of a man riding a red horse

Zechariah 1:18-21 records Zechariah's vision of the four horns

Zechariah 3:1-5 records Zechariah's vision of Joshua the high priest in filthy rags

Zechariah 4:1-14 records Zechariah's vision of the golden candlestick

Zechariah 5:1-14 records Zechariah's vision of the flying scroll

Zechariah 6:1-8 records Zechariah's vision of chariots and mountains

Luke 1:13-22 records Zacharias' vision of an angel confirming his wife's pregnancy

Matthew 3:16 records John the Baptist's vision of the Holy Spirit descending on Jesus like a dove; This is also recorded in Mark 1:10, Luke 3:22, and John 1:32-34.

Matthew 17:19 records the vision Peter, James, and John saw of Jesus transfigured, talking with Moses and Elijah; This is also recorded in Luke 9:28-36.

Acts 2:2-3 records the Upper Room disciples' vision of tongues like cloven fire falling upon them during the Baptism of the Holy Spirit on Pentecost

Acts 2:7:55-56 records Stephen's vision of Jesus sitting at the right hand of the Father in heaven

Acts 9:3-6 records Paul's vision of Jesus on the road to Damascus

Acts 9:10-11 records Ananais' vision of the Lord giving him instructions to find Paul and pray for him

Acts 9:12 records Paul's vision of Ananais coming to lay his hands on him to restore his sight

Acts 10:4 records the centurion Cornelius' vision of an angel telling him to call for Peter

Acts 10:9-18 records Peter's trance in which he saw a vision of unclean animals coming down on a sheet

Acts 18:9-10 records Paul's vision of the Lord telling him not to be afraid of preaching in Corinth

Acts 22:17:21 records Paul's vision during a trance in which Paul saw Jesus telling him to get out of Jerusalem quickly

2 Corinthians 12:1-6 record's Paul's vision of Paradise

Revelation 1:10-20 records John's vision of the golden candlesticks

Revelation 4:1 records John's vision of a door standing open in heaven

Revelation 4:2-11 records John's vision of the throne in heaven encircled by a rainbow, with 24 thrones, 24 elders, the sea of glass, and four living creatures

Revelation 5:1-5 records John's vision of the seven seals

Revelation 5:8 records John's visions of the four beasts and 24 elders with golden vials containing the prayers of the saints

Revelation 6 records John's vision of six seals being opened, including four horses, celestial events, and a quaking earth

Revelation 7:1-8 records John's vision of the seventh seal being opened and the sealing of the 144,000

Revelation 7:9-16 records John's vision of the multitudes who came out of the great tribulation

Revelation 8:1-6 records John's vision of what happened when the seventh seal was opened, how it was silent in heaven for one hour, and angelic activity around the throne

Revelation 8:7-13 records John's vision of the angel sounding the first four trumpets, hail and fire falling, a mountain cast into the sea, and a falling star

Revelation 9 records John's vision of the angel sounding the fifth and sixth trumpets, including the angel with keys to the bottomless pit, locusts, an army of horses and other vivid images

Revelation 10:1-7 records John's vision of a mighty angel clothed in a cloud with a rainbow on his head who had a little open

Revelation 11:1-2 records John's vision of the temple measurements

Revelation 11:3-12 records John's vision of the two witnesses, including their murder and resurrection

Revelation 11:4 records John's vision of two olive trees and two candlesticks

Revelation 11:7 records John's vision of the beast in the bottomless pit

Revelation 11:15-19 records John's vision of the seventh trumpet sounding, the temple of God opening, and the ark of the covenant with lightning, noises, thunderings and hail

Revelation 12:1-2 records John's vision of a woman clothed in the sun, with the moon under her feet and a garland of twelve stars who cried out in labor and gave birth

Revelation 12:3-6 records John's vision of a great red dragon with seven heads and ten horns

Revelation 12:7-9 records John's vision of the war in heaven

Revelation 13:1-10 records John's vision of the beast rising out of the sea with the name blasphemy

Revelation 14:1-5 records John's vision of the Lamb of God on Mount Zion with the 144,000

Revelation 14:6-7 records John's vision of an angel with the everlasting gospel

Revelation 14:8-13 records John's vision of an angel announcing Babylon's fall

Revelation 14:14-16 records John's vision of the Son of Man with a sickle

Revelation 14:15-20 records John's vision of an angel reaping the harvest, and the angel with authority over fire, and the great winepress of God's wrath

Revelation 14:17-19 records John's vision of the angel coming out of the temple with a sharp sickle

Revelation 14:18 records John's vision of the angel with power over fire

Revelation 15:1-8 records John's vision of the angels with the final plagues

Revelation 15:5 records John's vision of the temple of the tabernacle of the testimony of heaven opened

Revelation 16:2 records John's vision of the plague that comes upon those who take the mark of the beast

Revelation 16:3 records John's vision of the sea turning into blood

Revelation 16:16 records John's vision of angels with the seven bowls of wrath

Revelation 16:18 records John's vision of Babylon's destruction

Revelation 19:1-9 records John's vision of multitudes praising God

Revelation 19:11-16 records John's vision of Jesus riding a white horse

Revelation 19:17-21 records John's vision of an angel in the sun

Revelation 20:1-3 records John's vision of Satan being bound for one thousand years

Revelation 20:1-10 records John's vision of thrones of judgment, resurrection and Satan being loosed

Revelation 20:11 records John's vision of God's white throne

Revelation 20:12 records John's vision of the Book of Life opened

Revelation 20:14 records John's vision of death and hell

Revelation 21 records John's vision of the New Jerusalem

Revelation 22:1 records John's vision of the river of life

Revelation 22:2 records John's vision of the tree of life.

APPENDIX II

Every Dream in the Bible

The Bible records 21 dreams. Almost half—10—of those dreams are recorded in the Book of Beginnings, Genesis. Another six are recorded in the Book of Matthew.

Six of the dreamers in the Bible are kings and only one is a woman. It's noteworthy that not all dreamers were serving the Lord. Here is a list of the dreams in the Bible.

Read through them. Pay close attention to the symbols and how God speaks through dreams. If you want more information on how to interpret dreams, pick up my book *Decoding Your Dreams: What God May be Saying to You While You Sleep.*

God Warns Abimelech

Genesis 20:3-7, God came to Abimelech in a dream by night, and said to him, "Indeed you are a dead man because of the woman whom you have taken, for she is a man's wife."

But Abimelech had not come near her; and he said, "Lord, will You slay a righteous nation also? Did he not say to me, 'She is my sister'? And she, even she herself said, 'He is my brother.' In the integrity of my heart and innocence of my hands I have done this."

And God said to him in a dream, "Yes, I know that you did this in the integrity of your heart. For I also withheld you from sinning against Me; therefore I did not let you touch her. Now therefore, restore the man's wife; for he is a prophet, and he will pray for you and you shall live. But if you do not restore her, know that you shall surely die, you and all who are yours."

Notice how God spoke to this man directly in a dream. Sometimes God sends angels through dreams or lets events play out for your interpretation.

Jacob Sees Angels Ascending and Descending

In Genesis 28:11-13, we read: "So he came to a certain place and stayed there all night, because the sun had set. And he took one of the stones of that place and put it at his head, and he lay down in that place to sleep. Then he dreamed, and behold, a ladder was set up on the earth, and its top reached to heaven; and there the angels of God were ascending and descending on it."

God Tells Jacob to Go Home

Genesis 31:10-13 reads, "And it happened, at the time when the flocks conceived, that I lifted my eyes and saw in a dream, and behold, the rams which leaped upon the flocks were streaked, speckled, and gray-spotted.

"Then the Angel of God spoke to me in a dream, saying, 'Jacob.' And I said, 'Here I am.' And He said, 'Lift your eyes now and see, all the rams which leap on the flocks are streaked, speckled, and gray-spotted; for I have seen all that Laban is doing to you. I am the God of Bethel, where you anointed the pillar and where you made a vow to Me. Now arise, get out of this land, and return to the land of your family.'"

God Warns Laban

Genesis 31:24 reads, "God had come to Laban the Syrian in a dream by night, and said to him, 'Be careful that you speak to Jacob neither good nor bad.'"

Joseph Dreams of Famine

Genesis 37:5-7 reads, "Now Joseph had a dream, and he told it to his brothers; and they hated him even more. So he said to them, 'Please hear this dream which I have dreamed: There we were, binding sheaves in the field. Then behold, my sheaf arose and also stood upright; and indeed your sheaves stood all around and bowed down to my sheaf.'" This dream is connected with the next dream just a few verses down.

Joseph Dreams About Sun, Moon and Stars

Genesis 37:9 reads, "Then he dreamed still another dream and told it to his brothers, and said, "Look, I have dreamed another dream. And this time, the sun, the moon, and the eleven stars bowed down to me."

Notice how the two dreams are related. This is called a recurring dream. When a dream reoccurs, God is working to get your attention.

Cupbearer Dreams of Three Branches

In Genesis 40:9-11, we read, "Behold, in my dream a vine was before me, and in the vine were three branches; it was as though it budded, its blossoms shot forth, and its clusters brought forth ripe grapes. Then Pharaoh's cup was in my hand; and I took the grapes and pressed them into Pharaoh's cup, and placed the cup in Pharaoh's hand."

Baker Dreams of Three Baskets

Genesis 40:16-17 reads, "I also was in my dream, and there were three white baskets on my head. In the uppermost basket were all kinds of baked goods for Pharaoh, and the birds ate them out of the basket on my head."

Pharaoh Dreams of Seven Fat Cows

Genesis 41:1-4 reads, "Then it came to pass, at the end of two full years, that Pharaoh had a dream; and behold, he stood by the river. Suddenly there came up out of the river seven cows, fine looking and fat; and they fed in the meadow.

"Then behold, seven other cows came up after them out of the river, ugly and gaunt, and stood by the other cows on the bank of the river. And the ugly and gaunt cows ate up the seven fine looking and fat cows. So Pharaoh awoke."

Pharaoh Dreams of Seven Plumb Ears of Grain

Genesis 41:5-7, "He slept and dreamed a second time; and suddenly seven heads of grain came up on one stalk, plump and good. Then behold, seven thin heads, blighted by the east wind, sprang up after them. And the seven thin heads devoured the seven plump and full heads. So Pharaoh awoke, and indeed, it was a dream."

Unnamed Man Dreams of Bread Rolls

In Judges 11:13, we read: "And when Gideon had come, there was a man telling a dream to his companion. He said, 'I have had a dream: To my surprise, a loaf of barley bread tumbled into the camp of Midian; it came to a tent and struck it so that it fell and overturned, and the tent collapsed.'"

Solomon Dreams About an Invitation

In 1 Kings 3:5-15, we read, "At Gibeon the Lord appeared to Solomon in a dream by night; and God said, "Ask! What shall I give you?"

And Solomon said: "You have shown great mercy to Your servant David my father, because he walked before You in truth, in righteousness, and in uprightness of heart with

You; You have continued this great kindness for him, and You have given him a son to sit on his throne, as it is this day.

"Now, O Lord my God, You have made Your servant king instead of my father David, but I am a little child; I do not know how to go out or come in. And Your servant is in the midst of Your people whom You have chosen, a great people, too numerous to be numbered or counted.

"Therefore give to Your servant an understanding heart to judge Your people, that I may discern between good and evil. For who is able to judge this great people of Yours?"

The speech pleased the Lord, that Solomon had asked this thing. Then God said to him: "Because you have asked this thing, and have not asked long life for yourself, nor have asked riches for yourself, nor have asked the life of your enemies, but have asked for yourself understanding to discern justice, behold, I have done according to your words; see, I have given you a wise and understanding heart, so that there has not been anyone like you before you, nor shall any like you arise after you.

And I have also given you what you have not asked: both riches and honor, so that there shall not be anyone like you among the kings all your days. So if you walk in My ways, to keep My statutes and My commandments, as your father David walked, then I will lengthen your days.

Then Solomon awoke; and indeed it had been a dream. And he came to Jerusalem and stood before the ark of the covenant of the Lord, offered up burnt offerings, offered peace offerings, and made a feast for all his servants."

Nebuchadnezzar Dreams of an Image

In Daniel 2:31-35, we read, "You, O king, were watching; and behold, a great image! This great image, whose splendor was excellent, stood before you; and its form was awesome.

This image's head was of fine gold, its chest and arms of silver, its belly and thighs of bronze, its legs of iron, its feet partly of iron and partly of clay. You watched while a stone was cut out without hands, which struck the image on its feet of iron and clay, and broke them in pieces.

Then the iron, the clay, the bronze, the silver, and the gold were crushed together, and became like chaff from the summer threshing floors; the wind carried them away so that no trace of them was found. And the stone that struck the image became a great mountain and filled the whole earth."

Nebuchadnezzar Dreams of a Hacked Down Tree

In Daniel 4:10-17, we read: "These were the visions of my head while on my bed: I was looking, and behold, a tree in the midst of the earth, and its height was great. The tree grew and became strong; Its height reached to the heavens, and it could be seen to the ends of all the earth.

Its leaves were lovely, its fruit abundant, and in it was food for all. The beasts of the field found shade under it, the birds of the heavens dwelt in its branches, and all flesh was fed from it.

"I saw in the visions of my head while on my bed, and there was a watcher, a holy one, coming down from heaven. He cried aloud and said thus:

'Chop down the tree and cut off its branches, strip off its leaves and scatter its fruit. Let the beasts get out from under it, and the birds from its branches. Nevertheless leave the stump and roots in the earth, bound with a band of iron and bronze, in the tender grass of the field.

Let it be wet with the dew of heaven, and let him graze with the beasts on the grass of the earth. Let his heart be changed from that of a man, let him be given the heart of a beast, and let seven times pass over him.

'This decision is by the decree of the watchers, and the sentence by the word of the holy ones, in order that the living may know that the Most High rules in the kingdom of men gives it to whomever He will, and sets over it the lowest of men.'"

Daniel Dreams of Four Beasts

Daniel 7:1-8 records Daniel's dream of the four beasts:

"In the first year of Belshazzar king of Babylon, Daniel had a dream and visions of his head while on his bed. Then he wrote down the dream, telling the main facts."

Daniel spoke, saying, "I saw in my vision by night, and behold, the four winds of heaven were stirring up the Great Sea. And four great beasts came up from the sea, each different from the other.

The first was like a lion, and had eagle's wings. I watched till its wings were plucked off; and it was lifted up from the earth and made to stand on two feet like a man, and a man's heart was given to it.

"And suddenly another beast, a second, like a bear. It was raised up on one side, and had three ribs in its mouth between its teeth. And they said thus to it: 'Arise, devour much flesh!'.

"After this I looked, and there was another, like a leopard, which had on its back four wings of a bird. The beast also had four heads, and dominion was given to it.

"After this I saw in the night visions, and behold, a fourth beast, dreadful and terrible, exceedingly strong. It had huge iron teeth; it was devouring, breaking in pieces, and trampling the residue with its feet. It was different from all the beasts that were before it, and it had ten horns.

I was considering the horns, and there was another horn, a little one, coming up among them, before whom three of the first horns were plucked out by the roots. And there, in this horn, were eyes like the eyes of a man, and a mouth speaking pompous words."

Joseph Dreams About His Fiancé

Matthew 1:18-24 records the dream Joseph had concerning Mary, the mother of Jesus, after she told him she was pregnant:

"Now the birth of Jesus Christ was as follows: After His mother Mary was betrothed to Joseph, before they came together, she was found with child of the Holy Spirit. Then Joseph her husband, being a just man, and not wanting to make her a public example, was minded to put her away secretly.

"But while he thought about these things, behold, an angel of the Lord appeared to him in a dream, saying, "Joseph, son of David, do not be afraid to take to you Mary your wife, for that which is conceived in her is of the Holy Spirit. And she will bring forth a Son, and you shall call His name Jesus, for He will save His people from their sins."

"So all this was done that it might be fulfilled which was spoken by the Lord through the prophet, saying: 'Behold, the virgin shall be with child, and bear a Son, and they shall call His name Immanuel,' which is translated, 'God with us.'.

Then Joseph, being aroused from sleep, did as the angel of the Lord commanded him and took to him his wife."

Magi Receives a Warning Dream

Matthew 2:12 records the account of the Magi's dream after visiting the baby Jesus and presenting Him with gifts: "Then, being divinely warned in a dream that they should not return to Herod, they departed for their own country another way."

Joseph Dreams About Going to Egypt

Matthew 2:13-14 records the account of Joseph's dream about protecting Jesus: "Now when they had departed, behold, an angel of the Lord appeared to Joseph in a dream, saying, "Arise, take the young Child and His mother, flee to Egypt, and stay there until I bring you word; for Herod will seek the young Child to destroy Him.

"When he arose, he took the young Child and His mother by night and departed for Egypt, and was there until the death of Herod, that it might be fulfilled which was spoken by the Lord through the prophet, saying, "Out of Egypt I called My Son."

Joseph Dreams About Returning to Israel

Matthew 2:19-21 records the account of Joseph's dream about returning with Jesus to Israel: "Now when Herod was dead, behold, an angel of the Lord appeared in a dream to Joseph in Egypt, saying, 'Arise, take the young Child and His mother, and go to the land of Israel, for those who sought the young Child's life are dead.' Then he arose, took the young Child and His mother, and came into the land of Israel."

Joseph Dreams About Avoiding Judea

Matthew 2:22-23 records Joseph's dream with a warning to avoid Judea: "But when he heard that Archelaus was reigning over Judea instead of his father Herod, he was afraid to go there. And being warned by God in a dream, he turned aside into the region of Galilee. And he came and dwelt in a city called Nazareth, that it might be fulfilled which was spoken by the prophets, "He shall be called a Nazarene."

Pontius Pilate's Wife Dreams About Jesus

Matthew 27:19 reads, "When he was set down on the judgment seat, his wife sent unto him, saying, Have thou nothing to do with that just man: for I have suffered many things this day in a dream because of him." We don't know all the details of her dream, but we know it convinced her that Jesus was telling the truth.

Resources Used in this Book

Baker's Evangelical Dictionary of Biblical Theology
Britannica.com
Brown-Driver-Briggs
Easton's Bible Dictionary
Elliott's Commentary for English Readers
Gill's Exposition of the Entire Bible
Maclaren's Expositions
Matthew Henry's Concise Commentary
Merriam-Webster's Dictionary
Pulpit Commentary
Sciencing.com
Smith's Bible Dictionary
Strong's Concordance
Thayer's Greek Lexicon
The Encyclopedia of the Bible
The Geneva Bible
The International Bible Encyclopedia
The KJV New Testament Greek Lexicon
The KJV Old Testament Hebrew Lexicon
The NAS New Testament Greek Lexicon
The NAS Old Testament Hebrew Lexicon
The Spiritual Warrior's Guide to Defeating Water Spirits
Vine's Dictionary
Young's Literal Bible

About Jennifer LeClaire

Jennifer LeClaire is an internationally recognized author, apostolic-prophetic voice to her generation, and conference speaker. She carries a reforming voice that inspires and challenges believers to pursue intimacy with God, cultivate their spiritual gifts and walk in the fullness of what God has called them to do. Jennifer is contending for awakening in the nations through intercession and spiritual warfare, strong apostolic preaching and practical prophetic teaching that equips the saints for the work of the ministry.

Jennifer is senior leader of Awakening House of Prayer in Fort Lauderdale, FL, founder of the Ignite Network and founder of the Awakening Prayer Hubs prayer movement.

Jennifer formerly served as the first-ever editor of *Charisma* magazine. Her work also appeared in a Charisma House book entitled *Understanding the Five-Fold Ministry,* which offers a biblical study to uncover the true purpose for the fivefold ministry and *The Spiritual Warfare Bible*, which is designed to help you use the Bible to access the power of the Holy Spirit against demonic strongholds and activity. Some of Jennifer's work is also archived in the Flower Pentecostal Heritage Museum.

Jennifer is a prolific author who has written over 50 books. Some of her materials have been translated into Spanish and Korean.

Jennifer writes one of Charisma's most popular prophetic columns, The Plumb Line, and frequently contributes to Charisma's Prophetic Insight newsletter. Her media ministry includes her website; 500,000 followers on Facebook, Twitter and YouTube. Jennifer has been interviewed on numerous media outlets including USA Today, BBC, CBN, The Alan

Colmes Show, Bill Martinez Live, Babbie's House, Atlanta Live and Sid Roth's It's Supernatural, as well as serving as an analyst for Rolling Thunder Productions on a *Duck Dynasty* special presentation.

Jennifer also sits on the media advisory board of the Hispanic Israel Leadership Coalition.

Jennifer is affiliated with:

Network Ekklessia International, an apostolic network founded by Dutch Sheets

Forerunner Ministries, founded by Ken Malone;

"http://www.forerunner-ministries.org/"

Christian International Network, founded by Bill Hamon

Apostolic Network, founded by Chuck Pierce.

USCAL, the United States Coalition of Apostolic Leaders

The International Society of Deliverance Ministers.

Jennifer has a powerful testimony of God's power to set the captives free and claim beauty for ashes. She shares her story with women who need to understand the love and grace of God in a lost and dying world. You can also learn more about Jennifer in this broadcast on Sid Roth's *It's Supernatural.*

Other Books By Jennifer LeClaire

Angels on Assignment Again
Decoding Your Dreams
The Spiritual Warrior's Guide to Defeating Water Spirits
Releasing the Angels of Abundant Harvest
The Heart of the Prophetic
A Prophet's Heart
The Making of a Prophet
The Spiritual Warrior's Guide to Defeating Jezebel
Did the Spirit of God Say That?
Satan's Deadly Trio
Jezebel's Puppets
The Spiritual Warfare Battle Plan
Waging Prophetic Warfare
Dream Wild!
Faith Magnified
Fervent Faith
Breakthrough!
Mornings With the Holy Spirit
Evenings With the Holy Spirit
Revival Hubs Rising
The Next Great Move of God
Developing Faith for the Working of Miracles
Breaking the Miracle Barrier
Decoding the Mysteries of Heaven's War Room
Jezebel's Revenge

The Making of a Watchman

You can download Jennifer's mobile apps by searching for "Jennifer LeClaire" in your app store and find Jennifer's podcasts on iTunes.

GET IGNITED! JOIN THE IGNITE NETWORK

I believe in prophetic ministry with every fiber of my being, but we all know the prophetic movement has seen its successes and failures. With an end times army of prophets and prophetic people rising up according to Joel 2:28 and Acts 2:17-20, it's more important than ever that we equip the saints for the work of prophetic ministry. Enter Ignite.

Ignite is a prophetic network birthed out of an encounter with the Lord that set a fire in my hearts to raise up a generation of prophets and prophetic people who flow accurately, operate in integrity, and pursue God passionately. I am laboring to cultivate a family of apostolic and prophetic voices and companies of prophets in the nations who can edify, comfort and exhort each other as we contend for pure fire in the next great move of God. My vision for Ignite covers the spiritual, educational, relational and accountability needs of five-fold ministers and intercessory prayer leaders.

You can learn more at http://www.ignitenow.org.

AWAKENING PRAYER HUBS

The Awakening Prayer Hubs mission in any city is to draw a diverse group of intercessors who have one thing in common: to contend for the Lord's will in its city, state and nation.

The vision of Awakening Prayer Hubs is to unite intercessors in cities across the nations of the earth to cooperate with the Spirit of God to see the second half of 2 Chronicles 7:14 come to pass: "If My people, who are called by My name, will humble themselves and pray, and seek My face and turn from their wicked ways, then I will hear from heaven, and will forgive their sin and will heal their land."

For many years, intercessors have been repenting, praying, and seeking God for strategies. Awakening Prayer Hubs intercessors will press into see the land healed, souls saved, churches established, ministries launched, and other Spirit-driven initiatives. Awakening Prayer Hubs intercessors will help undergird other ministries in their city, partnering with them in prayer where intercession may be lacking. Although Awakening Prayer Hubs are not being planted to birth churches, it is possible that churches could spring up from these intercessory prayer cells if the Lord wills. You can find out more about this prayer movement at www.awakeningprayerhubs.com You can also join the Awakening House Church Movement at awakeninghouse.com or plant a house of prayer via Awakening House of Prayer.

Made in the USA
Coppell, TX
20 November 2021